Black and white elites in rural Rhodesia

This book is dedicated to the
Dominican Missionary Sisters
of Central Africa

A. K. H. Weinrich
(Sister Mary Aquina O.P.)

Black and white elites in rural Rhodesia

Manchester University Press

Rowman and Littlefield

Published by
Manchester University Press
316–324 Oxford Road
Manchester M13 9NR

ISBN 0 7190 0533 7

First published in the United States 1973
by Rowman and Littlefield, Totowa, New Jersey

Library of Congress Cataloging in Publication Data
Weinrich, A K H 1933–
    Black and white elites in rural Rhodesia.
    Bibliography: p. 233
    1. Rhodesia, Southern—Race question
2. Elite (Social sciences)   I. Title.
DT962.42.W44   1973   301.44′92′096891   72–12870
ISBN 0–87471–167–3

Printed in Great Britain by
Butler & Tanner Ltd
Frome and London

Contents

List of tables

List of figures

List of plates

(Plates I*a*, III*a* and *b*, and IV, are reproduced with acknowledgement to the
Rhodesian Ministry of Information)

Foreword

This book is not a structural anthropological study, but concerns Rhodesian European and African Elites and their attitudes in the rural areas of Rhodesia. It is a study of race relations; and in many respects it is also an exercise in psychological anthropology.

Those who have read Dr. Weinrich's previous writings, such as *Chiefs and Councils in Rhodesia* (Heinemann, 1971), will have been struck by the penetration of her fieldwork, her ability to persuade informants to yield material at the very heart of the matter. Such readers will not be disappointed in the present work, which presents data somewhat at variance with official statements on the tribal trust lands of Rhodesia during the 1960s.

Dr. Weinrich has handled the material in a systematic fashion, displaying categories of elite membership one by one, with their attitudes to one another and to various key issues. This is well suited to an examination and development of the race relations hypotheses with which the author deals. So comprehensive and clear cut are the data, however, that scholars with other frames of reference will find them readily applicable to the material; and here one particularly has role theory in mind.

A fascinating aspect of the data is that the two Rhodesian rural elites—European and African—are neither of them ostensibly integrated with one another, nor do they present any important internal cohesiveness among themselves. The stereotyped picture of a white Rhodesian elite bloc confronting an African one is thus in a sense untrue, except that each group would undoubtedly close ranks against the other in the event of an overt power confrontation.

The author has in effect presented two sets of elite roles, or role-clusters, between which there is both internal and external role dissonance. One-sided reconciliation between these rural clusters is achieved by the self-vindicating role model on which the Administration depends: the traditional/paternalistic one of the chief-like father and his tribal children. Inimical to this model is the presence in the rural areas of Europeans who do not act like chiefs or of Africans who are not tribal. Dr. Weinrich's analysis is full of cases which do not fit these idealized role categories.

It is instructive to contrast the Rhodesian District Commissioner as portrayed here with the former Tanganyikan D.C. as depicted in Tanner, 1966.[1] There are some points of similarity, such as overt seniority in the

[1]Tanner, R. E. S., 1966, 'European Leadership in Small Communities in Tanganyika prior to Independence', *Race*, 7, 3, 289–302.

administrative and judicial spheres; but the many areas of difference emphasize that the administrative system in Rhodesia today is by no means a British-type one. The district communities, if such they can be called in Rhodesia, seem far more scattered and diffuse than in Tanganyika, and not centred about the social club. The D.C.'s position is not merely tolerated by other officials in the Rhodesian district, and his staff is not outnumbered by technical specialists. The political policy in the Rhodesian tribal trust lands is not one of divided authority with a combination of checks and balances, but rather of hierarchical control, presumably somewhat influenced by South Africa's policies. The D.C. in Rhodesia does not have to conform to the ideals and social practices of those beneath him, but himself sets the pace. And finally the Rhodesian government's political plan to be carried out by the D.C. is not one of development towards independence, but is virtually a scheme of separate community development. All these factors make the Rhodesian D.C. far more of an undisputed, if sometimes a resented, leader than his former British counterpart in Tanzania.

At the time of writing, the Pearce Commission of 1972 has been and gone, the unexpectedly fierce opposition by both rural and urban Africans in Rhodesia to their understanding of the Proposals for a Settlement has been experienced, and the Administration have been widely accused of believing in their own mythology. It is earnestly to be hoped that this book will contribute to a better sociological understanding of the situation, on which future concord in Rhodesia must surely rest.

Department of Sociology　　　　　　　　　　　　　　D. H. Reader
University of Rhodesia
March 1972

Preface

This book was written in conjunction with another book, entitled *Chiefs and Councils in Rhodesia*, published by Heinemann in 1971, and provides a background to some of its data. Whereas the book on chiefs and councils deals with political processes in African rural areas of Rhodesia, this book is concerned with the interaction of Europeans who stand in influential and authoritative positions in African communities, and with the emergent African elite.

The main research for this book was done between 1962 and 1964 when most of the field data presented in Chapters 5–10 were collected. During those years, however, my main concern had been with the lives of the African people themselves, and although I had met many district commissioners, extension officers, missionaries and European farmers, all of whom strongly influence African communities, I did not study these Europeans systematically. I also had had few contacts with the more highly educated and wealthy members of the African elite, such as school inspectors and doctors.

Consequently, while I was lecturing at the University of Rhodesia, I engaged on part-time research during 1968 and 1969 in order to fill these gaps. I interviewed fifty Europeans. This number was not arbitrarily arrived at but was determined by my desire to meet a high proportion of district commissioners, a group of Europeans in Rhodesia whom my earlier research had shown to be most influential in African areas. There are fifty-two district commissioners stationed in the provinces of Rhodesia (twenty more are employed in the capital), and of these I interviewed fourteen, or 25 per cent. To facilitate comparison, I interviewed an equal number of extension officers, that is, agricultural experts, and also missionaries. The latter were taken from the Roman Catholic, Dutch Reformed and Methodist Churches. Later I added eight European farmers who, as the largest employers of African labour and often as friendly neighbours, also influence African rural life, though to a lesser extent than civil servants and missionaries. This brings the number of Europeans interviewed up to fifty.

The sample of fifty Europeans is small, but since few Europeans live in rural areas, as is shown in the first chapter of this book, and since all of those interviewed in this study occupy leading positions, their influence is very great. Time, and especially shortage of money, prevented me from choosing a larger sample. Even this limited number required me to travel some 3,000 miles to contact the men at their often outlying stations.

The small size of the sample was compensated for by very intensive interviewing. I spent on the average half a day with each of the fifty Europeans, sometimes a whole day. During this time we leisurely and informally discussed some fifty questions. Everywhere I was welcomed and a relationship of trust was almost invariably established. During these interviews I was competently assisted by Sister Mary Matthia Stigler O.P., who acted as secretary and recorded all conversations. Without her help the detailed record on which this book is based could not have been established.

During the same years, 1968 and 1969, I completed my study of the African elite, and interviewed in addition to the research carried out between 1962 and 1964 over twenty members of the emergent elite, especially doctors, hospital administrators, extension officers, school inspectors and school managers. Many of these positions were still filled by Europeans during the earlier period of research.

I wish to express my sincerest gratitude to all who helped me in the preparation and writing of this book, especially to the Reverend Mother General of the Dominican Sisters of Central Africa, who generously financed my early research, and to Professor D. H. Reader who contributed from departmental funds to assist me in carrying out the interviews during 1968 and 1969. I also gratefully acknowledge the stimulating comments of my colleagues at the department of Sociology and Social Anthropology at the University of Rhodesia.

Department of Sociology   A.K.H.W.
University of Rhodesia

Introduction

In his book *Race Relations*, Michael Banton describes himself as a 'writer who ventures outside the confines of conventional specialization'.[1] Banton's venture has stimulated me to the parallel exercise of arranging some of my own field data, gathered while conducting an anthropological investigation of the political and economic systems of the indigenous peoples of Rhodesia,[2] in a manner amenable for race relations analysis. This present book draws on some aspects of Banton's analysis as a framework within which the interactions of Africans and Europeans in the rural areas of Rhodesia are presented. The final chapter attempts, through certain deductions from the facts presented earlier, to make some contributions to current knowledge of race relations.

Among the hypotheses which Banton discusses are three which have gained general currency in race relations research, and which I have used as a framework for this study. These are as follows: (*a*) Race relations in a society are determined by historical events. The original encounter between two distinct racial groups frequently determines their relationship towards each other in subsequent decades. The first chapter of this book explores the validity of this statement for Rhodesia. (*b*) In societies in which one race dominates another race, the characters of members of both racial groups are formed by these unequal race relationships, and the freedom of both racial groups is restricted. Chapters two to four explore the relationships with Africans of those Europeans whose occupations bring them into close, often authoritarian, relations with members of the subordinate race. Sections of subsequent chapters study the reactions towards members of the dominant race of those Africans who have had most frequent contacts with Europeans.

[1]Banton, 1967, p. xiv.
[2]See my book *Chiefs and Councils in Rhodesia*, 1971, and a second study: *Old and New Peasant Societies in Rhodesia*, still in press.

1

(c) Racial cleavage gives rise to an elite structure among the subordinate race which parallels the elite structure of the dominant race. Chapters five to ten examine this statement at great length.

To set out Banton's interpretation in greater detail:
(a) *Race relations in a society are determined by the historical events surrounding the first extended contact between members of different races.*

Schermerhorn identifies as one of the most important variables in race relations the sequential pattern of interaction between subordinate and dominant ethnic groups.[3] In this area Banton distinguishes between first fleeting contacts between different races and more permanent contacts. First fleeting contacts are generally controlled by local leaders who mediate with members of the incoming group on behalf of their followers. At this stage few members of the two racial groups establish personal contacts across the colour line and those who do tend to occupy different roles in both their own and in the alien social system.[4]

Prolonged contact between the races has more far-reaching effects because it exposes large sections of both racial groups to interracial encounters. As many people of both races begin to interact, social changes occur in one or the other, or in both racial groups. Banton argues that in such situations the politically and economically stronger group tends to influence the politically and economically weaker group; if an industrialized nation confronts a pre-industrialized society, the latter is likely to accommodate itself to the expectations of the more powerful group and to accept many changes in its own social organization.[5]

Banton observes that such acculturation opens up two alternatives for future race relations. Either the more powerful race may conquer and subjugate the weaker race and so establish a dominative order, or a paternalistic relationship may be established.

Where the first alternative is chosen, race becomes a 'role sign' determining the economic, political and social privileges of the dominant group. A dominative order depends on force. Only if the power balance between the two races shifts, can this relationship be altered. If the two races continue to live in the same territory after the subordinate race achieves some economic, political and

[3]Schermerhorn, 1970, p. 15.   [4]Banton, 1967, p. 69.   [5]*Ibid.*, p. 70.

social influence, a plural society is likely to evolve. In a plural society race remains an important sign determining expected behaviour, but domination is replaced by separate development in which the races live side by side and try to reduce interracial contact to a minimum.

The second alternative, paternalism, results in colonial situations in which the government of a colonial power controls both the indigenous people of a territory and its own settlers. If the settlers increase in number, they may form an intervening body between the indigenous people and the government because their own interests generally diverge from those of the colonial administration. For whereas a colonial government may feel bound to advance the indigenous population, settlers are interested in a dominative order which preserves their own prerogatives. If the colonial government is strong enough to prevent these aspirations, paternalistic colonialism may in time give rise to an integrated society. But if the settlers increase in power, the colonial government may abdicate and leave the control to the settlers. Then a dominative order finally resulting in what Banton calls 'unequal pluralism'[6] and van den Berghe refers to as 'structural or social pluralism'[7] is likely to result. For an exact interpretation of the changes in race relations following prolonged contact, historical, demographic, political, economic and social factors must be considered.

(b) *The characters of members of both the dominant and the subordinate races are formed by unequal relationships, and the freedom of both is restricted.*

Banton states that racially composite societies are often characterized by racial antipathies, that racial antipathies form the characters of many people in such societies, and that the desire to keep the races apart limits the freedom of all. He illustrates this assertion by examples from the effects of slavery on the population of the southern United States, and then refers to Mannoni, a psychoanalyst, who studied race relations in colonial Madagascar. Mannoni uncovered the sources of unequal race relations on the one hand in the Europeans' desire for freedom which exposes them to feelings of insecurity and inferiority, compensated by a display of superiority *vis-à-vis* members of other races, and on the other hand in the Africans' desire for security which inclines them originally to recognize

[6]Banton, 1967, p. 75.
[7]van den Berghe, 1967, p. 133.

their dependence both on their own social environment and on an alien European government.[8]

Banton observes that a system which gives members of one race an exaggerated sense of their own importance,[9] engenders in them Superman attitudes. They feel obliged to guard their superiority jealously, even at the cost of personal freedom. Consequently they evolve an elaborate pattern governing race relations which assures all members of the dominant race of prestige, however lowly their occupation may be. Banton quotes the following comment of an American Senator before the outbreak of the Civil War: 'One of the reconciling features of the existence [of Negro slavery] is the fact that it raises white men to the same general level, that it dignifies and exalts every white man by the presence of a lower race.'[10]

This superior status, Banton observes, can only be maintained by a rigid conformity of all members of society to generally accepted norms. Any deviation, even by members of the dominant race, evokes sanctions forcing the deviant members back to conformity. Insistence on conformity is especially stressed by the less gifted members of the dominant race because their own position is threatened by the acquisition of skills and the presence of talents among members of the subordinate race. They regard racial solidarity as a duty through which they can preserve their ethnic honour, an honour which Max Weber calls *Massenehre* (honour of the masses).[11]

As a result of this insistence on conformity, contacts across the colour line become depersonalized, communication is impaired, and the knowledge which members of the separated races have of each other is generally confined to stereotypes.[12] Because freedom of association is greatly reduced for members of both racial groups, the freedom of the subordinate race and also the freedom of the dominant race is severely restricted.

The subordinate race suffers more than the dominant race because it is forced to accept subordinate positions in all social contacts.[13] Its members are treated as inferior by members of the

---

[8]Mannoni, 1968, pp. 39 ff., 97 ff.
[9]Banton, 1967, p. 123, and Mannoni, 1968, pp. 108, 120.
[10]*Ibid.*, p. 117.
[11]Weber, 1961, p. 308.
[12]Banton, 1967, p. 150.
[13]*Ibid.*, p. 147.

dominant race and many, especially the uneducated, begin to believe that they are truly inferior.[14] This acceptance of second-rate citizenship is essential for the smooth running of such a society, for otherwise its social stratification might be challenged. As a result of an accepted social inferiority, members of the subordinate race stress their dependence on their masters, and this dependence forms their characters. Because they are politically, economically and educationally at a disadvantage and lack the means, open to members of the dominant race, to compete with them on an equal basis, their freedom is very seriously limited. This applies also to certain racially composite societies which do not practise a system of slavery comparable to that of the southern United States before the Civil War.

(c) Racial cleavage gives rise to an elite structure among the subordinate race paralleling the elite structure of the dominant race.

To preserve their superior social status intact, members of a dominant race try to construct their society in such a way that colour becomes a rigid line, dividing the races from each other. It represents a status gap which no member of the subordinate race can cross.

During the first years of contact, all members of the dominant race are regarded as socially superior to all members of the subordinate race, but with increased interaction some members of the subordinate race may acquire certain status symbols which are superior to those possessed by some members of the dominant race. Banton, quoting Warner, represents in diagrammatical form the shift in social stratification which may occur when members of a subordinate race advance socially in a society which is opposed to racial integration (Figure 1).

The white areas in these diagrams represent the dominant race, the shaded areas the subordinate race, and the double line the status gap between the two racial groups. The dotted lines separate the different social strata or classes within each group. The diagrams represent the relative position of racial and class categories, not their size.

According to Banton, the originally superior social position of the dominant race is challenged as the subordinate race advances economically, politically and socially. In order to preserve intact the position of the dominant racial group, the other group is forced to evolve its own stratification system, paralleling that of the

[14]*Ibid.*, p. 155.

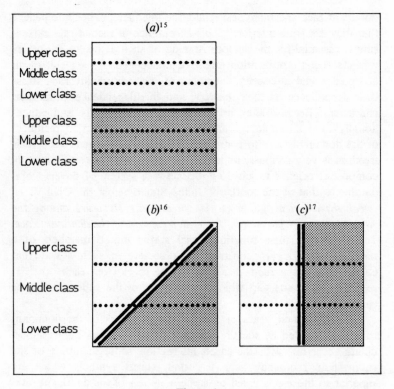

Figure 1

dominant group. Figure 1 illustrates this projected development: (*a*)
showing the initial phase in which the dominant race completely
controls the subordinate race, (*b*) the second phase in which the
subordinate race gains some of the more influential positions in
society, and (*c*) the hypothetical case, envisaged by advocates of
South African *apartheid*, in which both races become structurally
equal. This position, however, has not yet been achieved in any
society. It is postulated that as this parallel structure evolves, society
acquires a plural character; all social positions existing in one group
are duplicated in the other group, and yet no contact is established
between the two groups.

[15]Banton, 1967, adapted from p. 71.
[16]*Ibid.*, adapted from p. 144.
[17]*Ibid.*, adapted from p. 178.

Banton argues that this parallel development need not occur in a paternalistic society in which pressure from the home government forces settlers to accept members of the subordinate race into their own social system. In such societies the colour line dissolves and paternalism is replaced by integration.[18]

Banton's interpretation of race relations is of special interest to Rhodesia where a strong settler community rose in rebellion and declared itself independent of the British Government. The research on which this book is based took place in the 1960s when Rhodesia abandoned its policy of partnership which might have led to an integrated society and replaced it by a policy of separate development which aims at pluralism.

[18]*Ibid.*, pp. 256–7.

1. Origins of the racially composite society of Rhodesia

1. Historical and political background of racial domination

The country between the Limpopo and Zambezi rivers, which at the end of the nineteenth century was called Rhodesia, has a long history. Archeological as well as historical research suggest that the ancestors of the Shona speaking people, who at present constitute about four-fifths of the indigenous population, arrived about the year A.D. 1000. One of the immigrating clans, known as the Rozvi, extended its control over the remaining population and established its first administrative centre at Zimbabwe, a large fortress near the present town of Fort Victoria. The first walls of this fortress were erected about A.D. 1085 and during the thirteenth and fourteenth centuries its residents engaged in a lively trade with Arabs from the east coat. During the fifteenth century a political hierarchy was established which ruled the country until 1834.[1]

During the early sixteenth century the people of this central African kingdom made their first contacts with Europeans. In 1505 the Portuguese established themselves at Sofala on the east coast[2] and began to explore the interior. They traded with the central African rulers, but established no permanent contacts. Every attempt by the Portuguese to conquer the interior was foiled by the Rozvi who successfully maintained their independence.

Centuries later, however, the Rozvi suffered defeat, not by Europeans but by other Africans who moved northward from South Africa. In 1834 a Nguni army defeated the Rozvi and killed the last king on their northward migration to Malawi.[3] A few years later another South African tribe, the Ndebele, arrived and settled permanently to the west of the now shattered Rozvi kingdom. The

---

[1]Cf. Summers, 1960, 1961; Stokes and Brown, 1966, Abraham 1960, Davidson, 1964, Gann, 1965 *et alia.*
[2]Davidson, 1964, p. 146.
[3]Tindall, 1968, p. 63.

Ndebele kept their neighbours in subjection through frequent raiding parties. The once flourishing kingdom of the Rozvi disintegrated.

During these turbulent years other Europeans[4] came into the country. This time they arrived not from the east but from the south. They came not as conquerors but as isolated traders, hunters and missionaries. Soon they were joined by prospectors and concession hunters. Most of these early inter-racial contacts were of a fleeting nature. Because the early explorers did not make demands on their hosts, they were well received by the Africans.[5] Most of them begged for the favour to be allowed to engage in some economic enterprise or to teach a new religion to the people. All were utterly dependent on local rulers and paid them respect, even when they were repelled by local customs.[6] African rulers, on their part, welcomed the services rendered by the strangers, but reduced their contact with the people to a minimum because they were determined to preserve their traditional way of life.[7]

During these early contacts, therefore, no acculturation took place. Banton's observation that initially contacts are controlled by local leaders who mediate with the newcomers on behalf of their followers, is confirmed by the early interracial encounters in the country between the Limpopo and Zambezi rivers.

A change occurred in the 1890s when Europeans began a planned occupation of the country. Under the leadership of Cecil Rhodes, a pioneer column entered the country from South Africa in order to settle permanently. In 1893 the settlers came into armed conflict with the Ndebele and defeated them in battle. Soon the eastern neighbours of the Ndebele, whom the Europeans called Shona, also rose in rebellion and war continued for many years. Europeans gained a major victory over the Shona in 1896/7, but uprisings occurred intermittently until 1903.[8] Finally the conquest was complete and European domination was recognized by the indigenous population. The victory over the African people had been won through superior weapons, and military strength guaranteed the newcomers their subsequent political control over the country. They named the country Rhodesia.

[4]The word 'Europeans' in Rhodesia refers to persons of European ancestry, whether born in Europe, America or Africa.
[5]Selous, 1881.
[6]Cf. Gelfand, 1968, pp. 41, 138.
[7]*Ibid.*, p. 116.
[8]Ranger, 1968, p. 216.

The European population grew steadily in strength. Until 1923 Rhodesia was ruled by the British South Africa Company; then the country became a self-governing colony of Great Britain. Rhodesia, founded through conquest, was opened up as an economic enterprise. The control of the home government was always remote so that paternalism could never fully establish itself. Local settlers were strong and strove successfully to build up a dominative order. Throughout the 1920s and 1930s settler interests ranked first in Rhodesia.[9] During these years lasting racial attitudes were formed.

Due to the world-wide depression in the early 1930s, Europeans were fighting for their economic survival and jealously guarded their privileged position against African encroachment. Various Acts were passed to protect Europeans from African competition.[10] In town and country alike, Europeans lived in racially segregated areas[11] and certain occupations were in practice, though not by law, reserved for Europeans.[12] European farmers were given advantages over African producers[13] and these advantages prevented Africans from competing for restricted markets. These and other regulations ensured that a great cultural and economic gulf separated the races. Africans and Europeans lived in different worlds, although they inhabited the same country. During these years race became a role sign,[14] determining economic, political and social privileges, and a caste system crystallized in Rhodesian society.[15]

[9]Leys, 1959, pp. 70–1; and Palmer, 1968, pp. 47–51.

[10]*The Land Apportionment Act*, cap. 257, passed in 1931, severely restricted the right of Africans to purchase land and so brought about a division of Rhodesia into European and African areas. The most fertile land had already been allocated to European farmers (Palmer, 1968, pp. 20, 26, 28) and so the competition of African peasants for markets was greatly restricted.

The Industrial Conciliation Act, cap. 246, passed 1934, provided for the creation of industrial councils to protect the interests of employees. It explicitly excluded Africans from the definition of 'employee'. By fixing a standard wage, irrespective of the colour of the employee, it prevented Africans from performing skilled and semi-skilled work because no European employer willingly employed an African if he had to pay him the same wage as he would have to a European.

[11]*Land Apportionment Act*, 1931, amended 1941, Chap. 257.

[12]*Industrial Conciliation Act*, 1934, amended 1945.

[13]Cf. Maize Control Board and the segregation of the domestic market for maize during the depression, Leys, 1959, p. 71.

[14]I.e., a mark by which people are told the appropriate behaviour towards another person. Cf. *supra*, p. 3.

[15]This caste system, like the Indian caste system, was marked by the concept of pollution. Contact with Africans defiled the higher caste of Europeans. For a similar situation in American society cf. Davis, 1967, p. 385.

During the ten years between 1953 and 1963, when Rhodesia formed part of the Central African Federation, attempts were made to replace the dominative order, which had become firmly established south of the Zambezi river, by political partnership. Some Africans were admitted to parliament, some discriminatory laws were repealed, and efforts were made to reduce the social and economic gap between the races.[16] Some Rhodesians, and especially the British Government, expressed the hope that colour would lose its importance in Rhodesia and that a greater integration of the races might be achieved. This hope, however, was not shared by the vast majority of white settlers. A survey of racial attitudes, carried out in Rhodesia in 1959, revealed that although official government policy favoured racial co-operation, white Rhodesians did not. Rogers and Frantz found that if individuals were not compelled by government to accept the new policy of partnership, 'the direction of change would be toward an increasing amount of segregation and differentiation'.[17]

Rogers and Frantz concluded their work with pointing out three alternatives for future race relations in Rhodesia: (1) Biracialism, which seemed to be preferred by the majority of Europeans; (2) Uniracialism or non-racialism which was supported by very few Europeans indeed; and (3) Multiracialism, a concept which nobody was able to define but which seemed to imply a planned implementation of partnership between Europeans and Africans.[18]

With the defeat of the government party in 1962 which had led Rhodesia into the Federation, and the dissolution of the Federation in 1963, the policy of partnership was abandoned. Leys, who published his study on European politics in Rhodesia in 1959, observed that Britain's direct political role in Rhodesia had come to an end, that the immigrant settler community had effective power in the country, a power which was largely dependent on a discriminatory legal apparatus, and that there existed no possibility that the settlers would voluntarily share their power with the rest of the population.[19] This prediction was verified in the 1960s.

[16] *The African Land Husbandry Act*, cap. 103, passed in 1951, was implemented in the mid 1950s. It aimed at increasing African agricultural production by separating the African population into rural and urban dwellers, hoping that the men remaining in the rural areas would regard farming as a profit making vocation. Moreover, since the rapidly expanding industry of Rhodesia offered many jobs to urban Africans, government hoped that a permanent urban African community could be established.

[17] Rogers and Frantz, 1962, p. 238.   [18]*Ibid.*, p. 350.   [19]Leys, 1959, p. 294.

The new government party gradually withdrew its election
promises to allow members of all races to advance themselves
economically and politically in open competition.[20] In 1965 the
Prime Minister severed the country's ties with Great Britain and
declared Rhodesia an independent country. All pressure from the
home government to safeguard the rights of Africans was thereby
eliminated. Unexpected opposition by the world community to the
recognition of Rhodesia's illegal action isolated the country politically. Economic sanctions were imposed by almost all countries with
serious implications for continued economic growth in Rhodesia.

Under the double stimulus of the new government's policy, which
favoured separate development, and of economic hardship, Europeans quickly returned to their racial attitudes of the 1930s. Government declared community development, which had been started by
the previous government, to be a 'cornerstone of Government
policy'[21] by which African and European communities were to develop themselves along their own cultural lines, and according to their
own economic abilities. Segregation, especially in residential areas,
was to be intensified not only between Europeans and Africans, but
also between Europeans and other racial groups, such as Asians
and Coloureds.[22] Just as Government encouraged African culture
and separate development during the 1920s and 1930s,[23] so it did
during the 1960s. Government services were reorganized so that
one ministry[24] dealt with almost all aspects of African life, and African chiefs were given new powers.[25] As a consequence of these
changes, 'an "administrative" concept of race resulted in a dual division of government, partly to preserve the separate cultural communities and partly to minimize the possibility of competition and
conflict'.[26]

Such a return to the past required far-reaching constitutional

[20]The Prime Ministers frequently repeated the phrase 'advancement on merit'
during the early 1960s.
[21]Wrathall, 1969, p. 96.
[22]Cf. *The Rhodesia Herald*, 14.10.1968, regarding the Property Owners (Residential) Protection Bill. Coloureds are persons of mixed racial parentage, usually
of European fathers and African mothers.
[23]Rogers and Frantz, 1962, p. 334; Gray, 1960, pp. 3–42.
[24]The Ministry of Internal Affairs. Cf. *The Rhodesia Herald*, 14.3.1969,
1.5.1969, 8.5.1969; *The Sunday Mail*, 9.3.1969, 20.4.1969, 11.5.1969.
[25]*Tribal Trust Lands Act*, 1967, No. 9; *Tribal Law and Courts Act*, 1969, No. 24.
[26]This quotation comes from Rogers and Frantz, 1962, p. 334, writing about
the first half of this century. It is again applicable to Rhodesia in the 1960s.

changes. In 1965, the 1961 constitution was repealed. The new constitution made few alterations except those required by the newly independent status of the country. Yet many changes were planned. To prepare for these, a constitutional commission was appointed and instructed

to examine the provisions of the Constitution of Rhodesia, 1965, and . . . to advise the Government of Rhodesia on the constitutional framework which is best suited . . . and calculated . . . to ensure the harmonious development of Rhodesia's plural society, having regard to the social and cultural differences among the people of Rhodesia, to the different systems of land tenure and to the problems of economic development.[27]

The commission submitted its report in 1968 and in 1969 the government party published its 'Proposals for a New Constitution for Rhodesia', which were to a large extent based on the constitutional report. The same year the electorate voted in favour of the new constitution by an overwhelming majority of 72·5 per cent.[28]

The new constitution abolished the non-racial voters' rolls and fixed the number of African and European seats in parliament. In the future fifty of the sixty-six seats in the House of Assembly were to go to Europeans. The remaining sixteen seats were divided equally between the Ndebele and Shona speaking people, and in addition each of the two groups was to be further subdivided between African chiefs or their representatives and Africans elected by predominantly urbanized voters.[29] The 'Proposals for the New Constitution' state that the number of African parliamentarians can only be increased as the total amount of African income tax increases.[30] The probability of a rapid increase was practically eliminated when, a few weeks later, parliament presented its budget proposals which substantially increased indirect taxation to compensate for a reduction in direct taxation.[31] By 1969, therefore, Rhodesia was not merely divided between the different racial groups, but Africans were being divided along tribal lines and also according to residence; townsmen and rural inhabitants were to be separately represented in parliament.

[27]*Report of the Constitutional Commission*, 1968, para. 1.
[28]*The Rhodesia Herald*, 23.6.1969.
[29]*Proposals for a New Constitution*, para. 9.
[30]*Ibid.*, para. 10. This increase seems highly unlikely even under the most favourable economic conditions. Cf. *infra*, p. 25.
[31]*The Rhodesia Herald*, 21.7.1969 *et alia*.

European domination, first established in Rhodesia at the turn of the century, was again firmly entrenched in 1969. The terms of reference for the constitutional commission refer to 'Rhodesia's plural society'[32] and government policy in general stressed parallel development. Yet by 1969 Rhodesia could hardly be described as a fully developed plural society in Banton's terms because the power balance between the races remained unaltered. Internal stratification within the African community had merely begun. The relationship between Europeans and Africans in Rhodesia resembles that represented by Banton in his second diagram.[33] Europeans still controlled the political, economic and social life of the country and the new constitution was designed to preserve this power balance. It opens with the words: 'The Government believe that the present [1965] Constitution is no longer acceptable to the people of Rhodesia because it contains a number of objectionable features, the principal ones being that it provides for eventual African rule.'[34]

The 1969 Constitution ruled out even the possibility of a racially integrated society which was envisaged by some of the liberal leaders during the Federal period.

2. The demographic background of racial domination

(a) Growth in numbers

Apart from military conquest, European domination was promoted by certain demographic changes during the twentieth century. The country, covering some 150,820 square miles,[35] was thinly populated at the turn of the century. An estimate of the indigenous population in 1901 arrived at the figure 500,000. By that time some 11,000 Europeans and about 1,000 Asians and Coloureds had settled in the country.[36] This means that Rhodesia had a population density of three persons per square mile. Within seventy years the population grew to ten times its original size. The 1969 census counted 228,044 Europeans, 8,723 Asians, 14,809 Coloureds and 4,818,000 Africans; that is, Rhodesia had in that year a total population of 5,069,570.[37] During this period the proportion of Asians and

[32]Constitutional Commission Report, 1968, para. 1.
[33]Cf. Figure 1 (*b*) *infra*, p. 6.
[34]Proposals for a New Constitution, Introduction, p. 1.
[35]Rhodesia in Brief, 1969, p. 1.
[36]*1961 Census.*
[37]Provisional results: *The Rhodesia Herald*, 23.5.1969; 19.6.1969.

Coloureds in the population remained almost constant. Asians accounted for about 0·2 per cent of the population and Coloureds for about 0·3 per cent.

The proportion of Africans and Europeans in Rhodesia changed slightly in the course of time. In 1901 Europeans constituted 2·1 per cent of the population, in 1961 5·8 per cent, and in 1969 4·5 per cent. In 1901 Africans accounted for 97·8 per cent of all persons in Rhodesia, in 1961 for 93·7 per cent,[38] and in 1969 for 95 per cent. Throughout the century, therefore, Africans provided the majority of inhabitants, but their proportion declined slightly over the first sixty years of European rule when the country prospered, but increased once political uncertainty arrested economic progress.

The absolute number of Europeans in Rhodesia, which over seventy years increased to twenty times its original size, contributed to European political dominance. Table 1 sets out the population increase of the major races of Rhodesia since 1901.

Year	Europeans[39]	Africans[39]	Total population[39] (including Asians and Coloureds)	Proportion of Africans to Europeans
1901	11,032	500,000	512,000	45 : 1
1911	23,606	740,000	770,000	31 : 1
1921	33,620	860,000	900,000	26 : 1
1931	49,910	1,080,000	1,130,000	22 : 1
1941	68,954	1,400,000	1,480,000	20 : 1
1951	135,596	2,170,000	2,320,000	16 : 1
1961	221,504	3,550,000	3,790,000	16 : 1
1969	228,044[40]	4,818,000[40]	5,069,570[40]	21 : 1

Table 1. Population growth in Rhodesia

European population increase was especially rapid since the second World War and during the period when Rhodesia formed part of the Central African Federation. The more liberal government policies towards Africans during these years may have been influenced by the greater numerical strength of the European population. Numbers always mean power, but they are still more crucial in a situation where the dominant group is by far outnumbered by

[38]*1962 Census.*   [39]*1961 Census,* p. 3.
[40]*The Rhodesia Herald,* 23.5.1969; 19.6.1969. Between 1961 and 1969, the European population increased by 6,540 persons. During the period the natural increase of the European population, according to government statistics, was 21,000. Consequently, there has been a net loss of 14,460. *The Rhodesia Herald,* 31.10.1969.

an indigenous population. European confidence in its dominant position grew as its proportion in relation to the African population increased. At the time Members of Parliament anticipated that by 1984 Europeans and Africans might reach numerical parity through rapid European immigration, but this hope did not materialize. With a ratio of sixteen Africans to one European in the late 1950s and early 1960s, Europeans had reached the height of their demographic strength.

A reversal of this trend in the 1960s indicates a decline in European security. As the proportion of Africans towards Europeans reached the level of the 1930s, Europeans saw their dominant position endangered and embarked on an intensive campaign to attract European immigrants.[41] In many spheres of life the country returned to the conditions of the 1930s, for demographic trends and economic and political developments are closely linked.[42]

Throughout the century, European population increase has been due rather to immigration than to the rate of natural increase. In 1961 there were eighteen births per thousand European women. At the same time the European population had a death rate of six per thousand, and therefore a natural rate of increase of 1·2 per cent. At this rate of growth, the European population would double only once every sixty-five years. Between 1965 and 1969 Rhodesia attracted far fewer immigrants than in the preceding decade, and this accounts for the smaller percentage of Europeans in the total population. Because of the very low rate of natural increase, the importance of immigration, and the ease with which Europeans emigrate again,[43] European population growth depends to a very high degree on the political stability of the country.

African population increase, on the other hand, is almost exclusively due to natural increase and therefore independent of external circumstances. With a birth rate of forty-eight per thousand, death rate of fourteen, and therefore a natural rate of increase of 3·4 per cent, the African population doubles every twenty years. It is

[41] *The Rhodesia Herald*, 12.3.1968; 14.10.1968; 20.12.1968 *et alia*.

[42] Erikson notes: 'Where a group's socio-economic status is in danger, the implicit moral code becomes more restricted, more magic, more exclusive, and more intolerant, as though an outer danger had to be treated as an inner one' (1968, p. 55). This observation, together with the reference to separate development under the 1969 Constitution (*supra*, p. 14), indicate that race relations in Rhodesia are likely to follow stereotyped patterns.

[43] Especially to South Africa.

likely to grow consistently for the foreseeable future, irrespective of European policies. Consequently by their very numbers Africans present an ever greater challenge to European domination.

African immigration, mainly for the purpose of temporary wage labour, has not only dropped considerably since 1965, but many more Africans leave Rhodesia than enter it. Thus Rhodesia lost 33,500 Africans through net migration between 1965 and 1969,[44] and yet the African population increased greatly.

(b) Geographic distribution of racial groups

Neither absolute population growth, nor proportionate growth of the races in Rhodesia, give a complete picture of demographic power in Rhodesia. The geographic distribution of the racial groups is of key importance.

Between 1901 and 1969 the population density increased from three persons per square mile to thirty persons per square mile. Whereas at the turn of the century, therefore, the country was exceedingly thinly populated, by 1969 it was still underdeveloped in comparison with developed countries. The low average population density, however, gives a misleading picture because it assumes that the population is evenly distributed throughout the land. In fact, the population clusters in certain areas whereas others have still very few inhabitants. This uneven population distribution is the result of the Land Apportionment Act[45] which divided the country into areas reserved for the exclusive use of Africans, and into areas exclusively reserved for Europeans. Throughout this century blocks of land have been shifted from one land category to another; new land categories created and abolished again, but on the whole a consistent picture emerges which is set out in Table 2.

Unfortunately the rural—urban distribution of Africans and Europeans is not available for the early decades of this century. According to the general accounts, the figure of Africans in rural areas has always been below the figures given in Column 3 because many Africans lived always as squatters on European farms. But as the years passed ever larger numbers of Africans lived outside their villages. In the early 1960s, 23 per cent of all Africans lived in European farming areas and 18 per cent in towns.[46]

[44] *Migration Statistics*, 1969, p. 12.
[45] *The Land Apportionment Act*, cap. 257, amended 1941.
[46] *1962 Census*, p. 9.

Year	Persons per square mile	Land set aside for Africans[1] (square miles)	Population density in African areas		Land set aside for Europeans[1] (square miles)	Population density in European areas	
			(de jure)	(de facto)		(de jure)	(Europeans in European rural areas[3])
1901	3	*	*	*	*	*	*
1911	5	*	*	*	*	*	*
1921	6	33,900	25·4	*	76,600	0·4	0·3
1931	8	45,600	23·7	*	77,000	0·6	0·3
1941	10	46,200	30·3	*	74,400	0·9	0·6
1951	15	47,700	45·5	*	75,200	1·8	1·0
1961	25	65,800	54·0	31·8	56,000	4·0	1·0
1969	30	70,900[2]	67·9	45·8	70,900[2]	3·2	1·0

Table 2. Land distribution and population density in Rhodesia

* Not available.

[1] Derived from the Second Report of the Select Committee for the Resettlement of Natives, 1960, pp. 8 and 15.

[2] Derived from the Proposals for the New Constitution, 1969, para. 75.

[3] This is not the *de facto* population because it excludes African farm labour. In 1969, 918,000 Africans worked on European farms, that is, they increased the population density of European rural areas from 1·0 to 13·9. *The Rhodesia Herald*, 31.10.1969.

N.B. The total land surface of Rhodesia is 150,820 square miles. The remaining land, not contained in this Table, was until 1969 open for settlement by all races or consists of National Parks.

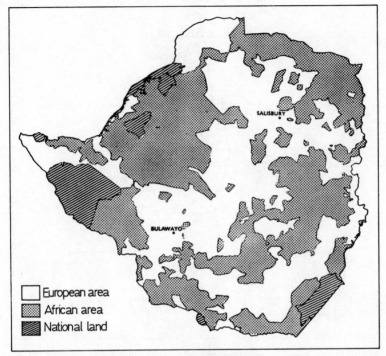

Figure 2. Map of the Land Tenure Act, 1969

Europeans too were more rural in the past than they are in the 1960s and 1970s. Whereas in the 1930s some 50 per cent of all Europeans lived in rural areas, in the 1960s only about 25 per cent lived in the country.[47] This rural–urban distribution of the races greatly affects the pressure on the land in African and European areas.

Table 2 shows that whereas European rural areas are still very thinly populated, African areas experience population pressure. Primitive agricultural techniques in African areas and modern farming techniques in European areas intensify the results of this uneven distribution of the people on the land and cause acute land shortage in half of Rhodesia.

In the rural areas Europeans are outnumbered by Africans by eighty to one.

[47]*Rhodesia: Its Natural Resources*, 1965, pp. 20–1.

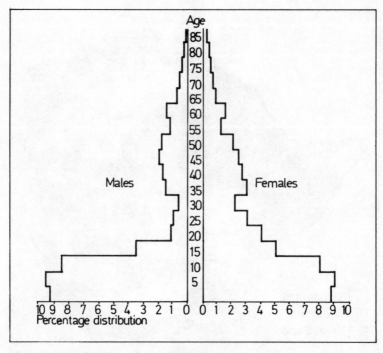

Figure 3. Population pyramid of indigenous population in tribal areas
(source of Figs 3 and 4: Kay, 1964, p. 17)

But even towns, which accommodate three-quarters of all Europeans, are predominantly black. Towns are the centres of industry and power. They are controlled by Europeans, but by Europeans who require a large number of African employees. The large African labour force with their dependants accounts for three-quarters of the urban population. In 1964 24·6 per cent of the total urban population was European and 73·4 per cent African.[48]

This geographical distribution of the races in Rhodesia shows that some areas are densely populated, others are thinly populated and that Africans, but not Europeans, suffer from land shortage. In spite of the uneven racial distribution in segregated areas, Europeans are everywhere outnumbered by Africans.

[48]*Rhodesia: Its Natural Resources*, 1965, p. 21. Asians and Coloureds, who are predominantly urban, account for the remaining 2 per cent.

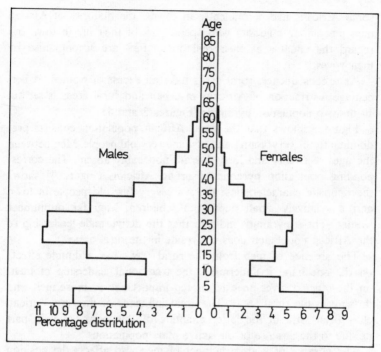

Figure 4. Population pyramid of absentees from tribal areas

(c) The social effects of the uneven population distribution in town and country

The centres of European power in Rhodesia lie in the towns where Europeans are outnumbered by Africans by only three to one. There, political and industrial power are concentrated and from those nodal points of power Europeans control the rest of the country in which they are outnumbered by eighty to one.

The influence of Europeans in rural areas depends on the backing they receive from the urban power centres. Yet even in the country Europeans exercise a dominant influence because they are well organized. Apart from farmers, the majority of Europeans in the rural areas are civil servants and missionaries, and by their profession these men occupy positions of leadership among their African neighbours. Their influence is further increased by the uneven sex distribution of Africans between town and country. For though some Africans live permanently in towns, the majority of African men are labour migrants who spend part of their life in town but regard the country as their real home. Few are accompanied by their wives.[49]

As a consequence, rural areas have an excess of women. A percentage distribution of Africans in urban and rural areas is set out in the two population pyramids (Figures 3 and 4).

Figure 3 shows that the rural African population consists predominantly of very young and of some very old people. Men between the ages of twenty and forty-five are noticeably absent. The corresponding population pyramid of urban Africans (Figure 4) shows the opposite characteristics: there are very few old people in town and a relatively small number of children. Men far outnumber women. These pyramids indicate that the active male leadership of the African population does not reside in the rural areas.

The absence of men from the rural areas has a double effect: on the one hand it undermines the traditional leadership of men; on the other it gives an exaggerated importance to those men who do stay in the rural areas. The great influence of the rural African elite, dealt with in the latter chapters of this book, may in part be due to the absence of the active male population.

The absence of a great number of men also affects the position of Europeans in rural African areas because the relationship between powerful outsiders and either a virile male population or a population consisting predominantly of women, children and old people who are unlikely to challenge their leadership, must obviously be different in character.

3. The economic background of racial domination

The economic system of a country can be arranged in such a way that a social order is created which keeps one group in constant dependence on another. Once such a system has been established subsequent legislation can perpetuate this dependence by granting special privileges to one group and by barring members of the other group from remunerative occupations. It has been mentioned

[49]The Africans' attitude towards town life is changing. By 1964 already 35 per cent of urban Africans were women. Whereas in 1958 the sex ratio of urban Africans was still one woman to 2·35 men (Rogers and Frantz, 1962, p. 15), in 1964 it had fallen to one woman to 1·85 men.

above[50] that during the 1930s legislation was passed which did not encourage the economic development of Africans and so preserved a wide gap in wealth between the races.

Partly because of the segregation of the races in special areas, partly because of unequal occupational opportunities and privileges, a dual economy evolved in Rhodesia which consists of a sector comprising African rural areas where the majority of peasants follow traditional farming techniques and produce an average annual gross output per family of less than £50,[51] and of a highly developed industrial sector, controlled by Europeans, in which all races participate but in which the average European earns an annual income of £1,360 and the average African of £138.[52]

These two sectors are not isolated from each other because at any one time 45 to 50 per cent of all rural African men are absent from their homes in search of European employment. Through their wages earned in the industrial sector they contribute substantially to the annual income of their rural families. Consequently many modern industrial goods find their way into rural African areas. The need of the industrial sector for African labour, and the need of rural Africans for additional income, keep the two sectors closely dependent on each other.

The two sectors make very uneven contributions towards the national income of Rhodesia. Table 3 sets out the contributions of

	African agriculture		Modern industries		Total gross domestic product	
Year	£million	Per cent	£million	Per cent	£million	Per cent
1954	14·6	8·7	153·9	91·3	168·5	100·0
1958	16·7	6·7	232·4	93·3	249·1	100·0
1962	19·3	6·4	282·2	93·6	301·5	100·0
1967	26·8	7·3	342·6	92·7	369·4	100·0

Table 3. Contribution of African agriculture and modern industries towards the gross domestic product[53]

[50] *Supra*, p. 10.

[51] Data derived from a sample of over a hundred peasant families in 1967. Yudelman states that in 1958 the gross output per peasant family in Rhodesia was £80. Consequently there has been a drop in productivity (1964, pp. 90 and 261). Cf. also Holleman, 1968, p. 59, for similar findings.

[52] Cf. Table 4, *infra*, p. 24.

[53] *Economic Surveys*, 1965, p. 48; 1967, p. 11.

African agriculture and of modern industry towards the gross domestic product since 1954.

Table 3 shows that although African agriculture almost doubled its output since 1954, its contribution towards the national economy remained as low as 7 per cent. It succeeded in providing the rural African population with their most basic foodstuffs, yet for any additional goods and food Africans remained dependent on the industrial sector. But for wage employment the rural population could not pay for vital goods and services.

In the industrial sector, too, Africans earn far less than Europeans so that even by working for Europeans in addition to cultivating their land they are unable to bridge the gap in income which separates them from Europeans and so prevents them approximating to European living standards. Table 4 sets out the employment opportunities and earnings of Africans and Europeans derived from the industrial sector.

	Africans		*Europeans*[54]	
Year	*Number in employment*	*Average earnings in £*	*Number in employment*	*Average earnings in £*
1954	555,000	65	64,400	884
1958	628,000	88	84,600	1,091
1962	616,000	110	88,500	1,186
1967	605,000	138	90,900	1,361

Table 4. Employment opportunities and average earnings of Africans and Europeans in the industrial sector[55]

Table 4 is characterized by three important differences:

(*a*) Africans by far outnumber Europeans in employment. This was already indicated by the previous demographic distribution of the races which showed that even in towns Africans outnumber Europeans by three to one. Throughout this period 87 to 88 per cent of the total labour force in the industrial sector were Africans. This means that the Rhodesian industry has been built up and is sustained by the joint effort of both races.

(*b*) Though Rhodesian industry relies on the contributions of both Africans and Europeans, the part which each race plays in the

[54]Includes a small number of Asians and Coloureds; separate figures for Europeans are not available.
[55]*Ibid.*, 1965, pp. 55–6; 1967, p. 11.

industrial sector is very distinct. The dominant position of Europeans and the subordinate position of Africans is shown by the wage gap in incomes between Africans and Europeans. Whereas in 1954 the average European earned £819 more than the average African, in 1967 he earned £1,223 more. In absolute amounts of money income the gap between the races widened. Yet if the income of Africans is expressed as a proportion of the European income, the gap may be said to narrow slightly, for whereas in 1954 a European earned fourteen times as much as an African, in 1967 he earned only ten times his income. Whatever view is taken, the figures indicate that the living standards between the races continue to differ very widely and the distribution of the national income preserves the dominant position of Europeans in the economic and political fields.[56]

(c) Table 4 also shows a constant drop in African employees since 1958. This decrease affects a large number of rural families whose husbands and brothers had contributed to their upkeep through sending them remittances. This fall in employment opportunities affects more than 23,000 families, as indicated in Table 4, because between 1958 and 1967 the African population increased by approximately 1·8 million people, and a significant proportion of these are potential wage labourers. Consequently in the 1960s there was a much larger number of African rural families living in great need than in the 1950s. Moreover, since the number of African employees has fallen, but the earnings of those still in employment has risen slightly, greater differences in living standards begin to appear in the African population than existed in the past.

Any stratification of Rhodesian society must take into account the great economic gulf between Africans and Europeans. In relation to the African people all Europeans form an elite. But even within African society economic differentiation marks a cleavage between rich and poor, as the above statistics indicate. Not only do Africans engaged in the industrial sector differ greatly in wealth from those engaged exclusively in peasant agriculture, but also Africans employed in the industrial sector earn greatly different incomes. The majority of African wage labourers do not earn much more than they do from their land, but if they cultivate land in addition to their wage employment, their wages double their annual income.

[56]Cf. *supra*, p. 13. Parliamentary representation depends on the amount of income tax paid by Europeans and Africans.

The reason for their low wages in the industrial sector is that 40 per cent of all African employees are engaged in European agriculture and 15 per cent as domestic servants, occupations which pay very low wages. In 1967 Government fixed the rate for African farm labourers at £3 per month, with an annual increment of ten shillings.[57] The typical annual income of a farm labourer is £48. Domestic servants earn on the average about £5 per month, that is, some £60 a year.[58] The great number of farm labourers and domestic servants reduces the average earning power of Africans in European employment. The average figure of £138 per annum is therefore misleading. Whereas the majority of Africans live in poverty, a few enjoy a relative affluence. The latter form a sub-elite or even an elite. The later chapters of this book are concerned with some of the men and women in these occupations.

In view of the uneven distribution of wealth, Rhodesian society can be viewed as a three-tier system. The top tier consists of Europeans, the middle tier of the new African elite, and the bottom tier of the African masses, whether they are in unskilled employment in the industrial sector or whether they live as peasants in the rural areas. The break between the second and the third tier is gradual and less significant than the break between the first and second tier which can never be bridged for, as Banton shows, the colour line cannot be crossed in a society in which one race dominates another, or in which two races live side by side because of an unwillingness to integrate.

4. The educational background for European economic domination

Apart from privileges and disabilities created by custom or law, the uneven distribution of the national income between the races is due to the different skills which Africans and Europeans bring to the labour market, and the differences in skills in turn are the result of different educational opportunities available to the two races.

Unequal educational opportunities are due to two factors: to the

---

[57]Government ruled that the total monthly wage paid out to an African farm labourer may not exceed £5. In addition to their wages, most farm labourers receive free food, some work clothing and accommodation, and occasionally free primary schooling for their children.

[58]A private survey of a Rhodesian town, including 25 per cent of all domestic servants, gives the average monthly wage as £5, plus free food, uniforms and accommodation.

government's claim that it is unable to spend large sums on education because the economy cannot afford it, and also to an unwillingness to expand African education because a greater influx of educated Africans into the labour market would upset the balance of power. If more educated Africans entered the labour market, pressure would be exerted to offer occupations, generally held by Europeans, to Africans, or the large number of trained but unemployed Africans could lead to political unrest. Consequently there is a tendency to gear the African educational output to the job opportunities which Europeans are willing to offer to Africans.

Approximately 2 per cent of the Gross Domestic Product are annually spent on African education, and an almost equal amount on European education.[59] This means that government spends annually some £8 for every African child in school, and some £120 for every European child. In 1969 the Minister of Education defended this policy in parliament by arguing that if the education votes for both races were added together and divided equally among all school children, only £9 extra could be spent on every African child, while every European child would be deprived of £98 a year. He concluded: 'The benefit to the African would not be great but the effect on the European would be disastrous.'[60] He expressed fear that if such a policy were introduced, Europeans would leave the country in order to assure a suitable education for their children. This would mean a decrease of the European population and therefore a decline in European power.

In spite of this policy, however, African education in Rhodesia has progressed faster than in most African countries. The contribution of Christian missions is to a large extent responsible for the development of the African education system, because by 1967 90 per cent of all African children were in private, mainly mission, schools and only 10 per cent in government schools. In the same year only 17 per cent of all European children were in private, but 83 per cent in government schools.[61] Government contributed to the running of private African schools mainly by paying teachers' salaries. Other contributions towards school maintenance were minimal. A substantial contribution towards African education has also

[59]In 1967 Government spent £6·6 million on Europeans and £7·5 million on African education. *Annual Report on Education for the year 1967*, p. 27; *African Education 1967*, p. 12.
[60]*The Rhodesia Herald*, 14.8.1969.
[61]*Annual Report on Education for the year 1967*, pp. 47, 58.

been made by African parents. The total investment in African education has therefore been greater than the government's education vote
indicates.

In 1969 government urged missionaries to hand over their primary schools to African rural councils[62] and expressed its intention
of taking over full responsibility for all African secondary education.[63] Missionaries as well as African parents were apprehensive
of this policy and resisted it as far as they could, for they realized
that the exclusion of missionaries from educational work among
Africans would greatly arrest the spread of African schools.

Europeans are divided in their attitudes towards African education. Many Europeans consider educated Africans a danger to their
own security,[64] and are therefore reluctant to encourage African
education. Missionaries, on the other hand, though themselves Europeans, generally press as hard for African education as Africans
do themselves. This split in attitudes towards African education
between missionaries and other Europeans, and its ramification into
other spheres of African advancement, is discussed in chapter three.

Extensive efforts are needed if Africans are to achieve an education equal to that of Europeans. The 1962 census revealed that 47
per cent of all African men born before 1946 had never been to
school; nor had 59 per cent of all African women of the same age
group.[65] A further large percentage had attended school for only a
few years and was practically illiterate. These men can fill none but
unskilled occupations. They provide a significant proportion of the
farm labourers on European farms and of domestic servants.

Different government policies for the education of African and
European children are reflected both in legislation and in school
facilities. In 1930 an Education Act was passed which made school
attendance compulsory for all European children between the ages
of seven and fifteen. School attendance is not compulsory for African children. Even in 1962 only 44 per cent of all African children
between the ages of seven and fifteen years were in school.[66] Some

[62]These councils are under the control of local Africans. They are the central
organ of the government's 'community development' policy which fosters the separate development of the races.
[63]*The Rhodesia Herald*, 22.8.1969.
[64]This has been thought throughout the century. Cf. for example Gray, 1960,
pp. 129, 138, 139 *et alia*.
[65]*Census 1962*, p. 28.
[66]*1962 Census*, pp. 17, 26.

of these had left school after a few years without completing their primary education, but others had never been to school. The 1967 annual reports for African and European education give the breakdown of final educational achievements for school leavers as contained in Table 5.

Education in years	Percentage distribution	
	Europeans[67]	Africans[68]
1–5	none	78·13
6–7	none	19·58
8–9	11·2	1·81
10–11	52·4	0·44
12–13	36·4	0·04

Table 5. Educational level reached by European and African school leavers

Table 5 shows that European children reach a very high average level of education. No child may leave school after primary education because all must be at least fifteen years of age. More than half of all European children attend school for ten to eleven years. This enables them to compete for most occupations in industry. Over a third of all Europeans complete a full secondary education which prepares them for university and future well-paid professions. Moreover, only some 4,000 to 5,000 European children annually leave school, and since all of them are well-educated and young adults they are easily absorbed into the Rhodesian economy.

Of the proportion of African children who are able to go to school at all, only a fifth complete primary education; less than 2 per cent are able to attend school for eight to nine years, less than half a per cent for ten to eleven years, and only 0·04 per cent complete secondary education. Most Africans with primary education are confined to unskilled, or at most to semi-skilled work. Those with junior secondary education, that is, those who attended school for nine years, try to find white collar employment, but few succeed. Those who have studied for eleven years are considered by the majority of Africans as 'educated people' and they themselves claim elite status. Since less than half a per cent of all students reach this level, their claim in relation to the African population is justified. In comparison with Europeans, however, they would never be regarded as members of an elite because almost all

[67]*Annual Report on Education for the year 1967*, p. 66.
[68]*African Education 1967*, pp. 21–2.

Europeans achieve an equal educational level. Only those who complete full secondary education and go on to university could claim elite status in Rhodesia. But as Table 5 shows, their percentage is very small indeed.

Annually some 40,000 African boys and 30,000 African girls leave school, and of these some 50,000 seek work. Only a few of them are successful, and the rest stay dissatisfied in the rural areas or swell the ranks of the unemployed in towns. Since even Africans with higher education experience great difficulty in finding employment, those who have received secondary education and secure appropriate employment are a very small minority. They are the more highly esteemed for their success because of the extreme difficulties encountered by Africans in improving their economic and social position.

5. Conclusion

The analysis of social stratification and opportunities for advancement presented in this chapter has shown that in Rhodesia race has become one of the most important factors determining a person's political rights, regulating his economic advancement and opening or closing to him educational opportunities. A European need exert little effort to hold down a well-paid job, but for an African to become a white collar worker indicates in most cases that he possesses ability and determination.

Through prolonged contact between the races, African culture has been modified. The introduction of a cash economy has drawn the African people into European employment. A western type of education has acquainted a significant section of the African population with European culture. As a consequence, the small minority of Europeans in Rhodesia has been able to influence the life of the African people. Its political and economic power has changed the African way of life. Yet this transformation has not integrated Africans into European society as equals but has kept them dependent on the dominant race. Banton's observations that a politically and economically stronger race will in situations of prolonged contact greatly influence a politically and economically weaker race, is borne out by the Rhodesian material.

In view of the partial transformation of the African way of life through cultural contact, it might be expected that Africans who have achieved elite status may become mediators in a nation-wide prestige hierarchy because they stand half-way between the European ruling class and the African masses. Through their early upbringing and family ties these Africans are still rooted in their traditional culture, but through their education they have become familiar with the values of western civilization, and through their higher income they are able to enjoy a living standard orientated towards that of Europeans.

But available literature shows that educated Africans are not generally accepted as mediators between Europeans and the African masses. In urban areas they are regarded with suspicion by members of the dominant race who have received little formal education themselves. Blumer writes: 'The entrance of members of a subordinate racial group as competitors in such arenas constitutes a challenge not merely to economic position but to social standing; hence such lines of competitive contact become focal points of racial discord.[69]

Little information, however, is available concerning the effect on race relations of an emergent African elite in the rural areas of a multiracial society. It might be argued that the few Europeans who stand in professional contact with Africans, such as administrators and missionaries, do not see their positions endangered by educated Africans and that they may therefore co-operate with them in their work. It might further be argued that the acquaintance of educated Africans with European values and their command of the English language be seized upon by administrators to facilitate their communication with the people they control. Moreover, since in the rural areas of Rhodesia, Europeans are outnumbered by Africans by eighty to one, it may be thought advisable for Europeans to cultivate friendly contacts with those Africans who stand closest to them in terms of cultural values. Since, finally, very few educated Africans reside permanently in rural areas, those who do are greatly respected by their own people and their influence is greater than it would be in an urban environment where more educated Africans live together. For this reason too it might be thought that the friendship of the African elite could appear desirable to Europeans whose function it is to communicate to Africans government policies and to enlist their co-operation for various purposes.

[69]Blumer, 1965, p. 229.

Seen from the angle of the African elite, such co-operation has also advantages. Europeans in rural areas provide a more effective reference group than do Europeans in town because contacts with them are more sustained, closer, and extending to more aspects of life than in towns where inter-racial contact, though more frequent, is impersonal and where roles are segmented. This holds true for contacts with missionaries as well as with civil servants and farmers. In the country, therefore, Africans have a better chance to get to know Europeans than do Africans in towns,[70] and if the new African elite should desire to model themselves on Europeans, as their behaviour often indicates, then inter-racial contacts in rural areas assume great importance.

[70]With the possible exception of domestic servants.

2. The European rural elite

1. The concept of elites for Rhodesian society

Chapter one showed that Rhodesian society forms a three-tier system in which the top tier consists of Europeans, the second tier of the emergent modern African elite and the bottom tier of the African masses. Most western societies are familiar with a class system, roughly falling into an upper class, a middle class and a lower class. Such a stratification, however, is not typical of the whole of Rhodesian society. A class system is an open system, allowing for mobility up and down the social hierarchy. Rhodesian society is not a real class system because no mobility is possible between the first two tiers though it is possible between the second and third tiers. On the other hand, Rhodesian society resembles in some respects a caste system because it keeps Europeans and Africans in exclusive social groups. But no caste barriers exist between the African elite and the African masses. In the strict sense of the word, therefore, Rhodesia does not qualify as either a class or a caste society; it is both and neither.

The difference in living standards and values of some members in the first and second tiers is smaller than the difference in values and living standards of some Africans in the second tier and the masses in the third tier. Moreover, Africans in the second tier are few in number. They accept Europeans as their reference group in many aspects of social life and are treated with great respect by the majority of the African people. Bottomore describes men of superior social groups as an elite.[1] It seems appropriate to use the term 'elite' to describe both Europeans in Rhodesia and those Africans who have acquired western values and prestige symbols.

According to Pareto, elites can be divided into governing and non-governing elites,[2] or into unified and divided elites. Bottomore

[1]Bottomore, 1964, p. 1.   [2]Pareto, 1935, pp. 1422–3 (Vol. 3).

33

describes the Russian elite and the elites of independent African countries as unified elites because in these countries the political office holders control all positions of prestige.[3] In contrast, Bottomore classifies the elites of western capitalist societies as divided elites because their interests diverge. In these societies members of the political elite are not necessarily members of the economic or religious elites.[4]

Rhodesian society may be viewed as a combination of both types of elite systems; when attention is focused on the black–white cleavage, all Europeans appear as a governing, unified elite, controlling the political, economic and social life of the country. There is a vast social distance between them and the African masses. A strict barrier exists which prevents members of the non-elite from joining their ranks.[5]

But when attention is focused on westernized Africans, that is, when the wider national picture is allowed to fade into the background and prestige positions in individual African communities are examined, some men and women stand out as a new elite, as a group of people who have acquired skills and talents differentiating them from the rest of the people. They enjoy positions of pre-eminence over all other Africans.[6]

These people, however, do not form a unified group. The strongest bond uniting them is their aspiration to European living standards and their frustration, if not at times opposition, to the caste barrier which denies them admittance into the reference group of their choice. But the forces dividing them are stronger than the forces uniting them. Their interests diverge. Highly westernized Africans with large salaries have different aspirations from Africans with less education. Members of the religious, educational, medical or civil service elites compete with each other for promotion. Their divergent interests prevent them from becoming a historical force.[7]

Of these two types of elites, the European elite is the more important, for, as Nadel writes, a governing elite is not just one among

[3]Bottomore, 1966, pp. 64, 70.

[4]*Ibid.*, p. 72.

[5]Nadel writes that there must exist barriers to guard the exclusiveness of an elite (1956, p. 415), but these barriers should not be absolutely insurmountable, lest the class system turns into a caste system.

[6]*Ibid.*, pp. 414–15.

[7]Cf. Mills, quoted in Bottomore, 1966, p. 29. To this may be added the dispersion of the African elite in rural areas. This too prevents them from becoming a coherent and powerful group. Cf. Lofchie, 1965, p. 90.

others, but its decisive pre-eminence lies 'in its fuller corporate
organization. It is first and foremost a ruling group, and only inci-
dentally an elite.'[8] Because it holds power in society, it is hostile
to the ideals and values of other elites. This description of a ruling
elite describes well the Rhodesian situation, and is examined in this
and the following chapters of this book. Later chapters analyse the
position and characteristics of the African elite.

2. The influential position of the rural European elite

If Europeans in general regard themselves as the governing elite
in Rhodesia, individual Europeans in rural areas are still more aware
of their leadership position because in their neighbourhoods they
constitute such an exceedingly small minority. Their experience as
a governing elite is fostered by their occupations. Apart from
farmers, whose sphere of authority is more limited and localized,
most Europeans living in the country fill positions of authority over
Africans. District commissioners from the ministry of Internal
Affairs are the direct representatives of government to the African
people; extension officers from the ministry of Agriculture[9] are civil
servants entrusted with the task of promoting the productivity of
African peasant farmers; missionaries do not rule in the same way
as do government officers, but they are very influential and highly
respected because practically all African education in the rural areas
has been in their hands. Different from these leaders, but also powerful,
are European farmers who employ 40 per cent of the African labour
force in Rhodesia. District commissioners, extension officers, missionaries and farmers represent four important groups of Europeans
whose occupations bring them into close contact with members of
the African race.

The scale of influence of these men differs and with this difference
in scale varies the objective power which members of this elite wield.

District commissioners have the widest influence because they
exert authority over a larger number of people than any of the other
members of this European elite. All but two district commissioners
of the sample survey,[10] including fourteen commissioners, were

[8]Nadel, 1956, p. 421.
[9]In 1969 extension officers working among Africans were transferred to the
ministry of Internal Affairs.
[10]Cf. Preface, pp. xi–xii.

entrusted with the administration of both European and African areas; two were in the exclusive charge of African settlements. The average district commissioner rules over some 89,000 Africans and 850 Europeans. The largest district included 175,000 people. The major administrative tasks of district commissioners are confined to African administration, and official administrative contacts with Europeans take up a relatively small portion of their working time.

Extension officers are in charge of smaller areas. The average extension officer in the sample holds himself responsible for the agricultural performance of some 7,000 peasant cultivators, that is, an African population of about 30,000 men, women and children. Only two of the fourteen extension officers interviewed regularly give advice to European farmers. Hence they too work almost exclusively for Africans. Their sphere of influence, however, covers less than one third of the sphere of influence of district commissioners[11] because their authority confines them to agriculture and does not extend to other spheres of the Africans' life, as does the authority of district commissioners.

The influence of missionaries is more difficult to gauge than the influence of civil servants. Half of those in the sample are engaged in teaching;[12] the others are engaged in full-time pastoral care. Each of these claimed to be in charge of some 12,000 Church members who live in a total population of about 110,000 Africans. This means that they work in an environment in which only 11 per cent of the people belong to their denominations. Most thought that their influence spread wider than Church membership. Only three, all of them Catholic missionaries, stated that they ministered to Europeans as well as to Africans. But the majority work most of their time for the African people, just as do most district commissioners and extension officers.

The European farmers' contact with Africans differs from the inter-racial contacts of civil servants and missionaries. Most of them meet Africans only as farm labourers. The average farmer in the area of study, owns a 10,000 acre farm, and employs some thirty

[11]The above figures indicate that the average district commissioner ruled over some 89,000 people and the average extension officer gave advice to peasants in a population of some 30,000 people.

[12]All missionaries surveyed in this study are ordained priests or ministers of their denominations, even if they are mainly engaged in teaching. Unordained missionaries, such as 'Brothers' in the Catholic Church who mainly work as craftsmen, or corresponding mission helpers in other denominations, are excluded.

Africans throughout the year, but doubles or even trebles their number during intensive labour periods. Yet the influence of farmers is not to be measured in relation to their employees. Several participate actively in the economic and political life of the European community as chairmen or other committee members of formal voluntary associations. One was a member of parliament. The farmers' life is wholly orientated towards the European rural community, however scattered it may be. Whereas civil servants and missionaries work directly for or with Africans, farmers work directly on their land, and African farm labour is one of the tools employed in their economic pursuit. On the other hand, their control over Africans living and working on their property is almost total. This different relationship to Africans puts farmers in a different category from civil servants and missionaries.

3. The self-evaluation of the European rural elite and their African stereotypes

Banton argues that members of a dominant race consider themselves inherently superior to members of a subordinate race, and Mills adds that 'people with advantages are loath to believe that they just happen to be people with advantages. They come readily to define themselves as inherently worthy of what they possess.'[13] It is possible that the Europeans' 'superman-attitude'[14] is due, as Mannoni argues, to a feeling of inner insecurity and inadequacy *vis-à-vis* fellow Europeans, but this is a question better answered by psychoanalysts. The present chapter examines the fact of the Europeans' belief in their superiority and its effects on race relations.

Each member of the European rural elite interviewed in this study was asked two sets of questions dealing with this topic. The first set dealt with their own view of the role they played in rural society and asked them to interpret their position. The second set included questions eliciting their views on the African character.

(a) District commissioners

Most district commissioners interpreted their role as that of administrator and added that they thought themselves efficient, firm and just. They considered that it was one of their most important duties to communicate government policies to the people, but several

[13]Mills, 1968, p. 14.　　　[14]*Supra*, p. 4.

added that these policies had originated with them, because the
higher echelons of the civil service relied on their information to
draw up new policies. Consequently they considered themselves directly responsible for the policies of their ministry. In addition some
district commissioners stressed their function as security officers
who guaranteed the peace of their districts.

Many emphasized the great mental strain under which they lived
due to the responsibility for the welfare of the people under their
charge. One said:

Our tremendous responsibility makes us nervous and worn out. A questionnaire sent round by the ministry found that 35 per cent of all district
commissioners suffer from stomach ulcers. I myself am riddled with all
tropical diseases. Worse than illness is that we are watched all the time.
Other Europeans can let themselves go occasionally, but a district commissioner is always obliged to act as a gentleman. As a result of these tensions
many of us have to retire before our time. It has been calculated that
40 per cent of all district commissioners die of a heart attack soon after
retirement. Our life expectancy is only sixty-four years, against the average
European's life expectancy in Rhodesia of seventy-two years.

A great number of district commissioners considered themselves
the most important men in their districts. One emphasized that he
was the Queen's representative at his outlying station and that his
house was called 'the residence'. This comment was made in 1968,
three years after Rhodesia's unilateral declaration of independence
and one year before the country voted for republican status. Only
a few held less elevated opinions of their own position and these
few generally lived in larger European communities, such as mining
districts. One district commissioner regarded himself as the odd man
out. He claimed to differ from his fellow Europeans because he felt
an obligation to re-think the moral values of modern times in order
to find a unique way in which to express himself in his work so
that he could leave an imprint on those who came under his charge.

The two most important characteristics emerging from the self-
evaluation of district commissioners which were revealed in the
interviews were therefore a great sense of responsibility which led
to the 'professional disease' of nervous tension, and a heightened
self-esteem. A feeling of mastery and deep satisfaction, which comes
from the recognition that an important task has been efficiently
handled, characterizes most district commissioners and marks them
as members of the ruling elite.[15]

[15]For a similar description of district commissioners see Holleman, 1968, p. 25.

By their own definition, therefore, as well as by virtue of their position, district commissioners are members of an elite, and this not only in relation to Africans but also in relation to fellow Europeans. Even the district commissioner who described himself as the odd man out considered himself superior to his neighbours, if not in terms of his social eminence then in terms of a moral code which he had evolved from his existential philosophy of life. He described himself as a prophet, an inspired man.

The image which district commissioners held of Africans was the very opposite of the image they held of themselves. Most district commissioners described Africans as happy-go-lucky, lazy,[16] fatalistic, afraid of change and over-concerned with their own security. One district commissioner said: 'The African has not yet become an individual. He is still totally submerged in his group.'

Most commissioners appreciated the Africans' good humour, their friendliness, courtesy, hospitality, cheerfulness and love of peace. But they complained about their lack of foresight, inability to think and to make decisions, their excuses for failure and their irresponsibility. One district commissioner summed up the list of African shortcomings by stating: 'Something seems to be missing in the African. He is unable to grow up.'

This African stereotype held by district commissioners reveals the value system of the district commissioners themselves: by describing Africans as lacking in responsibility and foresight they class them as lacking the very characteristics which they themselves claim to possess in a pre-eminent degree and to which they ascribe their high position. The statement that the African is 'unable to grow up' epitomizes their belief that Africans are inherently inferior to Europeans.[17] Because they regard Africans as yet immature people, they see themselves as guardians of African society whose welfare has been entrusted to them. One said: 'I have to carry the white man's burden.'

The district commissioners' stereotype of the African recalls the stereotype held by whites in the Southern States of America who regard the Negro as 'docile but irresponsible, loyal but lazy . . .

[16]One district commissioner answered: 'I suppose sociologists do not accept that a member of another race is lazy. They prefer the statement that Africans have a high leisure preference.'

[17]Cf. Lee, 1967, p. 126. In his study of the British Colonial Service in Africa Lee writes that colonial civil servants believed the native people to be incapable of learning.

his behaviour . . . full of infantile silliness and his talk inflated with childish exaggeration'.[18]

Similar behaviour has been observed among people of various races whose choices are severely limited.[19] The choices of Rhodesian Africans too are few. Stokes observes that the African south of the Zambezi is 'a regulated being'.[20] Hedged in by economic, political and social restrictions, it is very likely that the Africans among whom district commissioners work do in fact exhibit these characteristics and the district commissioners are accurate observers.

The relationship between district commissioners and Africans can be described as typical of a relationship between members of a dominant and a subordinate race. The distance between them is so great that direct association is almost exclusively limited to official contacts in which district commissioners are aware of their superiority. The general social distance between a senior administrator and ordinary people is here intensified by the different racial background of administrator and subject. Some district commissioners consciously dominate their surroundings, but the majority derive a feeling of responsibility from their high position and try to protect and guide Africans towards what they consider to be good for them. Most district commissioners claim that they 'like' Africans and appreciate their good qualities.

(b) Extension officers

Extension officers differed in their own role interpretation and in their attitudes towards Africans. The majority saw themselves as teachers and educators who have the duty to help Africans to raise their standards of living. Unlike district commissioners they did not make a bid for public recognition as community leaders, but rather stressed their role as technical advisers. Others stressed their supervisory functions over a team of African assistants. One of these called himself a personnel manager and another stated: 'I and my team link the African peasant with modern scientific research findings.' Most regarded themselves as one of the most underpaid sections of the civil service with no promotion possibilities. This reduced their self-esteem and so contrasted them strongly with district commissioners. Some reacted to their lack of social eminence

18Elkins, quoted in Banton, 1969, p. 129.
19*Ibid.*, p. 130.
20Stokes, 1964, p. 6.

by stating that they regarded themselves as rugged individualists who loved the life of the open veld and were unconcerned about social conventions.

The stereotypes that extension officers held of Africans over-lapped to some extent with the stereotype held by district commissioners. Several extension officers, however, emphasized the Africans' eagerness to learn. For them eagerness to learn meant an intellectual curiosity to know more about modern farming techniques. Consequently they disagreed with the district commissioners' judgment that Africans were unable to think. They agreed that Africans were very reluctant to implement what they had learned, but ascribed this less to laziness than to fear of the unknown. One stated: 'The African's conservation is a means of escape from the conflicting demands of modern life. The African is easy-going. But so am I. I would describe myself as an optimistic extrovert. Why should I exert myself if I can obtain my goals in life with less expenditure of energy? The African seems to think the same.'

Whereas some extension officers shared the district commissioners' evaluation of the differences between themselves and Africans, others stressed rather what they had in common. Consequently the attitudes of extension officers varied and no unified picture emerged, either of their own role or of their view of the African character.[21]

(c) Missionaries

Most missionaries regarded themselves as preachers, ministers of God, entrusted with the mission to save the souls of the African people. They thought of themselves both as teachers and servants of the people. Several stressed that they came as temporary visitors, ready to return to South Africa, Europe or America as soon as the indigenous Church had been established and their services were no longer needed. One stated with satisfaction that he worked under an African superior; he concluded that his goal in life had almost been achieved.

Missionaries, therefore, did not describe their role as one of dominance over the African people. They could not do so by virtue

[21]It is of interest to note that extension officers who claimed to be rugged individualists and emphasized their understanding of the Africans' dislike of exertion, were generally unco-operative with district commissioners. It is possible that their opposition to the administrators reduced the social distance between them and the Africans.

of their vocation, though in practice most filled positions of authority and all acknowledged their spiritual leadership among the Africans.

Their relationship with Africans is essentially different from that of district commissioners. Whereas the latter regard themselves as guardians of African traditions, missionaries by their vocation dedicated themselves to change the African value system. Many realize that to do this they have to change the social structure to which traditional values are closely linked.[22] To be conscious agents of change means that missionaries have to accept leadership positions. Their emphasis on service, therefore, does not obliterate the fact that they are members of the ruling elite, together with district commissioners and other Europeans.

Their role interpretation in African society, differing from that of district commissioners, gives rise to a different interpretation of the African character. It is difficult to discover a common stereotyped picture of Africans among missionaries. Most missionaries appreciate the African's cheerfulness, hospitality, optimism, eagerness to learn, his patience and his capacity for emotional response which, missionaries felt, is often lacking among Europeans.

When asked to state precisely which characteristics they thought described the African best, most missionaries emphasized the Africans' orientation towards their group without which they felt lost. Many added: 'Today the African has lost his dignity. We and all other Europeans are to be blamed for it because as grand paternalists we have constantly discriminated against them.'

Most missionaries were reluctant to admit any negative qualities in Africans. They admitted that Africans lacked responsibility, but ascribed this fault to a breakdown of their social system and consequent insecurity. Several stressed the African's lack of courage and his fear, but immediately excused these shortcomings by referring to the repressive laws of the country which held out restriction and detention to political dissidents. Their answers show that they concurred with the general stereotype of Africans, but tried to absolve Africans from moral responsibility for their character defects.

The missionaries' self-evaluation and their attitude towards Afri-

---

[22]Reformed missionaries differed in this respect from Catholic and Methodist missionaries. They did not intend to introduce any social change except in the religious sphere, though their teaching too had a transforming effect on African life.

cans imply a different relationship between them and the people than exists between district commissioners and Africans, or extension officers and Africans. A desire for domination, if it exists, is carefully concealed. Missionaries appear apologetic, blaming members of their own race, including themselves, for character faults they observe in the African personality. They seem more emotionally involved and to lack the detachment of the district commissioners in evaluating the people among whom they work. Many admitted this observation and claimed that they had identified themselves with the people and were determined to champion their cause.

(d) European farmers

If missionaries admitted to being emotionally involved with the people whose spiritual leaders they are, European farmers emphasized social distance between themselves and their African employees. Most European farmers saw themselves as paternal masters who looked after their African labour force well, but who in return for the wages they paid expected a fair share of work to be done. Only one, who grew up on his farm which his father had opened, had closer ties with his workers. He stated: 'I am their master, and yet I am one of them. I speak their language as well as they do, and as a youth I often accompanied them on beer drinks and hunts when I could escape my father's supervision. They don't forget this, and so I can ask more of them than most other farmers in the district.' But even he, as this statement shows, considered himself an exacting master.

This last farmer described Africans as dishonest, cruel and corrupt, but also as possessing a great sense of humour and a happy nature. He thought that this latter trait characterized Africans best. He observed: 'Sometimes, when I am with them, we laugh ourselves sick.' The other farmers agreed with his general evaluation. Most stressed the Africans' cheerfulness, their happy disposition and carefree life, but greatly deplored their utter laziness and irresponsibility. Some added that Africans were liars and thieves.

Since only one of them had contacts with Africans outside the labour situation on his farm, and since African farm labourers belong to the least educated section of the African people, none of the farmers was able to view the relationship between himself and Africans other than in terms of a master-servant relationship.

(e) Conclusion

The Europeans' definition of their own roles in rural Rhodesian society is that of leaders, whether in the administrative, economic or spiritual spheres. Most Europeans assumed explicitly, or at least implicitly, that they were superior to Africans. They recognized a great social distance separating them from the African people and often described Africans as possessing character qualities directly opposite to their own.

The African stereotypes held by Europeans were in agreement on the major characteristics attributed to Africans. But for the farmers' harsher judgments and the missionaries' excuses for African failings, all agreed that Africans were closely integrated into and identified with their social group and that individualism was unknown to them,[23] and that they were a cheerful[24] and friendly people, but a people that was lazy and irresponsible in its actions. This widely accepted stereotype governs Europeans in their contacts with members of the other race. Its consistency is not necessarily due to inherent qualities in the African character, as findings of other social scientists have shown,[25] but also, and to a great extent, to the subordinate position of Africans in Rhodesian society. In situations in which personal contacts are frowned upon, stereotypes regulate inter-racial behaviour and provide ready formulas on how to treat a member of the other race. Because stereotypes perform this useful function, they can maintain themselves even if personal experience contradicts the validity of the stereotype. For the individual who is better known will always be quoted as the 'exception' which confirms the rule that in general Africans are different.

[23]Cf. the missionaries' observation that Africans are group orientated and the district commissioners' claim that Africans were unable to grow up, that is, become individualized. But note also the observation that the African elite is divided (p. 34) and consists of members too individualistic to unite for a common purpose. This aspect of the African character is worked out in greater detail in the second half of this book.

[24]The interpretation of the Africans' cheerfulness, however, need not be accurate. Africans generally smile when they do not understand a European. They consider this the appropriate and polite behaviour. W. E. Abraham, writing about the African mind, states that laughter on the lips of Africans is evidence of their melancholy; that laughter is melancholy just as comedy is tragedy. Abraham, 1967, p. 102.

[25]*Supra*, p. 40.

(4) Relationships between members of the European rural elite

District commissioners, extension officers, missionaries and farmers differ in the extent to which they are in close contact with fellow Europeans. It may be assumed that their relations with Africans are affected by their exposure to the opinions of their white neighbours. The more isolated they are, the more independent they may be and the less affected by the sanctions imposed on them if they deviate from commonly accepted norms governing inter-racial contact. Table 6 sets out the geographical proximity of the fifty Europeans in the sample with each other and with Europeans in general.

Occupation	No European* neighbours	Some European* neighbours	Many European neighbours	Total
District commissioners	1	5	8	14
Extension officers	3	6	5	14
Missionaries	12	2	—	14
Farmers	—	—	8	8

* Apart from fellow civil servants or fellow missionaries respectively

Table 6. Geographical proximity of agents of change with fellow Europeans

Table 6 shows that apart from farmers, who live within completely European communities, though on isolated farms because of the low population density in their areas, district commissioners have the greatest number of white neighbours because their offices are frequently situated in larger European settlements, such as in administrative centres or mining districts. But some district commissioners are more or less confined to their civil service stations in predominantly African surroundings. The majority of extension officers live on such stations and almost all missionaries live in the centre of African areas. Very few missionaries have contacts with fellow Europeans outside their ministry.

Europeans who live in a community with members of their own race are dependent on their positive evaluation. Europeans who live as a small enclave in predominantly African surroundings may be expected to develop a strong group cohesion among themselves and to depend on the evaluation of their colleagues rather than on white opinion in general. The following data test this proposition.

Relations between members of the European rural elite are determined both by structural relations and by personality factors. In the eyes of Europeans, district commissioners occupy the most important positions in local communities. Consequently most hold clearly formed opinions about these administrators. The structural superiority of district commissioners gives rise to resentment and it also attracts further honours in the form of leadership positions in voluntary associations.

Resentment was most frequently expressed by fellow civil servants. Historical relationships between sections of the civil service are partly responsible for these strained relations. Until 1962 'Native Agriculture' formed a branch of the 'Native Affairs Department' and district commissioners were responsible for agricultural services. In 1962 both European and African agriculture came under one ministry, and the Department of Conservation and Extension took charge of African peasant cultivators. This removed extension staff from the control of district commissioners and gave them greater freedom. District commissioners lost control over African land use.

With the introduction of community development in the early 1960s and the Prime Minister's policy statement in 1965,[26] district conferences were established under the chairmanship of district commissioners. These conferences, which extension officers as well as all other civil servants have to attend, discuss local development projects and the co-ordination of available services. Many extension officers saw in these conferences a danger to their recently won freedom from the control of district commissioners. When in 1969 African agriculture returned to the Internal Affairs Department,[27] extension officers violently protested in the Rhodesian press and several left the service.[28]

To be effective in their areas, district commissioners must be able to obtain the co-operation of all civil servants at their stations. More than half of all district commissioners reported perfect co-operation, the others were less satisfied and some complained bitterly of opposition by extension officers.[29] They argued that the extension staff disregarded the general welfare of the district. They resented the extension officers' role concept as pure advisers and blamed them for deterioration in agricultural standards in African areas. One

[26]Prime Minister, 1965.
[27]Formerly called the 'Native Affairs Department'.
[28]*The Rhodesia Herald*, 14.3.1969, 1.5.1969, 8.5.1969; *The Sunday Times*, 9.3.1969, 20.4.1969, 11.5.1969.
[29]Cf. also Holleman, 1968, pp. 38–41, where he analyses the cause of the tensions between district commissioners and extension officers.

Plate I 47

Ia. A district commissioner discusses development plans with a chief and his council

Ib. An extension officer discusses a maize crop with one of his extension assistants

district commissioner stated: 'Extension officers won't punish Africans who do not follow their advice so that they can keep their white hands clean. They leave the dirty work to me.' Another was annoyed by the extension officers' emphasis on technology and their disregard for human problems and the traditional African social system. One district commissioner, commenting on opposition from extension officers, stated: 'The powers of destruction are at work.'

Extension officers felt even more critical of co-operation between themselves and district commissioners than did the administrators. Only two stated that relations were good, and three were indifferent about inter-departmental co-operation. The majority felt overtly opposed to administrators. Four were asked by district commissioners no longer to attend the district conferences because their presence was not desired. One extension officer summed up the general feeling: 'We are too lowly for district commissioners. They do not deign to associate with us.'

On small stations in rural areas district commissioners and extension officers[30] are often the only Europeans in an area and are therefore dependent on each other for their social life. If inter-departmental relations are strained, life on such stations becomes hard. District commissioners frequently regard themselves as fathers of their staff. One of them stated that he and his wife were clearly paternalistic towards their fellow civil servants, and another said that if any person at his station got sick, he would take him personally to the hospital because he held himself responsible for the well-being of all local Europeans. Most district commissioners regarded their homes as the social centres where other Europeans gathered for an evening drinking and sports.

The district commissioners' care for fellow civil servants was often resented by the agricultural staff. One extension officer commented: 'District commissioners take on more responsibility than they need and try to father us. We would rather look after ourselves.'

Where contacts with a larger number of Europeans are possible, for example, where nearby European farmers can be visited, district commissioners and extension officers are less dependent on each other and this eases possible tensions in their relationship. One extension officer said: 'District commissioners have much responsibility and have a standard to maintain. They are English gentlemen

[30]As well as some policemen.

who dress for dinner in the jungle. They have carefully built up their own image and now they must pay to maintain it. They cannot let themselves go or get drunk as we can.'

Relations between district commissioners and missionaries are less tension-ridden than relations between district commissioners and extension officers because the two groups do not have to associate as closely. Yet different ideologies between them sometimes lead to clashes. Most district commissioners stated that they had reasonably good relations with missionaries and one added: 'They have to co-operate with me; if they don't, they are the losers.' But some felt missionaries as difficult to deal with as extension officers. None of them regarded missionaries as very important. They thought that missionaries lived in a different, almost unreal, world.

Missionaries were divided in their attitudes towards district commissioners. About half of them felt indifferent towards them and regarded them as fair government officials with whom they had to co-operate whenever their work required. None had social contacts with them. The other half felt antagonistic towards them. A young missionary said: 'I dislike government and want no contact with any of its officials.' Another said: 'My people dislike district commissioners and so do I because I have completely identified myself with my people.' Others recorded past disagreements with district commissioners. One called them '*Gauleiter und Kommissare*', titles worn by German administrators during the Nazi government.

Just as the missionaries' evaluation of the African character showed great emotional involvement, so did their evaluation of district commissioners. Their geographical isolation in African areas as well as their missionary vocation may account for this. Missionaries seldom live close to civil servants and so are not involved in their social life. Most stated that their recreational life takes place within their own mission stations. Three missionaries seek occasional recreation with fellow Europeans, either by attending their social clubs or by visiting some European farming families. One occasionally travels twenty miles to the nearest town to enjoy leisure with other whites. A number have friendly relations with extension officers. But on the whole their contacts with Europeans are restricted. Several mentioned that other Europeans avoided them because of their championship of the African people.

The relationships between most district commissioners and

farmers were of a strictly offical nature. District commissioners claimed that many Europeans asked them for help even in those aspects of their lives which lay strictly speaking beyond the confines of their work. Most farmers emphasized a great social gulf between themselves and district commissioners. They stressed that their most frequent contacts with them derived from problems with their African labour force. They regarded district commissioners as too aloof and busy to approach easily. Even farmers who were very influential in their local communities felt that district commissioners looked down on them, and this they resented. They stressed that extension officers were much more sociable than district commissioners, and that even missionaries were easier to approach, especially if they belonged to their own denomination. Yet there were some district commissioners, living on lonely stations, who occasionally visited some white farmers for a game of bridge or for other social occasions.

These responses from Europeans in isolated communities give the impression that the European rural elite is divided among itself by tensions and divergent interests. Some of these tensions are reduced in larger communities whose individuals have a greater choice of social contacts.

In the larger settlements, district commissioners do not associate much with extension officers, nor do they seek out the company of missionaries. Most of them are social leaders, and outstanding Europeans such as mine managers and members of parliament vie with one another to invite them for dinner. One district commissioner reported that he was chairman of sixteen local committees and clubs. This enabled him to keep in close touch with the life of the European community. Another district commissioner in a similar position commented: 'Chairmanship on many committees enables me to keep my fingers on the pulse of the community.' Social leadership, therefore, appears to them at times to be both useful and subservient to their work as administrators.

These data of rural Europeans indicate that relations between the governing elite are hierarchically structured and that district commissioners occupy the command positions within the white rural elite. Their heavy involvements in voluntary organizations add a new dimension to their professional authority as senior civil servants, and their advice is frequently sought on important community issues. They form the upper stratum of the white elite.

The aloofness which district commissioners preserve in their contacts with other Europeans is reinforced by an intense *esprit de corps*. One district commissioner used no other name for his colleagues than 'my brothers'. Many referred to fellow district commissioners as 'we'. This terminology commonly used by members of certain high-ranking occupations, such as judges or regimental officers, indicates that many district commissioners set themselves apart as the very top elite in European rural society.[31]

All district commissioners stressed that although they were great individualists, they would always be able to pick out an unknown district commissioner, if such existed,[32] by his looks and behaviour. Several said: 'I would look for the most authoritarian person in a gathering and would be sure it would be the district commissioner.' Others said: 'He will be sure to talk shop, and be president or chairman of some committee.' Or: 'I would look for the man with the greatest frown.' Or: 'He will be the most lonely looking man because his job is one of such responsibility that he can never consult any of his staff, but must make all decisions personally and on the spot. This makes him very individualistic.' One district commissioner said with emphasis: 'The district commissioner is the inspired looking man who is often resented by the rest of his community.'

The high status accorded to district commissioners and their high opinion of themselves place them in a group apart. Not only they themselves, but also their wives are expected to live up to the ideal elaborated by their social circle. Whereas in most sections of Rhodesian European society it is common for wives to seek employment, none of the district commissioners' wives has taken up work. One district commissioner exclaimed in feigned horror when asked whether his wife was working: 'Consider her standing! She is the wife of a district commissioner. What would people say if she was working like an ordinary woman?' A district commissioner's wife is the first lady in many a European community. It is her function to entertain guests and, on smaller stations, to be responsible for a harmonious social life.

Extension officers claimed no special status in European society.

[31]For an excellent description of an outstanding district commissioner see Holleman, 1968, p. 229.
[32]In fact, all district commissioners in Rhodesia know each other well because the service is very small, including only fifty-two men in seven provinces.

They believed they possessed no characteristics which distinguished them from other Europeans and were unaware of forming a special group among themselves. They thought that they had often been together with other extension officers without realizing it. There exists no strong *esprit de corps* among them because many leave the service after a few years for employment in industries or to become farmers themselves. They consider themselves as 'ordinary' people who disappear in a crowd. Most of their wives work as secretaries to senior extension staff or to district commissioners. They often run African women clubs in which they teach African women cooking, sewing and hygiene. They often feel lonely at their stations and press their husbands to seek transfers to larger European settlements.

Missionaries fitted less easily into European life in large settlements than extension officers. They certainly did not occupy positions of prestige comparable to district commissioners. Some were well accepted by lay members of their own denominations. Others were directly excluded by fellow Europeans. One missionary commented: 'Whenever I come to the local European settlement to shop or to have my car serviced, I try very hard to establish friendly contact, but all whites withdraw from me because they know that our Church champions African economic and political advancement. I long for more contact with fellow Europeans but I cannot establish it.' Another missionary said: 'Long years in African areas without much contact with fellow Europeans makes one lose one's social graces.'

If missionaries are not fully integrated into white society because of their frequent identification with Africans,[33] they have intensive contacts with fellow missionaries with whom they share a common life and ideology. Through frequent visits between mission stations friendships are fostered and a deep mutal understanding, which contributes to the creation of a subculture among missionaries. This inward concentration goes still further in that missionaries of different denominations, such as Catholics, Methodists and Reformed missionaries, each evolved their own in-group culture. This is partly due to their particular interpretation of the Bible, partly to their national background, because the majority of missionaries from

---

[33]Reformed missionaries are different in this regard. They identify themselves with European, especially South African society, and are more often welcome in European homes.

each of these denominations come from different countries or even continents. Yet with the spread of ecumenism, differences between denominations have become less marked.[34]

European farmers live among fellow farmers. They form the majority of all Europeans in rural communities and so tend to determine the norms of inter-racial contacts and racial attitudes. They are not necessarily leaders because leadership positions tend to go to senior civil servants, but they are influential through their numbers.

The first part of the proposition that Europeans who live in a community with members of their own race are dependent on the positive evaluation of fellow Europeans can now be answered positively. Missionaries stand to some extent in a group apart. But because of their frequent isolation from fellow Europeans in predominantly African areas, they tend to develop a strong group cohesion and become more independent of the opinions of other Europeans. Civil servants, who temporarily live in small European enclaves in African areas, avoid such in-group tendencies because, as chapter four shows,[35] they are often transferred and so have many opportunities to mix with fellow Europeans.

The statuses of district commissioners, extension officers, missionaries and farmers in rural European society therefore differ widely, and the images which these groups have of each other coincide to some degree with the structural positions they occupy. When looked at from within their racial group, they do not form a coherent elite, though from the Africans' point of view these distinctions are not always as clearly visible. The question has therefore to be answered whether this internal differentiation is reflected in the relations of these Europeans with members of the African race, and whether members of the African race distinguish between members of the European elite in the same way as these do themselves.

5. Relations of the rural European elite with Africans

(a) The Europeans' evaluation of their relations with Africans

Most district commissioners judged their rapport with Africans as being reasonably satisfactory. Yet the young and old evaluated their

---

[34]Clergymen of the Reformed Church are an exception. They participate less in ecumenical activities than priests and ministers of other denominations.
[35]*Infra*, pp. 88–9.

relationships differently. The younger district commissioners emphasized their authoritative position more than the older district
commissioners and laid more stress on the Africans' duty to show
them deference. Many of the younger men stressed that they were
hard with Africans but that Africans appreciated their firmness.
They stated that they would not dare to find out what Africans
thought of them because this would be too discouraging. One said
frankly that he did not trust Africans and that they did not trust
him; another stated laconically that he had never yet had to carry
a weapon with him.

Most of the older district commissioners said with conviction that
they thought Africans liked and trusted them, and one stressed in
particular that he was well accepted by African chiefs. One was
more cautious. He said: 'They always say nice things to me, but
how do I know what they really think?'

In spite of their uncertainty about being accepted by Africans,
the younger district commissioners were generally convinced that
they made a tremendous impact on the African people and got them
moving in line with government policies. The older district commis-
sions stressed their successes more cautiously. They were reasonably confident that their work was slowly making an impact on the
people. The reason for the district commissioners' overall confidence
in influencing Africans lay in their power to back up their demands
by force should need arise. One district commissioner stated that
he had informed his chiefs that if they did not administer their areas
justly they would be deposed. Such gestures inspire fear in Africans
and most obey the district commissioners' orders, even if only reluc-
tantly.

All extension officers believed that they were trusted and accepted
by Africans. They thought that Africans appreciated their advice,
though they were less confident than district commissioners that
they made a great impact on the African people. Most thought that
they influenced strongly about 5 per cent of the peasant cultivators.
Unlike district commissioners they had no power to see that their
instructions were carried out. They were pure advisers and as such
could not directly order the implementation of better agricultural
techniques. This disengagement enabled them to take a more lenient
attitude towards Africans than administrators and made more cordial relations with Africans possible.

Most missionaries stated that their rapport with Africans was excellent. They believed themselves fully accepted and loved by the people who saw in them their priests and ministers. Several stressed that they thought Africans would go through the fire for them and added that so would they for Africans. Many considered Africans as their equals, and several felt bound to them by close bonds of friendship. No civil servant made a similar claim, but many civil servants denied that missionaries were as wholeheartedly accepted by Africans as they themselves claimed. But one Afrikaner missionary thought that his rapport with Africans was only moderately good; he was convinced that he would never fully understand men of another race. Another missionary of the Reformed Church stressed that there was such a basic inborn difference between Africans and Europeans that all that could be done was to accept members of the other race with tolerance and to make allowance for their differences.

The great majority of missionaries thought that they strongly influenced their people, and in order to prove their claim they pointed to increasing church attendance and the spread of voluntary church organizations; they also affirmed a deepening conviction of Christian truths among Africans. A minority was less optimistic. One believed that missionary work in Rhodesia had been a failure and that Africans would remain loyal to the Church only so long as they received social advantages from their membership. This latter is one of the oldest missionaries interviewed who has spent most of his life in Rhodesia. Since the authority of missionaries is supernatural rather than secular, it is difficult to compare its effectiveness with the authority and influence of civil servants.

Farmers thought of themselves as masters of their employees, or rather as feudal lords[36] who controlled the lives of their people and protected them when they were in need. Many considered themselves as the most important persons in their labourers' lives. They stressed that although district commissioners forbade them to try the court cases of their workers, they occasionally intervened to save their employees a trip to town. Their wives often assisted the Africans resident on their farms medically and frequently acted as midwives when their workers' wives were in labour.

Though all farmers stressed the social distance between themselves and their employees, most thought that they were reasonably

---

[36]An expression not used by the farmers but derived from their general statements.

accepted. All felt free to dismiss anyone who did not measure up to their expectations of a reliable and good worker. None thought that Africans worked on their farms in order to learn modern farming techniques which they might implement in their villages. The inability of any one employee to observe a complete work process may account for this lack of educational impact.

One farmer felt so close to his African employees and the people in an adjacent African area that in times of drought or financial loss he called on their diviners to tell his fortune, and occasionally he invited tribal elders to family feasts. He himself stated that he was exceptional in this respect and that no other farmer in the district followed his precedent. This farmer is widely known among local Africans and they praise him highly as one of the best Europeans they know.

The responses of almost all members of the European rural elite indicate that they think themselves accepted by Africans and fairly influential. Yet the degree to which they believe themselves accepted varies. Missionaries are most confident, followed by extension officers, district commissioners and farmers. Their believed acceptance therefore varies almost inversely with the degree of social distance they recognize between themselves and Africans. Those who minimize social distance feel more fully accepted than those who emphasize it. Their believed influence over Africans, however, is independent of these factors. It depends exclusively on their objective authority.

(b) The Africans' evaluation of the Europeans' prestige position

To complete the evaluation of the positions of the rural European elite, 104 Africans were asked to rank members of the European rural elite on a prestige scale. The scale measured positions as 'very high' (one), 'high' (two), 'average' (three), 'low' (four) and 'very low' (five). Sixty Africans of the sample were educated and forty-four uneducated. The educated Africans included teachers, hospital employees, agricultural staff and a class of thirty students of a teacher training college. Uneducated Africans included predominantly peasants, but also craftsmen with little formal education. A number of women were included in these samples. The average ratings given by these men and women are set out in Table 7.

This rating exercise was intended to measure the prestige attributed to the various occupations held by rural Europeans. Yet the

Occupation	Educated Africans	Uneducated Africans
District commissioner	2·7	2·6
District officer	2·9	2·8
Extension officer	2·3	2·5
Catholic priest	1·6	1·3
Protestant minister	2·2	2·2
Farmer	2·5	3·0

Table 7. Rating of European occupations, 1969

responses indicated that Africans were not measuring authority and prestige but rather social acceptance. Consequently the rank position 'very high' registers a very high approval of both the incumbents they knew who filled these occupations and of their usefulness to their society. 'Very low' registered rejection and extreme disapproval.

Table 7 lists the position of district commissioners who regard themselves, and are regarded by fellow Europeans, as men of great prestige, as 'high' to 'average'. The same exercise had been given to a group of Africans in 1963, and in that year educated Africans gave district commissioners the significantly higher average score of 2·0, and uneducated Africans of 2·1. The lower rank accorded to these administrators in 1969 seems due to changes in the political life of Rhodesia, and to a greater disillusionment of Africans with European government. The district commissioner's position was the only one of the European occupations which obtained a significantly different score in the two rating exercises.

Reasons given for the relatively low rating of the district commissioner were: 'We are afraid of him; he is "government" to us.' 'He imposes on us regulations which we do not like.' 'He is an important person, but there are others who are higher than he.' 'Too often he interferes unnecessarily in our affairs. He is a useless boss.' 'District commissioners frighten me. We Africans feel that we can never trust them.' 'When I go to his office I have to wait for hours, sometimes days, before I am admitted. When I finally stand before him I am so afraid that I can hardly speak. Then he shouts at me and I become still more frightened.'

The personality of known administrators often influenced the rating. One peasant stated: 'Our district commissioner is not so bad; sometimes he even helps us.' But a highly educated African said: 'Our district commissioner forces me to speak to him in the African language. I have to address myself to his interpreter although I speak English much better than this man. It seems that the district commissioner thinks that he would lose prestige if I were to speak to him directly.'

The score given to district commissioners by Africans is therefore less an evaluation of their rank than a rejection of their authoritarian attitude towards the people, and perhaps also a rejection of the government they represent. The fact that many expressed fear *vis-à-vis* district commissioners implies that they regarded them as very powerful.

District commissioners are assisted by district officers. None of these were personally interviewed for this study, but many were known to the investigator during the research. District officers share many of the attitudes with the younger district commissioners who have just been promoted. Africans in general show a slightly greater aversion for district officers than for older district commissioners. The rating of the two positions, however, comes very close.

Extension officers, though ranking lower in the estimation of Europeans, are rated higher by Africans. Africans know that district commissioners are more powerful than extension officers, yet they gave a higher score to the latter because they are 'more useful to us'. Again, therefore, Africans did not measure prestige but social acceptance. Some said: 'The extension officer teaches us better agricultural techniques so that we can make more money.' 'He sees to it that we have enough food. Without food we would die.' But others regarded his occupation as utterly 'useless and superfluous'. Only one used a criterion measuring prestige. He said: 'Extension officers are in charge of the African agricultural staff and therefore they have great authority in rural areas.'

These responses show that Africans took a pragmatic view of extension officers. Political aversion played less a role in their relation to these civil servants than in their relations with district commissioners. The difference is most likely due to the absence of compulsion in the extension officers' relationships with Africans.

In contrast to civil servants, missionaries were rated exceptionally high, especially Catholic priests. The distinction between priests and Protestant ministers in the rating is in part due to the higher education of Catholic priests, and in part to the Church policies of the various denominations. Ministers of the Dutch Reformed Church were often regarded by Africans as belonging to those Europeans who wanted to preserve the dominant position of the white minority in Rhodesia and were therefore rated lower.

The following reasons were given for the high rating of missionaries: 'They guide us to God.' 'They save our souls and help us to go to heaven.' 'They preach the word of God.' 'They help all the people, rich as well as poor.' 'We all have spiritual aspirations. Priests are the specialists who mediate between us and God.'

These comments refer almost exclusively to the spiritual functions of missionaries and give the impression that Africans are very spiritual. But this need not necessarily be the case. In their daily lives Africans frequently turn to missionaries in many needs. In the past they often asked missionaries to mediate between them and government officials, though this occurs less frequently in the 1960s because district commissioners insist that Africans see them personally. Since because of the religious bond Africans call Catholic priests 'Fathers', they often act towards them with the love and confidence they bear towards their own fathers. If missionaries do not live up to their expectation of a 'father', the disappointment is acute. One African reported a serious disagreement with a missionary and admitted shouting at him: 'If you act like this you are no longer my father but just a European.'

The Africans' high rating for missionaries seems to reflect a high degree of social acceptance and confirms the missionaries' own positive evaluation of their relationship with Africans. Missionaries are the Europeans with whom Africans have most personal contacts. Again, therefore, personal considerations, not objective prestige criteria, influenced the Africans' rating of missionaries.

European farmers were evaluated very unevenly by the African people. Some stressed their great wealth and rated them high. One African said: 'Most of them come to town in dirty clothes, but then they go to the bank and draw much money. Other Europeans respect them highly.' Another commented: 'Government considers European farmers important and gives them big loans. Government seems to depend on their support and consults them often.'

On the other hand Africans were very critical of farmers. One said: 'Farmers do not respect Africans. They treat us with contempt. Therefore I rate them very low.' Another said: 'Farmers underpay their African workers. How, therefore, can I respect them? If they would pay more, I would not mind working for them.' One negative comment referred to European thriftiness. A man said: 'Some European farmers drive their tractors personally. This shows that they have not enough money to employ labourers. Such men rank very low.'[37]

In their evalution of European farmers, therefore, human relationships as well as wealth determined the Africans' responses. Some mentioned both aspects simultaneously and found it difficult to decide on one of the five rating positions.

Because of the different criteria employed, Africans rate occupations differently from Europeans. It seems that whereas Europeans measure objective authority, Africans measure human acceptance and usefulness. Europeans recognize objective superiority even if they feel personally resentful to the incumbents of an office, such as extension officers feel *vis-à-vis* district commissioners. Africans do not do this. They look at total human relationships and pay respect and honour to persons they trust.

6. Conclusion

The above analysis has shown that the European rural elite is not as homogeneous a group as it appears from the outside. The members clearly distinguish between the rank positions they occupy, and those most closely identified with government, that is, those who are most visibly part of the 'governing elite', occupy the highest prestige position. This governing elite and 'ordinary members' of the European community, such as extension officers and farmers, form the standard pattern of white behaviour towards Africans. In spite of internal divisions they are superficially united by the knowledge that they are members of the white race, living in little islands among a sea of Africans.[38]

But missionaries are marginal to this European community. Though they are Europeans, their contacts are often more intense with Africans than with fellow Europeans. For this reason, the 'ordinary European' often looks askance at them, sometimes almost as a traitor of white society.

The evaluation by Africans of members of the European elite shows that the subordinate race does not share the values of the

[37]Africans regard most manual labour as degrading because in Rhodesia it is almost exclusively performed by Africans.

[38]Cf. Huggins, quoted in Gray, 1960, p. 152: 'The Europeans in this country can be likened to an island of white in a sea of black.'

dominant race. They esteem most highly those Europeans who are most marginal to their own racial group. Consequently, since association with these atypical Europeans is easiest for Africans, they may not receive a generally valid picture of Europeans by using missionaries as their reference group.

Banton observed[39] that members of a dominant race regulate race relations in such a way that all members of their own race enjoy a superior status and that, in order to maintain this status, restrictions are imposed on members of their own group if they wish to associate with members of the subordinate race. Banton stressed that any deviation of the generally accepted norms calls forth sanctions on the offenders in order to bring them back to conformity. For their deviations from the standardized pattern of inter-racial behaviour might evoke in the subordinate race the aspiration to be accepted as equals in a unified social system, and this would threaten the dominant race's superior status.

Many missionaries constantly deviate from the norms governing race relations in Rhodesia. Instead of following a standard ritual in their contacts with Africans they often accept them as equals. This arouses resentment among many other Europeans and they react by refusing them admittance into their social circles. This exclusion may be intended as a sanction calling them back to conformity. But in many instances it merely intensifies the missionaries' contacts with fellow missionaries and Africans, and causes them to challenge more strongly still the current European ideology of racial superiority. Thus missionaries are becoming ever more marginal to white Rhodesian society.[40] This split within the ruling elite of Rhodesia, between those members who insist on white supremacy and those who deny the Europeans' inherent superiority, is of greater importance for race relations than rank distinction within the white elite. The following chapter analyses in greater detail the different attitudes held by Europeans towards Africans.

[39] *Supra*, pp. 3–6.

[40] Several missionaries have been declared prohibited immigrants by the Rhodesian Government because they challenged the Europeans' racial ideology. The most outstanding cases are those of Bishop Dodge of the American Methodist Episcopal Church (cf. *The Rhodesia Herald*, 1.8.1964) and the Catholic priest, Father Traber (*The Rhodesia Herald*, 10.3.1970).

3. Social profiles and racial attitudes of Europeans

The previous chapter sketched the setting of the rural European elite in Rhodesia and indicated what kind of stereotypes they held concerning Africans. This chapter analyses their attitudes in greater detail. In order to evaluate these attitudes correctly, the section on racial attitudes is prefaced by the social profiles of members of the European elite, and followed in the next chapter by a scrutiny of the character of their occupations in order to determine the role which various factors play in attitude formation.

1. The social profiles

Because the sample of fifty Europeans is too small to draw valid statistical conclusions from it, general profiles are presented here which draw mainly on the fifty interviews with agents of change, but also include data collected during several years of fieldwork and contact with other district commissioners, extension officers, missionaries and farmers.[1]

(a) District commissioners

District commissioners fall roughly into two age categories: about half are in their thirties and half in their fifties, with a very few men in their forties. This age gap is due to recruitment difficulties during the second World War. The attitudes maintained by these two groups of administrators towards Africans differ significantly.

Most of the administrators joined their ministry straight after completing their formal education, either in their late teens or early twenties. Only one joined later after some years of service with the police.

Almost all district commissioners attended school for eleven or twelve years, which is typical for the average European in Rho-

[1]For statistical data, see Appendix, pp. 230–32.

desia,[2] but a few obtained a university degree before they joined their ministry. Their degrees were all of a general, non-technical, nature, such as a Bachelor of Arts or Honours degree in English. As junior members in their ministry they received an intensive inservice training.[3] On the average, district commissioners spent some seven years as cadets and eight years as district officers, that is, assistants to commissioners, before they were themselves put in charge of districts. This means that they spent some fifteen years in the service before they reached their present rank.[4] During these years they studied privately to pass examinations in law, administration, African customs, and written and oral African language.

The average district commissioner receives a salary of some £2,800 per annum. This is considerably above the average earning of Europeans in Rhodesia[5] and shows that their services are highly regarded by society.

Most district commissioners belong to the Church of England, though a significant number of these stated religious affiliation as 'C. of E., but', that is, they claimed to belong nominally to the Church, but did not participate in Church activities. A certain number claimed to be agnostics.

The great majority of district commissioners were either born in England or in Rhodesia. Only a few were born in South Africa and Commonwealth countries. Some of those who were born in other countries arrived in Rhodesia in the 1920s and 1930s, others only in the 1950s. These last belong to the younger district commissioners who differ in their attitudes towards Africans from many of those who were born in this country or arrived several decades ago.

Almost all district commissioners come from families with long connections with the civil service, the army, police or the Church of England. Only a very few come from farming or working-class families. This is especially true of those born in Rhodesia. Of these three were sons of district commissioners, one the nephew of a

---

[2]Cf. *supra*, p. 29, Table 5.

[3]In 1969 cadets for the ministry of Internal Affairs attended formal courses for the first time in the history of the ministry. The courses extended over several weeks each, fitting the men for their future work as district commissioners. *The Rhodesia Herald*, 18.11.1969.

[4]Holleman, 1968, pp. 26–7, gives a corroborating account, stressing the 'mental inbreeding' caused by the department's training policy.

[5]Cf. *supra*, p. 24, Table 4.

provincial commissioner and one had a cousin and two brothers in the same ministry. These men, as well as those whose fathers and grandfathers had served in the army, were very proud of their family connections.

All district commissioners are married and have on the average two children, most of them still of school age.

(b) Extension officers

Extension officers are on the average younger than district commissioners. Most of them are in their twenties and thirties. Almost all joined their ministry relatively recently, during their mid-twenties, because they had to undergo technical training after completing their secondary schooling and before they would be accepted by the ministry of Agriculture.

About half of all extension officers took a diploma in agriculture, the other half a university degree. This prolonged training prevented them from joining their ministry as early as did district commissioners, and, as a consequence, extension officers have undergone a longer formal training than administrators.

Extension officers also receive an inservice training, but it is of a different nature from that of district commissioners. They are immediately appointed to the rank of extension officer and then continue throughout their career to attend special courses in extension work and African culture which aim at acquainting them with the most recent developments in their profession. The majority of extension officers attended between ten and twenty courses each. This means that the technical staff has a relatively high level of formal training which is constantly kept up to date by refresher courses.

Their higher education, however, is not reflected in their salaries. Those with only a diploma in agriculture receive a salary of about £1,000 a year, those with a university degree of about £2,000. They are therefore paid less than administrators, and their lower remuneration places them socially below district commissioners.

The large majority of extension officers are Protestants, only a few are Anglicans and one claimed to be an agnostic. Most indicated that they practised their religion regularly and contrasted their participation in Church activities with that of district commissioners.

Extension officers come from a large number of countries, and the mother tongue of most is either English or Dutch. Some were born in Rhodesia, some in England, others in Holland or the East

Indies, some in the Congo or in Tanzania. Apart from those born in Rhodesia, all arrived in the country since the second World War, some as late as in the 1960s. Consequently the great diversity of their origin is still very marked in their behaviour. They have not yet adopted typically Rhodesian attitudes. The fact of their recent arrival distinguishes them significantly from district commissioners.

Just as extension officers come from many countries, so they come from different family backgrounds. Their fathers are either professionals, businessmen, civil servants, craftsmen or farmers. Yet in spite of this diversity, almost all can trace some link with agriculture: one is the son of a botany professor, two have brothers in the ministry of Agriculture, one comes from a family in which all members but his own father are farmers. Like district commissioners, therefore, most extension officers have chosen an occupation which is not far removed from their childhood milieu.

All extension officers are married. But because they are much younger than district commissioners they have only very small children and are still building up their families.

Their social characteristics class extension officers as young, enterprising Europeans who have no great stake in the country because most of them are recent immigrants. They are well educated, but not too well paid. Consequently they look for occupational advancement, if necessary outside their ministry.

(c) Missionaries

The profile of missionaries is more diversified. Their ages range from the early twenties to the mid-sixties, with a heavy clustering of men in the mid-forties. They joined the religious societies in which they work as missionaries straight after school, or alternately embarked on their theological studies straight after school and volunteered for the missions as soon as they had completed their studies. Like district commissioners, therefore, they were exposed to the influence of their present profession since early youth.

Missionaries distinguish themselves from all other agents of change through their very high education.[6] All of them completed secondary school and then either attended universities or seminaries. Their post-school fulltime training lasted on the average between six and seventeen years, varying with denomination and religious order. Jesuit missionaries of the Catholic Church, for example, had,

[6]Cf. *supra*, p. 36: only ordained missionaries are included in this study.

of all missionaries, the longest training in philosophy and theology.

Because of their highly specialized training, missionaries received less inservice training than civil servants. Some specialized in addition to their formal training in philosophy and theology also in agriculture, economics, journalism, pedagogy or linguistics, and most attended courses in the African language and local customs after their arrival in Rhodesia.

Because of their special religious commitments, no missionaries receive a salary corresponding to their education. Protestant missionaries receive a money grant from their Churches varying between £600 and £1,600 per annum, depending on the number of children they have to support. Catholic missionaries, who are all unmarried, receive no salary at all; they live in community and share all they have in common. In some missionary societies individual missionaries receive a small amount of pocket money. One priest stated that he used about £4 a month; but another said that on arrival at his present mission station he had received from his superior ten shillings, and at the time of the interview, six months later, he had still eight shillings left. Money earned by individual missionaries through regular salaries as teachers is immediately put at the disposal of the mission and used for the upkeep and expansion of the various missionary enterprises.

The missionaries interviewed in this study belong to the Catholic, Methodist and Reformed Churches. Most Catholic missionaries come from either England or the continent of Europe, Methodists from America, and Reformed missionaries from South Africa. Most of them arrived in Rhodesia during the 1950s, some earlier and a few later.

The typical family background of missionaries is that of middle-class families in western societies. Most of their fathers were themselves ministers of religion, or engaged in business and the teaching professions. Some of their parents were wealthy, including the manager of a large shipping company. None of them, however, placed much importance on his father's occupation.

Most missionaries come from deeply religious families. Several have relatives engaged in the ministry or in mission work. Most Catholic missionaries come from families that had sent many of their members to various missions; one of these has eight relatives working as missionaries in three different continents. Consequently, a family tradition can be as clearly discovered in the case of missionaries as in the case of district commissioners and extension officers.

The private life of missionaries varies. Apart from the celibate Catholic missionaries who live in communities of fellow missionaries, most Methodist and Reformed missionaries are married. But whereas the latter tend to send their children to schools in South Africa, Methodists send their children to local schools, and one missionary family tries to teach its children privately in order not to expose them to the racial prejudices widespread in many Rhodesian schools. In this respect this Methodist missionary family differs significantly from those of other European families.

The profiles of missionaries reveal them as a highly educated, idealistic group of men. In the pursuit of their goal to spread the Christian religion among the African people, they disregard considerations of wealth and at times even of the social convention regulating the upbringing of children in Rhodesia. Catholic celibate missionaries, still more than the others, stand in a group apart from other Europeans.

(d) Farmers

Farmers belong to all age groups, though a slightly larger proportion is elderly. All except one, who in his late forties retired from mining, began farming in their youth. Several inherited a farm from their fathers; others were given their farms by government after retirement from military service after the second World War.

Farmers have less education than any of the other agents of change. None has more than eleven years' schooling, some less. Most stated that as boys they just were not interested in learning, nor did they see any need for it since they knew they wanted to become farmers.

Farmers were unwilling to state their annual agricultural profit. But considering that the average farmer owns some 10,000 acres, of which he uses approximately 10 per cent for crops and 50 per cent for ranching—the average farmer has a herd of over 1,000 head of cattle—their annual profit is unlikely to be low.

Like extension officers, most farmers are Protestants. But whereas extension officers belong predominantly to the Presbyterian or Methodist Churches, many farmers belong to the Dutch Reformed Church. A few claimed no religious affiliation.

Most farmers were born in Rhodesia, some came from South

Africa. But since the fathers of most Rhodesian-born farmers had come from South Africa, most are Afrikaaner. One younger farmer had immigrated from England after the last war, and there was a retired civil servant. As Leys observes, farming is a prestige occupation for Rhodesian Europeans and outstanding public figures run farms next to their other economic pursuits.[7] Most farmers interviewed come from farming families. Locally the most important farmers are the sons of pioneers whose fathers had received their farms for the services they had rendered in the occupation of the country. These farmers with longest family traditions in Rhodesia claim local elite status in their communities and consider themselves typical members of Rhodesian European society.

(e) Conclusion

The social profiles of district commissioners, extension officers, missionaries and farmers reveal quite distinct social groups. They seem to be typical of Europeans in rural Rhodesia,[8] but not of white Rhodesians in general because all of them belong to what may be called 'higher income groups'. Missionaries are atypical in this respect because of their voluntary religious poverty. But for this commitment they too would receive high salaries.

Rogers and Frantz in a sample of 500 Europeans, drawn from a cross section of Rhodesian society,[9] found that people with little education were more opposed to African advancement than people with more extensive education;[10] that people with lower salaries were more suspicious of African advancement than people with higher salaries;[11] that Reformed Christians were more opposed to it than Anglicans, Anglicans more than Catholics, and Catholics more than agnostics.[12] By country of origin, they found South Africans more conservative than the English,[13] but noted that length of residence affected racial attitudes: those who were longer in Rhodesia were less willing to see African advancement than recent arri-

---

[7]Cf. Leys, 1959, p. 98. He mentions two former prime ministers of Rhodesia, one a doctor and one a missionary, who opened up their own farms.

[8]No mention has been made in this study of European businessmen in rural areas. Many of them are farmers; most have their stores attended by local Africans.

[9]Rogers and Frantz, 1962, pp. 53–4. 500 people were chosen at random and asked to fill in a questionnaire eliciting racial attitudes.

[10]Rogers and Frantz, 1962, p. 129.

[11]*Ibid.*, p. 128.

[12]*Ibid.*, p. 130.

[13]*Ibid.*, p. 122.

vals.[14] According to occupational classification, Rogers and Frantz found professionals and technically trained people most willing to welcome African progress, followed by civil servants. Farmers were found to be more reluctant.[15]

According to this more extensive survey it may be anticipated that district commissioners are relatively favourably disposed towards African advancement, and among them those with no religion and a university degree more so than their colleagues. Extension officers may be expected to welcome African advancement even more than district commissioners, and missionaries most of all, apart from Afrikaner missionaries of the Reformed Church. Farmers, owing to their South African origin and low education, may be expected to be more opposed to African advancement than the other agents of change. Yet even these, as the size of their properties indicates, belong to the affluent section of Rhodesian Europeans and may therefore be more liberal than the average European.

If this assumption, derived from the findings of Rogers and Frantz, proves true, then race relations in rural Rhodesia ought to be more cordial and less tension-ridden than race relations in urban areas where European artisans and other less qualified persons interact most frequently with Africans.

2. Attitudes of the European rural elite towards African advancement and racial integration

(a) Attitudes towards the political advancement of Africans

The key question in the minds of many Europeans in Rhodesia during the 1960s and 1970s is the political advancement of Africans. To study the opinions of rural Europeans on this topic, two questions were asked: 'What is your attitude towards majority rule?' and 'How do you visualize the political situation of Rhodesia in a generation's time?' The first of these questions aims at determining what future members of the European elite desire, and the second what they consider the future likely to be.

(i) District commissioners

The majority of district commissioners thought that majority rule would be detrimental for Rhodesia and several added that it would mean the economic ruin of the country. They pointed to independent

[14]*Ibid.*, p. 124.
[15]*Ibid.*, p. 125.

African territories and expressed the conviction that in the event of a drastic political change the majority of Europeans would leave Rhodesia. One added: 'This would be the end of us,' and another: 'It is my task to postpone it for as long as possible.' Since the great majority considered the present civil service the most efficient Rhodesia could ever have, they could only see retrogression in change. Several hoped that separate development along South African lines would bring political stability to Rhodesia. Only one pleaded that Africans be given a chance to participate politically in the building up of a great nation in Central Africa.

Their hopes differed only slightly from their expectations. Some district commissioners thought that majority rule must and will come one day, being convinced that Africans, even peasants, were satisfied with nothing less. But they projected this possibility into the distant future. The majority were confident that Rhodesia was competent enough to control any political agitation. None seriously expected an African uprising, but rather envisaged a gradual adoption of the South African pattern of separate development.

The majority of district commissioners therefore rejected African political advancement. They thought it to be both unlikely and undesirable. As a group they opted for separate development and thought this the most likely course Rhodesia would take.

(ii) *Extension officers*

Extension officers as a group showed a conspicuous lack of interest in politics. This may be due to the fact that many are aliens in Rhodesia. Almost half of them had no opinion at all on these questions. The majority of those who did hold some opinion thought that full participation of Africans in the political life of Rhodesia would be desirable, a small number thought it disadvantageous, but held no strong convictions. One clearly opted for separate development.

Most extension officers expected the present situation to continue for a long time because they believed Africans to be neither interested in politics nor able to make a bid for power.[16] A small minority saw the country faced by bloody uprisings.

The greatest difference between district commissioners and exten-

---

[16]Just as extension officers projected their own attitude towards work on Africans, cf. *supra*, p. 41, so they here project their political indifference on Africans. In contrast district commissioners stree polar attitudes in themselves and Africans. Cf. *supra*, p. 39.

sion officers in regard to African political advancement was that administrators had carefully considered the consequences of alternative policies and had overwhelmingly rejected majority rule, whereas extension officers were more apathetic. Perhaps because they had less stake in Rhodesia than the senior civil servants, they were more willing to allow for African political participation.

(iii) *Missionaries*

Missionaries were split in their attitudes towards majority rule according to their religious affiliation. Reformed missionaries rejected majority rule as a serious impediment to the wellbeing of the country. The others thought that majority rule was urgently needed to avoid a major disaster. They claimed that Africans had a right to freedom and self-determination just as every other human being. Some of these, nevertheless, saw dangers in a sudden change and pleaded for a gradual but steady increase of African participation in government.

Reformed missionaries felt pessimistic about the future; some even expressed despair. They believed that majority rule would come and prepared themselves to accept it with fatalism; but they were convinced that it would not work. One of them was less pessimistic and thought that if the government succeeded in repressing tribalism, democracy might be preserved through a gradual inclusion of Africans into parliament.

Methodist and Catholic missionaries fall into two groups: a smaller section believed that the present government was so strong that no major changes could be expected because the Africans were too disunited to rise up in revolt. They themselves felt helpless to bring about a change and hoped against hope for a change of government. The great majority, however, saw a racial war as inevitable, being convinced that Africans would not remain satisfied with second-class citizenship.

Apart from Reformed missionaries, therefore, this group of Europeans most strongly favoured African political advancement, justifying their anticipation by the basic human right of self-determination. Their hopes to an extent dictated their expectations. Not that they looked forward to racial wars, but that they considered them as an inevitable step towards majority rule. Some Reformed missionaries even concurred with this judgment.

Missionaries, except those of the Reformed Church, differ radically from civil servants: they differ from district commissioners in that most of them hope for a future differing greatly from the future district commissioners look forward to, and they differ from extension officers in that they are keenly interested in the political development of the country. They regard apathy towards politics as morally reprehensible and irresponsible. All hold clearly formulated views on African political advancement.

(iv) *Farmers*

Almost all farmers rejected majority rule as evil. A few hoped for a very gradual integration of Africans into the political life of Rhodesia. Only one had no objection to African political advancement and pleaded that Africans be allowed to advance themselves in any direction they desired.

But farmers were very unsure whether what they desired would actually happen. Most of them expressed great fear of the future. One well-established farmer said: 'Africans are so many in number that they can easily burn down Salisbury in one night and take over the country by force.' Several felt that African political advancement was bound to be fast and stated: 'We need African chiefs to protect us from African competition in parliament.' Others thought that Rhodesia stood at the brink of disaster and many admitted that they prayed earnestly that bloodshed might be averted in the country. Only one farmer, a younger man from England, felt confident; he thought Africans incapable of rising in rebellion. It was he who pleaded that Africans be allowed to advance themselves.

The reaction of farmers has the closest affinity with the reaction of Reformed missionaries. Their common South African origin may contribute to their almost identical views towards African political advancement. Though they hope for the same as what district commissioners expect will happen, they fear that what missionaries hope for, may happen.

(*b*) *Attitudes towards the economic advancement of Africans*

Again two questions were asked to determine the attitudes and expectations of Europeans towards African economic advancement: 'Do you think it desirable that Africans should advance economically?' and 'How do you visualize the Africans' economic position in a generation's time?'

(i) *District commissioners*

A significant minority of district commissioners did not like to see any African economic advancement; one stated it bluntly and others said that economic advancement had no meaning to Africans. The great majority, however, thought that economic advancement of the African was essential for the wellbeing of the whole country and that everything possible must be done to achieve it, though many thought that it would take a long time to achieve any economic improvement in African areas.

Half of the district commissioners thought that African living standards would rise over the next generation because African agriculture would become more productive. Others felt doubtful about the economic future of Africans, attributing any change to the Africans' willingness to work harder on the land and to adopt modern farming techniques. Several thought that African living standards would fall considerably. They gave the following reasons or comments: 'The African will withdraw into the uterus of tribal custom.' 'He will be more frustrated and unhappy than he is now, and be completely overcome by witchcraft and superstition.' 'He will starve himself to death as he deserves.' And 'In twenty years' time there will be no more Africans in Rhodesia; as they increase their families, their living standards will fall and they will die out.'

There was a clear division in the attitudes of district commissioners. Those who disliked a rising African living standard expected it to fall; those who hoped for improved living conditions were more optimistic. With a few exceptions these answers coincided with the age groups of district commissioners, the young men being more pessimistic and the older more optimistic.[17] The older district commissioners based their optimism on their years of experience in African areas during which they claimed to have seen great economic progress.

(ii) *Extension officers*

Extension officers differ from district commissioners in that all of them favour African economic advancement. It is their professional duty to contribute to such an improvement.

Yet if they desired African economic progress, they were more pessimistic than district commissioners about its possibility. Half of them expected an inevitable decline in African living standards, and an ever-widening gap in income between rural and urban Africans.

---

[17]There were two exceptions to this general pattern: one older district commissioner was most opposed to African advancement and one young commissioner did all in his power to stimulate it.

Unlike district commissioners, they thought that African progress
could come only from industrialization; the rural environment,
which they knew well, seemed incapable to them of great improvement. Most of the other extension officers doubted that any changes
would take place, and a few anticipated a very gradual improvement, but an improvement which would be so slow that it would
be hardly visible within a generation.

Extension officers offered several reasons for their pessimistic forecast of African economic improvement: rapid population increase
which outstripped the growth in agricultural production; separate
development which prevented European money being invested in
African areas; and a transfer of agricultural responsibility from the
ministry of Agriculture to the ministry of Internal Affairs.[18]

(iii) *Missionaries*

Missionaries shared the extension officers' desire for African progress. Their actual forecast of future development was given by the
majority in a conditional way, depending on political and other
developments. They believed that if Africans were given a fair
chance to progress, if equal educational opportunities were provided
between the races, if the land of Rhodesia were re-distributed, then
Africans would advance fast because of their ability to improve
themselves. But if present conditions continued they saw no hope
for African economic progress. Reformed missionaries expected little
change in the Africans' economic position. One stated that their
economic progress would depend on the Europeans' prosperity and
on the judicious help given to Africans by Europeans.

(iv) *Farmers*

All European farmers stressed the need for African economic
advancement. They realized that their own security depended on it,
for with a frustrated African population they saw their own position
endangered.

Most of them had little contact with Africans apart from their
labour force, but some gave help to Africans in adjoining tribal
areas and were familiar with the economic situation in African villages. These foresaw a steady fall in African living standards and
pleaded for the introduction of individual land tenure among Afri-

---

[18]Though this had not yet taken place at the time of the survey, many indications
in this direction had been given. Especially in that African chiefs had been given
great powers over the land and extension officers had to work through chiefs;
chiefs have always been directly controlled by district commissioners.

cans, a plea also made by extension officers and missionaries, but vigorously rejected by all district commissioners as undermining the traditional African social system.

(v) *Conclusion*

All agents of change, except some district commissioners, hoped for an improvement of African living standards, but most were exceedingly doubtful whether such improvements could be achieved. The greatest optimists were district commissioners. Their optimism may derive from their political conviction which favours the continuation of the present social set-up in Rhodesia, and also separate development. Should they foresee a deterioration of African living standards under this system, their highly developed sense of responsibility might force them to query the very *status quo* of which they are proud. The district commissioners who favoured African economic regression were an embarrassment to some of their colleagues.

(c) *Attitudes towards African social advancement*

District commissioners, extension officers, missionaries and farmers were asked two questions concerning African social advancement: 'Do you subscribe to advancement on merit, and if so, what should be the criteria by which the Africans' readiness to advance is to be measured?' and 'What is your attitude towards educated Africans?'

(i) *District commissioners*

A few district commissioners stated that they were unwilling to see any African advance socially, with merit or none. Others thought that educational certificates were not enough to prove ability; merit had to be proved in action; yet since a job depended on proved ability it was difficult to see how a first job requiring ability could be offered to Africans. The majority, however, wholeheartedly subscribed to promotion on merit, but did not care to define what they meant by it.

Half of all district commissioners held negative views about educated Africans. Some considered African university graduates 'barbarians with a degree'.[19] Others stressed that they disliked nothing

---

[19]Cf. Wilson and Mafeje, 1963, p. 142: 'The white attitude, in its extreme form, is expressed in the familiar phrase: "You may have a B.A. but you still remain a Kaffir with me."' The authors write about European attitudes towards Africans in South Africa.

more in Africans than education because it made Africans irresponsible towards their own people and utterly selfish, and that it
deprived them of that concern for the common good which currently
only the old chiefs still possessed.[20]

A smaller number of district commissioners, however, greatly
approved of educated Africans. They claimed that they were delight-
ful men and much easier to deal with than the uneducated, that
they could reason more clearly, understand the content of a conversation, and were less destructive than uneducated Africans. These
commissioners were willing to use educated Africans as mediators
with their people; the half who held negative views about educated
Africans, however, would never consult them and dealt directly with
African peasants. Some district commissioners sympathized with
education Africans because they found them caught between the
African traditional way of life and the values presented to them by
European culture; they realized that this caused them much suffering.

Those district commissioners who refused to allow for any social
advancement of Africans were the same as those who greatly
objected to educated Africans. The majority of these belonged to
the younger age group. The older men were more willing to see
Africans advance themselves and found it easy to converse with
educated Africans.

(ii) *Extension officers*

All extension officers subscribed to promotion on merit. Several
added that their own promotion was often hindered for lack of a
university degree, however successful they were in their work. Consequently they sympathized with Africans. They stressed that 'merit'
ought not to be measured exclusively by educational qualifications
but also by the successful performance of occupational duties.

The great majority of extension officers greatly appreciated educated Africans and preferred them to the less educated. They
stressed that educated Africans shared their values and spoke the
same language, by which they meant not merely English, but also
that these Africans expressed similar views and attitudes. Most of
them had worked with African colleagues and so spoke from experience. Only a few took exception to educated Africans. These described them as dishonest, snobbish and of sullen insolence. One
commented that educated Africans ought to learn their subordinate
place in Rhodesian society.

[20]Cf. Weinrich. 1971: *Chiefs and Councils in Rhodesia.*

District commissioners and extension officers alike fall therefore into two opposed categories in their attitude towards African social advancement, but the significant difference is that the proportion that opposes African advancement is much smaller among extension officers than among district commissioners.

(iii) *Missionaries*

All missionaries subscribed to advancement on merit, though different groups qualified their consent in different directions. Reformed missionaries believed that Africans ought to make a collective effort to improve themselves as a group, and they were confident that this would take place, however long the process might take. Missionaries of other denominations believed that individual capable Africans ought to be given much help and encouragement to take over leading positions, preferably at first as assistants to well-qualified Europeans, so that they could be trained on the spot to take over positions at present filled by Europeans. All of them stressed that equal opportunities ought to be provided for Africans and Europeans, otherwise the frequent statements by the Prime Minister of advancement on merit would remain empty slogans. Some were willing to see Africans given promotion to positions for which they would not yet qualify if objective measurements were used, because 'they ought to be given a chance' and helped as much as possible. This means that some missionaries were willing to lower standards of performance to hasten African social advance.

The missionaries' responses towards educated Africans fell into line with their attitudes towards advancement on merit. Reformed missionaries felt that educated Africans ought to open their eyes to their own cultural values and not use Europeans as their exclusive reference group. They saw much that was beautiful in African culture and believed that even though Africans might take over outward forms of western culture, they would always fill them with an inner meaning that was typically African. They admitted knowing some very fine educated Africans, but found it hard to get on with those who were very politically conscious. Since most Africans with secondary education fall into this group, they found educated Africans generally difficult to deal with. Some complained of their arrogance.

The other missionaries accepted educated Africans as their equals and found them pleasant companions. They were very conscious of the difficulties in which educated Africans find themselves. One said: 'Old Africans had an easy life because things changed slowly in the past. Our young men are caught up in rapid social change and are not sure of either their traditional values or those of Europeans. Because Europeans have often discriminated against them, they now doubt both the honesty of Europeans and the values they uphold. This makes communication often difficult.' Another, referring to his African teachers, commented: 'Educated Africans are fine if they are treated justly; but if treated unjustly they cause serious trouble.'

Missionaries thought that they held more positive attitudes towards educated Africans than other Europeans and one, contrasting his attitude with what he believed to be the attitude of district commissioners, explained: 'District commissioners only like uneducated Africans who are afraid of Europeans and never argue with them. I like to discuss matters with Africans.' Since most educated Africans have graduated from mission schools it is natural that missionaries who trained them should feel sympathetic towards them.

(iv) *Farmers*

Farmers, who themselves had received less formal education than any other group of rural Europeans and whose contact with Africans is exclusively confined to uneducated Africans, regarded educational certificates as inadequate to prove an African's merit. They recommended that Africans be apprenticed to skilled Europeans and learn from them as much as possible.

On their own admission, the farmers' views on educated Africans were inadequate since they had met few. Half of them shrugged them off as corrupt, unpleasant and useless. One admitted: 'Supposedly Africans have got to be educated', and a small number thought that educated Africans could be fine men.[21]

(v) *Conclusion*

Responses to these questions show that most Europeans subscribe to advancement on merit, though they differ in the interpretation of merit. They differ still more in their attitudes towards educated Africans. District commissioners and farmers are most sceptical of educated Africans, and extension officers and missionaries,

[21]Mphahlele, a South African writer, made the following observation about European attitudes towards Africans: 'There are whites who say naïvely: "I like Africans". Some, especially those who cannot conceive of Africans as anything but servants, will say they hate the educated blacks. "He's an educated boy, but you wouldn't think it," some liberals say. "So humble and respectful."' Mphahlele, 1962, pp. 94–5.

who have most contact with them, are most favourably disposed towards them. District commissioners and farmers may therefore be said to constitute the more conservative element of the rural European elite, and extension officers and missionaries, at least those of the Methodist and Catholic Churches, the more liberal element.

(d) Attitudes towards racial integration

Again two questions were asked to elicit the Europeans' attitudes towards the topic: 'Would you like to have African colleagues in your profession?' and 'What is your attitude towards social integration of Africans and Europeans in Rhodesia?'

(i) District commissioners

District commissioners overwhelmingly rejected the possibility of Africanization in their ministry. They gave reasons for the inability of Africans to fill their posts which closely reflect their own self-evaluation and their African stereotypes.[22] They claimed that district commissioners had to make many decisions and were burdened with great responsibilities: Africans were irresponsible and unable to make decisions and therefore unqualified for the post; district commissioners were security officers and responsible for peace in their districts: Africans could not be trusted to keep information of a security nature from fellow Africans and could therefore not be appointed to the position; district commissioners, as senior civil servants, were the centre around which social life on their outlying stations revolved: if an African were to take over their position, social life at the station would disintegrate and the remaining European staff would feel lost because they could not associate socially with a man of another race. District commissioners also argued that African peasants would not place the same confidence in an African district commissioner as they placed in a European because they doubted whether any African could be impartial.

A small number of district commissioners had no strong objections to African colleagues and stressed that up to the present Africanization had been the policy of their ministry. As proof they pointed to one African district officer stationed at head office who had joined them many years ago. They pointed out that several African youths had joined as cadets, but that all of them had left again because the demands of their service had been too harsh for them. Even these district commissioners admitted that

[22]Cf. *supra*, pp. 39–40.

Africanization might be discontinued if separate development were accepted as official government policy.[23]

The question about social mixing in private life was still more strongly rejected. Some called social intercourse with Africans 'revolting' and leading to a lowering of moral standards in Rhodesia. Others stressed that Europeans had no right to disturb Africans in their way of life and that attracting them to their culture would 'turn them into driftwood' and ruin their character. Others stated plainly that they did not want to mix and considered multiracialism objectionable. A few, however, thought that social integration might take place in the future as African living standards rose, and admitted that they had some African friends who occasionally came to visit them in their homes; they greatly appreciated these men for what they had achieved in life.

(ii) *Extension officers*

Africanization has been effectively practised in the ministry of Agriculture and all extension officers interviewed had worked with African colleagues. All of them accepted them as equals, and the majority praised them as being better able than Europeans to understand the difficulties of African peasants; they readily stressed the excellent work done by African extension officers. They welcomed an increase in African colleagues, though one was unwilling to have an African superior, and some who had only a diploma looked askance at African extension officers who were studying privately for a degree.

Extension officers were less opposed to social mixing than district commissioners.[24] One reason might be that they occupy the same houses at transfers which an African officer may have occupied before them. Most maintained that integration was fine if both sides agreed, if the African had reached the European's cultural level, and above all if the educated African's wife was herself socially advanced to mix as an equal with Europeans, because on the stand-

[23]This observation is likely to be correct, for in 1968 an African school manager, who had returned from America after taking a university degree in social administration, applied to his district commissioner to forward his application to join the ministry of Internal Affairs. He thought that as district commissioner he could best serve his country. He received the answer that the Rhodesian civil service had no vacancy for him.

[24]Consequently the district commissioners' argument that the social life of a government station would disintegrate should an African be appointed district commissioner, might not be true.

ing of the woman a home atmosphere depended. One insisted that
for moral reasons integration ought to be speeded up since racial
discrimination was immoral and contrary to his Christian conviction.[25] A small minority, however, expressed aversion to social intercourse with Africans and one added: 'I am a Rhodesian. How could
I want social integration?'

Again, therefore, district commissioners and extension officers fall
into two categories in regard to race relations but also again the
size of the categories favouring or disapproving of a change in race
relations varies inversely.

(iii) *Missionaries*

All missionaries stressed the importance of an indigenous clergy,
but members of the three denominations differed in the evaluation
of the success of the Africanization of their ministry.

Methodist missionaries were convinced that an indigenous Methodist Church had already been established and they felt confident
that should European missionaries have to leave the country, the
Rhodesian Church could stand on its own feet. Owing to the efficient guidance of their Church by their late bishop, who was
expelled from Rhodesia by government,[26] they had a large number
of ordained ministers, and teachers with university degrees, many
of whom had studied in Europe and America.

Reformed missionaries actively pursued a policy of indigenizing
their Church and stressed that the local synod had a majority of
African members so that, when policy decisions had to be taken,
the African vote already counted. Yet they felt that European assistance was still needed for a long time because too few African
ministers had been trained. By 1968 the Reformed Church in Rhodesia counted twenty-eight ordained African ministers. European
missionaries of this Church thought that they co-operated well with
their African colleagues.

Catholic missionaries, who demand a much higher education
from their priests than Protestants, felt less confident about the Africanization of their clergy. By 1968 there were thirty ordained
African priests, constituting 10 per cent of all Catholic priests in
Rhodesia. The general opinion of Catholic missionaries was that
candidates for the priesthood had to be chosen very carefully and
that their training had to be constantly improved until it reached

[25]Cf. *supra*, p. 64. Most extension officers claimed to be practising Christians.
[26]Cf. *supra*, p. 61.

the same level as that of European missionaries. During the 1960s it was lower: candidates were accepted after eleven years' schooling, and then underwent a six-year course in theology and philosophy.

Missionaries also differed, according to denomination, in their views and practices regarding racial integration. Reformed missionaries desired that educated Africans form their own third culture and abstain from seeking acceptance into European society. On their mission stations African and European families live in different houses and do not mix socially, though when on district duties black and white ministers associate more closely and eat from the same lunch box.

On Catholic mission stations African and European priests live in one community and share food and accommodation in common. No racial distinctions are made in any aspect of life. On Methodist stations married couples with their children have their own houses and bachelors live together in one house. Again race plays no role and social interaction is equally intense between Europeans and Africans as between members of each race. Methodists gave the impression of being 'colour blind'.

Missionaries of these two denominations looked forward to an integrated society and claimed that political, economic and social integration had to go hand in hand. They expressed the wish that government leave people free to associate with whom they desired and not regulate race relations by law. They believed that only if the races began to mix socially would they begin to understand each other and avoid an otherwise inevitable revolution.

(iv) *Farmers*

Farmers were very divided in their opinion whether to accept African farmers as neighbours. Some welcomed the suggestion, some were doubtful whether Africans could run large farms, but thought that with the help of extension officers they might succeed. These farmers asked for the abolition of the Land Apportionment Act. Others rejected the idea out of hand, fearing that their cattle would catch diseases from African-owned cattle.

Farmers were also divided in their attitude towards social integration, though less evenly than on their willingness to accept African neighbours. Half of them refused even to consider the possibility; some thought it might happen in the very distant future. Only one, who considered himself exceptional in his community, welcomed social integration warmly and deplored any delay because this might cause needless tension in the country.

(e) Conclusion

The above analysis of the responses given by the various agents of change to questions of African advancement and social integration shows that district commissioners are most cautious in regard to African political, economic and social advancement, and are especially opposed to social integration. Their answers suggest that they are generally satisfied with current race relations in Rhodesia and reluctant to see any alterations. Because of their influential position in society their views carry much weight.

Extension officers are dedicated to the economic advancement of Africans, but occupy a middle-of-the-road position in regard to African political and social advance, and in regard to racial integration.

Missionaries are more eager to see African advancement and rapid integration in all spheres of social life than any other group.

Farmers are predominantly against African political advancement because they fear for their own safety, but welcome African economic progress. They generally refuse to accept Africans socially.

Since the sample on which these findings are based is small, it is now compared with the findings of Rogers and Frantz's study. If the overall conclusions of the two surveys are the same, the present findings may be considered representative for a greater number of Europeans than were actually interviewed.

This is a tentative comparison because Rogers and Frantz asked different questions which, however, touched on the same problem. Also, their survey included urban as well as rural Europeans, whereas the present study is purely rural, and, as shown in the earlier chapters, the position of Europeans *vis-à-vis* Africans differs significantly in towns and in rural areas.[27]

It has also been stated above[28] that all rural Europeans belong to the upper stratum of Rhodesian white society. The responses of poorer Europeans, most of whom live in towns, should be very different. In Table 8, which sets out the findings of Rogers and Frantz, the category of craftsmen is included to show the distance in racial

[27]Cf. pp. 31–2 above, *et alia*.
[28]Cf. p. 68 above.

Occupational group	Political Advancement[29]	Occupational Advancement[30]	Educational Advancement[31]	Social Mixing[32]
Professional and technical	2·25	3·01	4·74	1·89
Administrative	1·74	2·54	4·13	1·32
Farming	1·48	2·26	3·66	1·06
Crafts	1·15	1·36	2·89	0·48
Mean	**1·57**	**2·21**	**3·71**	**1·17**

Table 8. Scores relating to a sample of 500 Europeans of attitudes towards African advancement and racial integration.

attitudes expressed by these Europeans from those surveyed in the present study.

A further slight difficulty derives from the occupational classification. Rogers and Frantz class together professional and technical occupations. For comparative purposes these are loosely equated with missionaries and extension officers. Rogers and Frantz's categories of administrators and farmers ought to correspond more closely with those of district commissioners and farmers surveyed in the present study.

All in all, then, a strict comparison between the two studies is difficult and only tentative deductions can be drawn. Nevertheless, certain similarities stand out clearly.

The findings of the larger sample, in which higher scores indicate a greater approval of African advancement and of social mixing than lower scores, show a significant gap both between the professional and technical occupations and others, and also between administrators and farmers on the one hand, and craftsmen on the other. The mean scores show that farmers score very close to the mean of the total European population in Rhodesia in all their responses, but that administrators, professionals and technical workers are much more ready to see changes in racial attitudes than any other section of the European population.

In broad outlines, the two studies reach similar conclusions. Differences occur in that some farmers hold more 'liberal' views towards African advancement, especially in the economic sphere, than district commissioners, that is, administrators. The more positive

[29]Rogers and Frantz, 1962, p. 165.
[30]Ibid., p. 175.
[31]Ibid., p. 174.
[32]Ibid., p. 277.

attitudes of farmers are due to their financial position. Many of them are second generation Rhodesians whose fathers came up with the pioneers. Their farms are therefore large and their families well established in Rhodesia. This gives them a security which people who are less willing to see African advancement often lack.

Because of the broad similarities of the present sample with the larger sample of Rogers and Frantz, its results may be accepted as reliable and applicable to a larger number of Europeans than was actually interviewed.

4. The influence of the occupational milieu on racial attitudes of Europeans

1. Occupation as a determinant of racial attitudes

If the racial attitudes expressed by district commissioners, extension officers, missionaries and farmers are compared with their social profiles, little correlation can be established between many of the personal characteristics and race relations. Age, for example, which seemed to play a role in connection with younger and older district commissioners, seems irrelevant in connection with the other occupations, for extension officers, who are almost all young, are much more willing than young district commissioners to see African advancement.

Prolonged formal education, as against inservice training, seems to have some effect in broadening Europeans' attitudes towards African advance, but again there are notable exceptions, for some of the district commissioners least willing to welcome African progress have a university degree.

Salaries too play no determining role. Rogers and Frantz's finding that men with higher incomes are more liberal than men with lower incomes[1] was not clearly demonstrated in the above study, for district commissioners, who earn the highest salary, formed not the most liberal section of the European rural elite.

Religion too proved less important than is generally believed. Rogers and Frantz found that people without religion were most broadminded in their racial attitudes, followed by Catholics and Anglicans, and that Reformed Christians were most conservative in regard to race relations; other Protestants occupied an intermediate position.[2] Yet district commissioners, most of whom claimed to have no religion or to be Anglicans, were not distinguished by pronounced liberal views. Protestant extension officers were more liberal than Anglican or agnostic district commissioners. Only

[1] Rogers and Frantz, 1962, p. 128. [2] *Ibid.*, p. 130.

among missionaries did a different racial attitude coincide with religious denominations. Reformed Christians generally expressed greater reluctance than other Christians to envisage African political progress and social integration.

Family status may have played a part in racial attitudes. Married men with children were generally more concerned about the future than single men. Consequently celibate missionaries welcomed African advancement and even social integration more fully than married people. But again, Methodist missionaries, most of whom are married, did not differ in this respect from Catholic missionaries.

Since, therefore, personal characteristics seem to contribute little towards the racial outlook of agents of change, it may be suggested that racial attitudes are formed by occupations. This suggestion is based on Mead's observation that what is internal in the mind is learned from the outside.[3] Since men spend most of their time in the pursuit of their occupations, their occupational environment is likely to influence them most deeply.

(a) District commissioners

The social profile of district commissioners has shown that many come from civil service families and that they entered on their occupation early in life, generally just after completing eleven years' schooling. At this age their minds were still open and ready to be formed by the values of their senior colleagues. Moreover, their family background made it easy for them to internalize the norms of the civil service.[4]

District commissioners gave the following reasons for their choice of occupation: poverty in the family forced one to interrupt his schooling and seek work; another, who had just completed a general university degree, came to Africa by boat on which he met an older district commissioner, was fascinated by this civil servant's description of his life, and joined the ministry. Others were dissatisfied with occupations they had attempted, such as serving in the police force, and left because they hoped for better promotion prospects in the ministry of Internal Affairs. Several stated that they preferred other occupations in their youth but lacked professional training facilities; one of these wanted to become a civil engineer, another

[3]Cf. Mead, 1967.
[4]Cf. Holleman, 1968, p. 231. He argues that most district commissioners grew up under very similar circumstances and developed similar personalities.

a magistrate. Many admitted that when they first joined their ministry they were unaware of the importance of their chosen occupation, but that they came to appreciate it later.

At first sight these responses suggest that district commissioners drifted into their present occupation. But a closer examination shows a certain similarity in their positions: their parents provided them with an incomplete or very general education. None has undergone a specialized training.[5] Few of them were highly motivated to choose a professional career. Their initial unawareness of the importance of their occupation indicates that they lacked ambition and were satisfied with the life they knew. More important still, they soon found that their early life experience did not contradict their occupational values. Consequently they were not exposed to internal conflicts when they underwent their long inservice training. African cadets, on the other hand, whose home background differed greatly from that of the present district commissioners, were exposed to great strains and resigned.[6] The political situation of Rhodesia, and the Africans' image of the ministry of Internal Affairs, may also have contributed to their resignations.

The district commissioners' lives can therefore be seen as undivided wholes without alien intrusions. In the civil service they merely entered more deeply into those values which they knew from childhood. Consequently they were easily set in certain ideas. Their long inservice training confirmed them in their views and led to their thorough internalization of their ministry's ethos.

The long inservice training cultivated certain character qualities in district commissioners. It turned them out as practical men, able to handle problems, proud, responsible and incorruptible. Weisman's dictum that 'responsibility does not bestow authority; it confers authenticity'[7] is well borne out by Rhodesian district commissioners.

The district commissioners' occupation is characterized by frequent transfers which do not allow them to strike roots in any community. Most district commissioners served in all the provinces of Rhodesia, and throughout their careers they have been stationed in some ten to twenty districts. Their transfers had been more fre-

---

[5] A B.A. Honours degree is here classed as a broad, general, non-specialized education.
[6] Cf. *supra*, p. 79.
[7] Weisman, 1965, p. 184.

quent in the early years of their careers, but even as senior officers they are transferred about every two years. They judged that transfers were useful to young men because they provided opportunities to get to know the various regions of Rhodesia and the different tribal groups and problems facing administrators in these districts, but they preferred fewer changes once they were in control of a district. They thought that frequent changes of district commissioners made efficient administration difficult and caused discontinuities in social planning.[8]

The frequent changes which force a man to take over the job of one colleague, and after a year or two pass it on to another, contribute to a strong group cohesion among members of the ministry and a corresponding degree of social isolation from wider European Rhodesian society. This in turn helps to foster a distinct set of values among district commissioners.

Other characteristics of their occupation also contribute to a common outlook of life among these administrators. Their work differs from that of most Europeans. The great majority of district commissioners spend half of their working time in African areas, visiting their people, holding meetings and familiarizing themselves in detail with the life in their districts. A minority visit African areas only once a week and spend the rest of the time in their offices. But even in the office most of the district commissioners' time is filled with attending to requests by Africans.

Most district commissioners stressed that they loved their occupation, mainly because of its many-sidedness: they were trying court cases, initiating development schemes, guiding chiefs, and administering large districts. The older district commissioners especially liked the open air life and the many opportunities it provided to deal with people. Many of these placed a high value on personal contacts. Consequently they felt the routine work of the office burdensome and the endless red tape which, they stated, only began in recent years, exasperating. Many also resented the ever greater pressure under which they had to work because of an over-bureaucratization demanded by head office and the needless meetings with fellow civil servants and Africans, which swallowed up much of their time. Younger district commissioners did not object to routine office work as strongly as did the older district commissioners.

[8]Transfers seem to have been less frequent during the first decades of this century. Cf. Holleman, 1968, p. 35.

On the whole, district commissioners liked their occupation and frequently added that it was a vocation to which they were utterly dedicated. None of them seriously considered leaving the ministry for some other type of employment and they often added that they were not qualified for any other but administrative work.

These occupational characteristics show that the post of district commissioner in the past attracted independently-minded men who liked an ill-defined job which gave them scope to define it themselves. These characteristics, however, are a-bureaucratic. Today district commissioners are working in a bureaucracy. The different characteristics of younger and older district commissioners are a reflection of the changes which are taking place in the ministry of Internal Affairs.

Early during this century, commissioners in Rhodesia were given charge of large districts and instructed to preserve peace among the indigenous people, to supply European farmers and miners with labour, and to collect taxes.[9] Apart from these orders, few positive instructions were given them. Their relations with their superiors were often haphazard. In their districts they were the men on the spot and their word was law.

Consequently the older district commissioners are more personalistic rulers than true bureaucrats and their relations with Africans are easy. Africans understand this type of relationship.

Over the years positive instructions have become more and more frequent. Certain policies have to be implemented and these have to take precedence over what individual district commissioners might prefer to do. The ministry of Internal Affairs itself has become a fully fledged bureaucracy. The older district commissioners feel this extensive bureaucratization burdensome and do not fully fit into the new mould. They yearn for the past.

The younger men, however, who have been brought up under the new system, fit smoothly into this bureaucratic framework. A thoroughly structured ministry, with great emphasis on seniority, the demand for co-ordination with other ministries, all this is what the younger men expect. They fully accept the impersonal relationships of bureaucracy and the many directives which have to be complied with. They are ready to implement distinct policies so that their ministry can run like a well-oiled machine.

In relation to Africans, these different attitudes of younger district

[9]Cf. Leys, 1959, p. 291; Gann, 1965, p. 147 *et alia*; Palmer, 1968, p. 15.

commissioners often cause tensions. The younger commissioners must be hard because everything under their control must go according to plan.

The younger men's impersonal and bureaucratic relations are alien to Africans. Consequently the distance between these men and members of the other race is much greater.

The young bureaucrats, moreover, are very conscious of their position in the civil service hierarchy and unwilling to lower their own status. Because they have only recently been promoted, many still feel insecure in their position and therefore depend to a greater extent on the exercise of their authority than do the older men.

This insecurity is most easily overcome by ritualizing their relations with others and emphasizing strongly values generally accepted in European society. They are far less individualistic than the older district commissioners.

The findings of this study indicate that as the character of the district commissioners' position changed, the type of men who fill it changed also. This accounts for the different racial attitudes entertained by younger and older district commissioners.

(b) Extension officers

Extension officers, as pointed out above, entered their profession later than district commissioners and not before they had undergone a specialized training in agriculture. They differ therefore from district commissioners in that they had a focused technical rather than a broad general education when they joined their ministry. All stressed that from childhood onwards they had been interested in agriculture and that agriculture was for them a way of life. The earlier section also showed that most had experience with agriculture through their own families or close relatives.

All extension officers stated two major attractions which they found in their occupation: an open air life and great freedom to plan their work as they thought best. To a secondary degree they expressed an eagerness to help others to improve their farming techniques and to draw Africans into Rhodesia's cash economy. One said: 'I want to do something useful for mankind.'

All of them greatly dislike office work and spend at the most one day a week in their offices. The rest of their time is devoted to practical extension work in African villages and fields. Consequently they know their areas and the peasants very well, and are well informed about local events.

Their familiarity with their areas is increased by their longer stay in any one district. The average extension officer is transferred every four to five years, a period which most judged ideal because more frequent changes would arrest development, and a longer stay would result in routine work. Since, therefore, the extension officers' stay in any one area is about two to three times as long as the district commissioners', and since the areas of which they are in charge are only about a third of the size of the district commissioners', they know their people more intimately. This personal contact is likely to contribute to their more ready acceptance of Africans because knowledge often leads to appreciation.

The absence of prolonged inservice training leaves individual extension officers freer than district commissioners to form their own outlook on life, since many short courses have less power to form a man's outlook than some fifteen years of dependence on senior officers. Moreover, their courses are technical and do not aim at rounded professional socialization. When district commissioners emerge from the long tunnel of training, their outlook on life has been formed. Extension officers experience no such occupational pressures moulding their views.

Other professional characteristics also contribute to the individualism of extension officers. All are younger men and many of them are adventurous. A significant number have been in other continents, or countries of Africa. Several do not speak English as their mother tongue. Few intend to stay permanently in Rhodesia, and still fewer feel fully committed to a lifetime's service in their ministry. In fact, a year after the survey took place about a third of the men interviewed had either left the country because they disagreed with government policies, or they had left their work to find employment in industry or to open up farms of their own. To many, therefore, their position in the ministry of Agriculture was a stepping stone to some more remunerative occupation.

It may be said that both the ministry of Internal Affairs and the ministry of Agriculture attracted independently minded candidates—at least the ministry of Internal Affairs did so in the past. Yet less conformity is expected from extension officers than from administrators. Extension work attracts individualists and continues to foster their individualism. No group pressure exists to make them conform to a distinct professional ethos.

As civil servants, extension officers are by definition working in a bureaucracy just as are district commissioners. Yet the nature of their work and their own characters predispose them to act as individualists rather than as bureaucrats. Their attitude towards Africans seems to a large extent to be influenced by their individualism. Unlike district commissioners, extension officers seem to be men who lack strong convictions but who are able to adapt themselves to new situations as requirements arise. Nothing seems to be static or fixed about them.

(c) Missionaries

The influence of occupation on the racial views of missionaries differs according to the way their denominations interpret their work. It is most broadly conceived by Catholic missionaries, and most narrowly by missionaries of the Reformed Church.

All missionaries gave as the reason for their work a vocation to bring the true religion to non-Christians. Catholic missionaries stated that since early childhood they wanted to be missionaries, that they had been fascinated by what they had read about missionary work in Church magazines, and that they wanted to imitate the great missionaries they had come to admire.

Catholic missionaries stressed the pastoral aspect of their work, but they also emphasized their obligation to contribute to the social development of the people, to provide them with good recreational facilities, with schooling and health services, to stimulate their economic enterprises and to teach them better farming techniques and encourage them to form credit unions to improve their living standards. One of the Catholic missionaries was engaged full time in organizing sporting facilities for Africans, another in stimulating African voluntary organizations, especially those of an economic nature. They claimed that the Gospel could not be received unless the whole human being was confronted with Christ and enabled to live in an environment in which Christian morals could be practised, because it provided social facilities worthy of human beings. They considered their social activities not as paternalism but as pre-evangelization.

Methodist missionaries emphasized the spiritual aspect of their mission more than Catholic missionaries. They talked about having been called by God to save the souls of Africans, but stressed that this could be done best by educating them to as high a level as possible. Their main attention was therefore concentrated on the expansion of schools. One of them, however, had taken a degree in agriculture to assist his people with technical advice. The main aim of Methodist missionaries seemed to be the training of indigenous people to take over leadership positions in the Church. This meant that they tried consciously to work themselves out of their jobs.

Reformed missionaries saw their vocation most narrowly. One of them said: 'I see myself as an ambassador of Christ. It is my sole duty to teach the Christian truth and the Christian way of life to Africans. It is not my task to familiarize them with western culture. In fact, this would be harmful to Africans since they should live according to their own customs as long as these are not morally objectionable by Christian standards.' Social, political and economic questions, which are eagerly discussed by Catholic and Methodist missionaries with the African people, are very rarely mentioned by Reformed missionaries. These aspects of life fall outside their interpretation of the vocation of ministers of the word of God. The only exceptions Reformed missionaries recognized to this rule are concern for education and health because these are seen as directly preparing the way for the acceptance of the Gospel.

From these interpretations of their mission, it can be deduced that missionaries' interaction with Africans as well as their racial attitudes are influenced by their denominationally distinct views of their vocation.

In spite of a distinct interpretation of their vocation by Catholic, Methodist and Reformed missionaries, most shared certain characteristics of their daily lives. All work within a territorially narrowly circumscribed area, generally as large as a province of Rhodesia. In this area their denominations have several mission stations, and individual missionaries are transferred about every four years from one mission to another. However, since all missionaries of a denomination or a missionary society[10] keep in close personal contact through frequent visits and bonds of friendship, such transfers do not uproot them as do transfers of civil servants.

Their prolonged stay in any one place allows them to form intimate ties with the local African population and their frequent visits enable them to keep in touch with many of their African friends. Especially missionaries who are not tied to a particular mission,

[10]Catholic missionaries belong to various religious orders or societies.

but who are in charge of certain activities throughout a mission area, have a large circle of African friends, many of whom are local leaders in one of the voluntary associations they organize. These personal contacts not only create personal attachments but they also account for the missionaries' frequent identification with the African people and their championship of African rights. Whether missionaries are mainly engaged in pastoral work or whether they also teach, all of them are ordained ministers and therefore 'Fathers' of their people; they have a personal love and affection for them.

All missionaries stated that they were very happy in their vocation, that it measured up to their expectations and that they would never choose another type of work. They claimed that their vocation was not an 'ordinary job' but a religious task undertaken for the glory of God. Methodist and Catholic missionaries claimed that their racial attitudes were formed by their religious convictions and therefore morally compelling. They stated that as Christians in a world in which social injustice was widespread they could not conform to public opinion. Reformed missionaries took a different stand. To an outsider it appears that Reformed missionaries regard religion and secular life as unconnected and that they do not acknowledge that their attitudes to one determine their attitudes towards the other.

(d) Farmers

Apart from one farmer who had spent most of his life in the mines, all had either inherited their farms from their fathers, bought them many years ago, or obtained them from government after retirement from the army at the end of the second World War. Yet even the last mentioned had spent their childhood on farms. All of the farmers had therefore grown up in an agricultural milieu and knew no other way of life. Many were second generation Rhodesians whose fathers had immigrated from South Africa. All were well to do and thought themselves important members of their local communities.

The farmers' main concern was to make a profit from farming, and if farming in one district proved less satisfactory than they had anticipated they sold their farms and bought others in more fertile districts. Several of the farmers interviewed had made such a change. This economic attitude also influences their relationship to their African labour force.

The farmers' interactions with their African labourers are standardized. They demand a good day's work from their employees and in return are willing to assume feudal responsibilities for their workers' families. Often their wives care for sick Africans on their property and they themselves frequently intercede for their labourers with local district commissioners when their men are involved in technical breaches of the law.

Of all rural Europeans, farmers are least involved with Africans. On the one hand, their contacts in the work situation emphasize the social distance between the races, on the other, their own working force is well known to them and they often take a personal interest in their wellbeing. Consequently many farmers have a double relationship with their workers: that of employer, and that of personal guardian. This accounts, in part, for their sometimes contradictory views towards African advancement.

2. Evaluation of the occupational milieu

Whereas no correlation was found to exist between the personal profiles and racial attitudes of district commissioners, extension officers, missionaries and farmers, a close correlation seems to exist between the racial attitudes of these agents of change and their occupations. It appears that the ethos of each occupation, and the role expectations characteristic of them, come to influence greatly the incumbents of these occupational roles.

However, care has to be taken not to jump to conclusions too hastily. Because members of a profession show a certain unanimity in their expressed attitudes towards African advancement, it has been inferred that correspondence derives from the character of their recruitment and occupational socialization. Yet the occupational ethos of the four groups has not itself been studied directly. It has merely been assumed that the similarity in attitudes derives from the character of the four occupations and circumstantial evidence has been adduced to support this contention. What other factors may influence racial attitudes, it is as yet impossible to determine. More information must be gathered on what these groups of agents of change expect from their work and from their colleagues, and how step by step certain values and attitudes are inculcated into them during their training and the performance of their duties.

District commissioners, who receive the longest inservice training, and missionaries, who undergo a long professional training, often in religious houses—which has the same effect as long inservice training—express the greatest unanimity of opinions. Extension officers and farmers, who are less exposed to the constant teaching of certain values, show consequently a greater divergence of view.

Moreover, the degree to which members of these occupations are kept apart from other Europeans further strengthens their uniform outlook towards members of the other race. Social separation is strongest among district commissioners because of their high social position, and among missionaries because of their marginality to Rhodesian European society.[11] The loneliness of these positions, whether due to authority and power or due to geographical isolation from all but their colleagues, further contribute to common value systems shared by members of these four occupational groups.

3. The place of the African elite in the lives of European agents of change

Having examined the social and occupational characteristics of the European rural elite, their relations with each other and their position in the European community, and especially their attitudes towards Africans, a final question remains to be answered: Through which channels do agents of change receive their information about the African society? Do they appeal particularly to educated Africans to mediate a contact with the African people or do they contact the African peasantry directly?

District commissioners, who hold positions of honour in the European society and whose authority among Africans goes unquestioned, do not generally use the emergent African elite as mediators but go directly to the ordinary people, by-passing Africans with modern prestige criteria. On their own admission, most district commissioners gained their information either through direct conversation with ordinary peasants and attending their meetings, or through chiefs, the traditional leaders of the African people. Only a small number mentioned junior African civil servants employed

[11]Reformed missionaries are also marginal to Rhodesian European society, but are closely integrated with their society of origin; they maintain their ties with South Africa by regular visits, sending their children to South African schools and listening to South African mass media.

in their ministry as a main source of information. District commissioners seemed to have no connections with African teachers, businessmen or doctors who hold positions of great esteem in the African community.

Extension officers, who mix easily with fellow Europeans and have more informal relations with Africans, quoted two major sources of information: direct contact with African peasants, but more important still, information from their African agricultural staff. The African agricultural staff, members of the emergent African elite, stand to extension officers in the same official relationship as do junior civil servants to district commissioners, though the relationship of extension assistants with the African people is characterized by a slightly greater confidence than the relationship of Africans employed by the ministry of Internal Affairs.

Missionaries, who are marginal to European society because of their conscious identification with Africans, claimed to get most information through personal contacts. The men with whom they had most intense contacts were African ministers of religion and teachers, because these men stood closest to them occupationally. But like civil servants, missionaries did not confine themselves to these intermediators; they too frequently visited the ordinary people of their Churches.

Farmers acted similarly to the other Europeans living in rural areas. They claimed to know what went on among their workers but relied heavily on the information given them by their 'boss boys', that is, Africans they had placed in charge of work gangs.

All Europeans, therefore, used two main channels for obtaining information: members of the emergent elite who stood closest to them occupationally, either because they served in the same ministry or were employed by them, and direct personal contacts. Of all agents of change district commissioners seemed least inclined to rely on intermediaries.

Because members of the European rural elite frequently use members of the emergent African elite to communicate with the African masses, members of the African elite stand in a key position to interpret to their fellow Africans the expectations and ways of Europeans.

Yet rural Europeans and the African elite stand on either side of the colour line in Rhodesia and so are separated by a status gap which few find it possible to cross, and which prevents Africans from mixing socially with Europeans outside the work situation.[12] It is therefore mainly through occupational contacts that the European and African elites of Rhodesia associate. Consequently race relations in the work situation are of great importance.

Race relations seem to be smoothest between administrators and Africans in their civil service branch, between extension officers and their African assistants, and missionaries and their fellow African clergymen and teachers. But relations crossing these occupational boundaries are often strained, for example between district commissioners and teachers.

The knowledge which members of the African elite acquire through association with Europeans in rural Rhodesia is coloured by the Europeans' position in their own racial community. In cases where the contact is closest, as in the case of missionaries, the typicality of the reference group for the wider European society is least, so that the Africans' image too is often distorted.[13] Extension officers, whom Africans find it relatively easy to contact, present a more typical picture of Europeans. The few district commissioners who, also, are willing to accept some select Africans into their homes and so serve as their model of behaviour, present Africans with European leadership personalities. Only farmers, who stand completely outside the social range of educated Africans, never serve them as a reference group.

Only those Europeans who appreciate educated Africans are likely to become important models for the emergent African elite in rural areas. Since some district commissioners, several extention officers, and a great number of missionaries welcome members of the African elite, but because the typicality of the Europeans decreases in inverse proportion to their readiness to meet Africans, rural Africans experience some difficulties in acquiring a typical picture of European life.

In spite of some contacts across the colour line, the evidence of this chapter indicates that, apart from missionaries, most Europeans in rural areas feel relatively independent of the African elite.

---

[12]Van der Horst's observation that where government policy seeks to curtail contacts between the races, many whites are intimidated and fear to act in opposition to official policy, even when association is not illegal, may account for this lack of social contacts. Cf. van der Horst, 1965, p. 139.

[13]My survey of racial attitudes taken in a Rhodesian town repeatedly recorded the comment of disillusioned townsmen: 'I thought all Europeans were as kind and helpful as missionaries. I am very disappointed.' Publication forthcoming.

They do not conspicuously try to win their confidence. They remain self-contained islands of whiteness in a sea of black people.[14] Their contact and co-operation with the African elite are dictated by their professional duties and seldom extend to the social sphere. Most of them consciously preserve the image of racial superiority.

Though many Europeans have contacts with members of the African elite, they frequently seem unaware of the full extent of the changes going on in African society. This may be due to their strongly held views, or even stereotypes, of Africans. According to Mphahlele, the privileged class of Europeans in Southern Africa knows little about the Africans among whom they live because of the emotional circumstances surrounding their contacts, circumstances which allow Europeans to see Africans only as a group, not as individuals.[15]

Many Europeans consider the emergent African elite as unrepresentative of African society. In doing so they overlook one of the dynamic factors working for the transformation of the country in which they live. For African society is changing rapidly in spite of government policies which try to arrest social change and to foster the traditional African life.[16] The following chapters examine the types of African elites which have emerged and their position in African society. Only in understanding this African elite can the role of rural Europeans be correctly interpreted.

[14]Cf. Huggins, as cited in Gray, 1960, p. 152.
[15]Mphahlele, 1962, pp. 96, 111.
[16]*Tribal Trust Land Act*, 1967, No. 9; *African Law and Tribal Courts Act*, 1969, No. 24.

5. The African rural elite

1. Introduction

The first part of this book ended with a reference to the willingness or unwillingness of Europeans to use members of the emergent African elite as their intermediaries with the African people, and the observations that Europeans generally seem to underestimate the influence of the emergent elite in African society. The following chapters try to give an interpretation of the African elite as seen by themselves and by fellow Africans.

(a) Ties of the emergent African elite with Europeans and their own people

The emergent African elite forms the second tier of Rhodesian society and in their own eyes, as well as in the eyes of other Africans, they are the link between the great majority of the African people and Europeans. Africans are proud of members of their own race who have succeeded in filling occupations generally filled by Europeans, because the success of these men appears to them as a proof that there exists no essential difference in ability between the races, and that Africans are capable of doing the same work as Europeans.[1]

Though the emergent African elite has ties with both the first and the third tiers of Rhodesian society, their links with the African people are stronger than their links with Europeans. They have accepted many European values, yet their total set of values is still less different from that of fellow Africans than the total set of values held by Europeans.

[1]My survey of an African township, carried out in 1969, recorded that almost the only difference recognized by Africans between themselves and Europeans is the difference in privileges and wealth; otherwise Africans regard the two races as equal. Publication forthcoming.

The ties which unite members of the African elite with the bulk of the African people differ substantially from their ties with Europeans. With the African people they are connected through the values which they inherited from their past and which gave meaning to their traditional way of life. With Europeans they are connected through their acceptance of many new values which they learnt in cultural contact situations, mainly through their schooling and university studies which initiated them into the inner meaning of western culture.

Different sections of the African elite, however, have been initiated to different degrees into western culture. For some the contact has been intense and these have closely identified themselves with western values. For others contact has been of a more fleeting nature and these have internalized only superficial aspects of western culture. These men and women stand still closer to traditional African culture than do the highly educated Africans. Between these two extremes lies a whole spectrum of different modes of adaptation.

The degree of cultural contact varies both with the type of occupation, whether Africans work in the religious, medical, educational, agricultural or business spheres, and also with the extent of their formal education. Both these subdivisions lead to different interests among the emergent African elite, and because no Africans occupy top executive positions in government which would enable them to co-ordinate diverse interests, the Rhodesian African elite—unlike the elites of independent African states—constitutes a divided elite.

(b) Social differentiation within African society

Within African society a new stratification is evolving. Africans have a strong sense of hierarchy. In the past people were born into the position they would fill throughout their lives. Members of a chief's family were assured of higher status than members of a commoner's family. Status was ascribed.

Because people lived at subsistence level, their economic situation was more or less equal. A chief might have larger fields and larger herds of cattle than a commoner, but he could only eat sufficient to satisfy his hunger; he had no means of storing his surpluses for long periods. What he produced in excess, or what was brought to him as tribute, he had to re-distribute among his followers. Consequently the standard of living among the people did not differ significantly. This uniform living standard in traditional society has given rise to the belief among Africans in the second half of the twentieth century that their society had in the past been an egalitarian society. In fact, there was equality in economic scarcity, but inequality in social and political rank.

Today, ascribed status is rapidly losing its importance in African society. Men with higher education rarely care for traditional status, but they rather invest their assets in modern status symbols. Consequently achieved status comes to take precedence over ascribed status in many aspects of life. Different earning capacities in the cash economy play a leading role in differentiating African society and a great disparity in living standards appears between the various sections of the African people. The traditional myth of social equality is severely challenged.

With lack of emphasis on ascribed status, traditional prestige positions undergo a revaluation. Chieftainship, which in the past constituted the highest cultural goal, has become one of the most controversial of African social institutions. European-trained African priests, doctors and teachers claim a prestige, and are accorded it by most of their fellow Africans, which greatly surpasses that of traditional tribal leaders.

With the complexification of Rhodesian society, social mobility becomes for the first time possible on a wide scale. Smelser and Lipset write that the less differentiated a social system is, the more difficult it is for individuals to move with regard to a single role, because to do so they have to move in regard to all roles, political, economic, religious, and so on. Yet in a highly differentiated system individuals can easily move upwards or downwards in any one aspect of social life without altering all their other social positions. For example, men can become occupationally mobile without becoming politically or religiously mobile.[2] This mobility by individuals in distinct social roles is now taking place in Rhodesia and accounts for the emergence of a modern elite in the spheres of religion, health, education and business.

Achieved status enjoys particularly high esteem among Africans[3] because it is exceedingly difficult for Rhodesian Africans to

[2]Smelser and Lipset, 1964, p. 11.
[3]Ngcobo notes three criteria accounting for the high social status of educated Africans: (1) they are regarded as 'civilized'; (2) their command of English has a utilitarian value; and (3) they may obtain white collar jobs and so escape the toil of common labourers. Ngcobo, 1956, p. 435.

complete higher education. As shown above,[4] less than 2 per cent
of all African students complete nine years' schooling, less than half
a per cent eleven years—which is the average standard of education
reached by all Europeans—and only 0·04 per cent complete full
secondary education. Davis's observation that the less opportunity
for upward mobility exists, the greater is the merit of success,[5]
applies fully to the modern African elite.

Most members of African elites all over Africa move to the towns
so that W. E. Abraham could write that there is a division between
the modern African elite in the towns and the traditional African
elite in the villages.[6] But to this general trend there are exceptions.
A significant number of educated Africans do stay in the villages,
and those members of the modern elite who stay in rural areas
are at times honoured quite out of proportion to their rank in the
wider society. For example, African primary school teachers, who
already among urban Africans are accorded only moderate prestige,
are ranked exceedingly high in rural areas.[7]

(c) Definition of an African elite

Since the economic diversification among Africans is still pro-
gressing, it is difficult to draw a line between those men and women
who form the elite in the proper sense of the word, and those who
form an intermediate category between the newly emergent elite and
the African masses. The transition from the second to the third
tier of Rhodesian society is very gradual and no single characteristic,
such as skin colour which marks the distinction between the first
and second tier, is applicable. As a working aid, Lloyd's suggestion
that the term 'elite' be used to denote those who are western educated and wealthy, and who earn an annual income of at least
£250,[8] is here adopted because a definition of the African elite by
education and wealth is acceptable to most Rhodesian Africans.[9]

In addition to members of the elite proper, certain occupational
groups are included in the present study whose members are poorer
and less well educated than the elite itself, but who are structurally
important and fill occupations either newly introduced by Euro-

[4]Table 5, *supra*, p. 29.
[5]Davis, 1967, p. 388.
[6]Abraham, 1967, p. 30.
[7]Results of my urban survey. Publication forthcoming.
[8]Lloyd, 1966, p. 2.
[9]Yet cf. *infra*, pp. 105, 109.

peans, or greatly influenced by contact with western culture. Lloyd classes such groups as 'sub-elites'[10] and comments that they may be more important reference groups to the African masses than the elite proper because they stand closer to the majority of the people than do the few highly educated Africans.[11]

2. Social ranking of African occupations

Benoi lists five chief criteria for measuring prestige: 'A person of high prestige is: (*a*) an object of admiration, (*b*) an object of deference, (*c*) an object of imitation, (*d*) a source of suggestion, and (*e*) a centre of attraction.'[12]

In the discussion of the Africans' evaluation of European prestige positions it was noted that Africans tend to rank positions less according to such prestige criteria as education, income and extent of authority, than according to the degree that the incumbents of these occupations are socially acceptable to the African people, and that their work is judged to be useful. That is, Africans want to admire their elite and emulate it.

The same group of Africans who rated occupations filled by Europeans were asked to rate occupations partly or exclusively filled by Africans. Occupations which were filled by both Europeans and Africans, such as priests and ministers of religion or extension officers, are included in both Tables 7 and 9. The attention of the men and women who were interviewed for the exercise was drawn to the fact that these positions could be filled by members of either race. The great majority answered that the race of the occupants made no difference to their evaluation. In averaging out the responses the differences due to those who did make a distinction according to race was so small that it is ignored in the tables.

The occupations listed in Table 9 had already been rated in 1963, but no significant differences emerged between the results of the first and second exercise.

With the exception of the Catholic priest, doctor and carpenter, educated Africans rated all occupations slightly higher than did the uneducated, but the difference is nowhere very great. It is most notice-

[10]Lloyd, 1967, p. 153.
[11]Lloyd, 1966, p. 13.
[12]Benoi, 1966, p. 78.

Occupation	Educated Africans	Uneducated Africans
Religion:		
Catholic Priest	1·6	1·3
Protestant Minister or Pastor	2·2	2·2
Health:		
Doctor	1·4	1·3
Nurse	2·5	2·8
Teaching:		
School Inspector	1·2	2·3
School Manager	2·3	2·5
Headmaster	2·3	2·9
Teacher	1·6	2·1
Agriculture:		
Extension Officer	2·3	2·5
Extension Supervisor	2·5	2·6
Extension Assistant	2·7	2·8
Peasant	3·3	3·7
Business/Craft:		
Big Trader	2·6	2·9
Small Trader	3·6	4·0
Carpenter	3·2	3·1
Builder	3·3	3·5

Table 9. Rating of African occupations, 1969[13]

able in the occupations of teachers and headmasters, and this may be due to the high proportion of teachers and teacher trainees in the sample of educated Africans:[14] these men over-rated their own positions.

Occupations connected with mission work, either those directly concerned with religion or those originally, and still today to a large extent performed by missionaries, rate high. To these belong occupations concerned with health and education. Occupations generally filled by civil servants rank lower. To these belong agricultural occupations. Businessmen and craftsmen rate lowest, and some of these can no longer be included in the elite proper but must be assigned to the sub-elite.

Africans gave the following reasons for their rating:

[13]Cf. Foster, 1967, p. 269, for a similar rating exercise undertaken in Ghana. Its result is similar to that of the present survey.
[14]Cf. *supra*, pp. 56–7.

(a) Religion

Priests, ministers and pastors were rated high because of their religious vocation. People stressed that priests, ministers and pastors guided them to God, saved their souls and prevented them from going to hell. A typical comment ran: 'A priest is a man whose sole function it is to preach to us and to remind us of what Jesus said: "Be worthy in the eyes of my father." The priest therefore is important to our souls. We may not forget that one day we will die and after death we ought to be ready to lead a new life in heaven.'

A clear distinction was made between Catholic priests and Protestant ministers and pastors. The majority of Africans thought of their local ministers and pastors as men with an education of eight to ten years, and of Catholic priests as highly educated men. An educated African commented on the African Protestant clergy as follows: 'They are only respected by those who lack education.'

(b) Health

Doctors were rated very highly because they preserve life and restore health and help people to live their lives with a minimum of pain. Respondents argued that since everybody at one time or another is sick, everybody had great need of a doctor. Many admired the skills of doctors and the many inventions of the medical profession. One stated: 'It is imposing to watch a doctor operate.'

The occupation of nurse was esteemed because nurses assist doctors in serving and caring for the sick. Many stressed the kindness of nurses, others regarded them as proud.

(c) Teaching

The position of teachers was rated exceptionally high by educated Africans, higher in fact than the positions of school managers and headmasters because, people argued, before a man can become either he must first be a teacher. The occupation of teacher was regarded most essential to Africans because without teachers progress would be impossible. Comments ran: 'A teacher ranks very high because he helps people to modernize their lives and to become educated.' 'A teacher widens our horizons so that we are able to distinguish what is good and what is bad in the leaders of our country.' 'The teacher opens the world to the child.' 'He brings

knowledge to the people, develops their abilities and fights ignorance.' 'Every other profession depends on the work of teachers.
Teachers are the cornerstone of our new society.'

In contrast to the high value placed on the elementary work done
by teachers, the administrative work done by certain members of
the educational professions was downgraded. Africans stated that
school managers and headmasters were just there to organize
schools, look after teachers and help government to check on regular class work. Several concluded that school managers and headmasters had no more knowledge than ordinary teachers. School
inspectors formed an exception. They are seen to live the life of Europeans and were rated high, especially by uneducated Africans. One
said: 'He is a big shot and earns much money. When a teacher
causes trouble, he can dismiss him.' Another commented: 'An
inspector has been a teacher for many years and understands the
teachers' difficulties.' A third observed: 'I am surprised to see that
there are now African school inspectors. We parents fear inspectors
because they can close our schools. When headmasters tell us of
an inspector's visit we work hard so that he cannot find fault
with our schools.' A fourth said: 'An inspector is a very big man.
Wherever he goes he is accompanied by a government messenger who
serves him and sees that he has all he needs.' But a teacher observed
with some bitterness: 'I would rank an African school inspector
as average because he shows off with his position. He bosses us
around and is very domineering.' Another teacher said: 'I feel free
with headmasters and school managers, but inspectors frighten me.'
The school inspector's image among Africans is therefore marked
by the recognition of their authority in African education.

The responses of educated and uneducated Africans alike reflect
a widespread distrust of administrators in the field of education.
This mistrust is recognized by many people. The monthly African
newspaper, *Moto*, for example, recorded in October 1969: 'Teachers
and parents often regard school managers with mixed feelings.
Teachers dread their visits and liken them to executioners. Likewise,
parents think of them as extortionists, because they recommend certain school improvements requiring money.'[15]

(d) Agriculture

Civil servants were generally esteemed rather lowly. This also

[15]*Moto*, vol. 11, no. 10, October 1969.

applies to those engaged in agriculture, though the ministry of Agriculture was more positively accepted in rural areas during the time of study than other ministries, such as the ministry of Internal Affairs. When teachers were asked why they rated extension officers, who had more education and earn a higher salary than themselves, so much lower, they answered: 'Education and income in themselves are of no importance. What counts is the love and respect people have for an occupation. The extension staff does nothing these days and people do not care for them. But teachers are greatly loved. When a teacher comes to a village, people fetch him a chair and offer him the biggest cup of beer.'

Some Africans indeed regarded the occupations of all extension staff as utterly useless and would prefer to be left without agricultural advice. But others were more willing to accept extension workers, stressing that no family could do without food, and the extension staff greatly helped them to increase their food production. One man stated: 'Agriculture is the mother of life.' Several stressed the great educational influence of extension workers.

Even the occupation of African peasant farmers was rated as average, and slightly higher by the educated than by the uneducated section of the African population. Europeans in Rhodesia generally believe that Africans are fleeing from the land and flocking to towns because they desire white collar employment. This belief is not borne out by the value given to African peasants. Respondents commented that the work of a farmer was most essential for the community. Without his production of food, nobody could live. The esteem connected with farming is also shown by the eagerness with which even white collar workers, such as teachers, try to obtain a right to cultivate land in their chiefdoms or to possess title deeds to larger farms in purchase areas. Successful farmers are esteemed by fellow Africans.

(e) Business and crafts

The relatively low rating of businessmen is surprising in view of the relative wealth enjoyed by many traders. Most people agreed that local businessmen performed a useful function in their communities by providing people with goods which could not be obtained otherwise; traders also provided their neighbours with transport to the nearest towns. They stressed the traders' role in developing the country and importing essential goods into their local communities, such as clothes, special food and some agricultural equipment.

But people criticized traders for selling their goods at too high prices and of often cheating buyers. Others stressed that businessmen pay for their licences to government and so contribute more than other people to the country's revenue; consequently they helped Europeans more than their own people.

Craftsmen were appreciated for their useful services, such as building houses and making furniture.[16] Several men stressed that the services of builders and carpenters introduced modern items into the rural areas and so narrowed the gap between town and country life, making rural life more attractive than it was in the past.

Apart from these elite or sub-elite occupations concerned with religion, health, education or economics, there are some with either a strong traditional or a political association, or with both. Ngcobo, writing about South Africa, states that in rural areas the modern elite exists side by side with the traditional elite.[17] This is equally true for Rhodesia. But the esteem of the traditional and modern elites vary greatly. Unlike the occupations discussed above, those connected with the past and, or, politics, underwent a significant change in rating between the years 1963 and 1969. The rating of these occupations is set out in Table 10.

	Educated Africans		Uneducated Africans	
Occupation	1963	1969	1963	1969
Police	2·6	3·2	2·2	3·1
Chief	1·5	2·9	1·3	3·7
Sub-chief	2·2	3·8	2·7	4·1
Village headman	2·4	3·8	2·9	4·2
Diviner/herbalist[18]	2·4	4·2	2·8	4·9

Table 10. Rating of African political and/or traditional occupations, 1963 and 1969

All these occupations were heavily down-graded during the six-year interval, and this down-grading is no doubt connected with the political development of Rhodesia. In 1963 uneducated Africans

[16]Less essential crafts, such as painters, were rated very low.
[17]Ngcobo, 1956, p. 432.
[18]The Shona word for both diviner and herbalist is *nganga*; most *nganga* perform both functions.

stressed that the occupation of a policeman required much courage and inspired fear and admiration. Educated Africans were less fear struck by the police and rather saw in them government agents with whom they did not want to be associated.

By 1969 there was hardly a discrepancy between the rating of the police given by educated and uneducated respondents. People stressed that the police were entrusted with the task of keeping peace in the country and arresting criminals. Many expressed their attitude towards the police by calling them government agents, charged with the duty to 'maintain law and order', a phrase frequently used by government ministers in their campaigns against African independence movements. No African respondent expressed admiration for the police in 1969.

More significant still is the decline in the prestige given to chiefs between 1963 and 1969. Whereas in the early 1960s chiefs ranked almost on par with priests, doctors and teachers, by the late 1960s they were ranked with craftsmen and peasants.

In the early 1960s, African nationalism had reached the peak of its power in Rhodesia and was extolling traditional African culture. By 1964/5, after the nationalist party had split into opposing factions, many Africans became disillusioned. When, finally, the Europeans who control government began officially to upgrade the position of chiefs and to restore to them powers which they had possessed in the past,[19] even drawing them into parliament,[20] Africans began to turn away from their chiefs and the chiefs' prestige fell rapidly. Africans came to see their chiefs as an extension of a government whose policies they bitterly resented. This change of attitudes towards chiefs is clearly expressed in their comments. Sub-chiefs and village headmen are associated with chiefs and share their loss of esteem.

The comments of educated and uneducated Africans alike reveal why chiefs have lost prestige. In 1963 many answered that chiefs were their leaders who looked well after them and kept order and peace. Chiefs were considered important men. By 1969 Africans either stressed that chiefs were there to keep law and order in their areas—that is, they did the same work as the police—or they

[19] *Tribal Trust Land Act*, 1967, No. 9; *African Law and Tribal Courts Act*, 1969, No. 24.

[20] Cf. *supra*, p. 13. *Proposals for the New Constitution for Rhodesia*, 1969, para. 9.

rejected them outright. Some answered: 'Chiefs, sub-chiefs and village headmen are good for nothing and utterly useless.' 'The chiefs today rule blindly according to government instructions because they are uneducated.' And 'Chiefs form a bridge between the district commissioners and the people.'

Whereas the position of chief dropped from high to average and low, the position of diviner and herbalist dropped from high to low and very low. In the 1969 exercise diviners and herbalists obtained the lowest score of all occupations listed.[21] Already in 1963 the standard deviation for this occupation had been much higher than for any of the other occupations; some had rated diviners and herbalists as very high and others as very low. By 1969 diviners and herbalists were almost unanimously classed as very low. Those who still partially accepted them stressed their function as herbalists. Very few rated their divining skill high. Most stressed that diviners deceived people, told them lies, cheated them of their money and were generally unable to help them in any way. It is likely that the constant emphasis by government on the traditions and customs of the people has adversely affected this traditional occupation as well as that of chiefs.

Table 10 shows that even by 1969 all traditional occupations were still rated higher by educated Africans than by the uneducated. The difference in rating between the two groups of respondents is much greater in regard to traditional occupations than in regard to the occupations listed in Table 9. To educated Africans these occupations still remain a symbol of their traditional society towards which they have an ambivalent attitude.

3. Conclusion

The social rating of occupations followed by Africans shows that traditional prestige positions have lost in influence, but that many new occupations, which require higher education and familiarity with western culture, have acquired great popularity among Africans and those who fill them are respected by their neighbours. The incumbents of modern and traditional prestige positions differ in important characteristics, especially in regard to age and education.

---

[21]All in all, thirty-three occupations were tested, including domestic servants, petrol attendants, street sweepers and other occupations not practised in rural areas; many of these carried low prestige.

Since traditional office holders are generally poorly educated, may not even have attended school at all, and tend to be very old,[22] tensions are likely to exist between the traditional and the modern elites. Special attention is therefore given in the following chapters to the relationship between members of the modern elite and chiefs.

Of equal, if not greater, importance is the relationship of the modern elite with Europeans. The first part of this book analysed the attitudes of members of the European rural elite towards educated Africans. It showed that many members of the European rural elite have contacts with some members of the emergent African elite. It now remains to study the emergent African elite's self-interpretation of their role in Rhodesian society.

Because of their intermediate position between traditional African society and modern European society, members of the African elite may be marginal men, belonging fully to neither group. Merton describes marginal men as those who are poised on the edge of several groups, but who are fully accepted by none.[23]

In spite of their strong ties with traditional society, members of the modern African elite have chosen Europeans as their reference group. Traditional African society remains their in-group because Europeans refuse to accept them fully. By using European society, to which they do not belong, as their reference group, members of the modern elite orientate themselves towards an out-group. According to the degree to which they do this, and even affirm their out-group orientation in word and action, they may create a gap between themselves and their in-group and progressively widen it.[24]

The marginality of the African elite towards European society is clearly recognized because of the caste barrier separating Africans from Europeans in Rhodesia. Yet the marginality of the African elite in relation to their own people is not proved. Ngcobo warns not to over-emphasize the extent of estrangement between educated Africans and the African masses. He writes:

While the educated African is aware of being different in outlook and mode of living in several respects from the rest of his people and conscious of his position, he nevertheless maintains contact with them. He has ties of blood and family loyalties with his relatives and kinsmen; he speaks the

[22]Cf. Weinrich: *Chiefs and Councils in Rhodesia*, 1971.
[23]Merton, 1964, p. 265.
[24]*Ibid.*, p. 265.

language of his people and feels proud to know the important elements of their tribal culture. He also lives among his people, knows their difficulties and problems, suffers their disabilities and sympathizes with their hopes and aspirations.[25]

The relationship between the African elite and the majority of the African people is therefore of great importance.

Should sections of the emergent elite prove truly marginal to their own people, their elite status and leadership qualities might be queried. Those Europeans will then be right who regard educated Africans as unrepresentative of the African people. Seligman claims that an elite must be both symbolically and functionally representative.[26] Should the elite be marginal, then educated Africans would not be objects of emulation within their society[27] and other Africans would not be proud of them.[28]

Yet whether members of the African elite are marginal men and women or not, they are definitely poised between two cultures. This intermediate position turns them into keen critics of both traditional and modern society. For education has sharpened their intelligence and instilled in them liberal values which are not fully accepted by their surroundings.[29]

In addition to examining these issues, the following chapters also pay attention to the recruitment of the modern African elite, for Merton considers it essential to determine who the people of an in-group are who orientate themselves towards an out-group.[30]

[25]Ngcobo, 1956, p. 435.
[26]Seligman, 1966, p. 335.
[27]Cf. Ngcobo, 1956, p. 435.
[28]Cf. *supra*, p. 101.
[29]Cf. Parkins, 1966, p. 176.
[30]Merton, 1964, p. 268.

6. The African religious elite

1. Catholic priests

(a) Recruitment

Catholic priests come predominantly from peasant families. Though many members of the emergent African elite are the sons of peasants, the proportion of Catholic priests coming from peasant families is perhaps still greater than among other groups of educated Africans. The reason is that missionaries give special help to poor but religious-minded and intelligent young men to study for the priesthood. One of the African Catholic priests interviewed was an orphan, brought up by missionaries. Another related:

My father was an ordinary peasant and all the members of my family were pagans. My elder brother went to a mission school. When I was twelve years old my mother died and my brother came home to help the family. He sent me to school for the first time in my life. After six years' schooling I decided to become a priest. The missionaries then gave me all the help I needed.

Though economic considerations rarely prevent African youths from becoming priests, long years of study often form a barrier. The average education of African priests includes some six years of philosophical and theological studies after secondary schooling. Many young men drop out during this long training course. The few who persevere are greatly esteemed in their communities.

Most African Catholic priests serve near the chiefdoms in which they were born because, apart from foreign missionaries, dioceses are staffed by local clergy. Consequently all African priests are well known among the African people, even if they are not stationed in the very chiefdom of their birth.

(b) Relations with Europeans

African priests receive a salary of £10 a month, of which £2 are subtracted for their pension fund. Thus they have more money at their disposal than European priests who receive no regular salary. Because they live in community with other priests and are clothed, fed and lodged from common funds, this money is pocket money and not needed for their upkeep. Many use it to assist their families.

Their life in community with European missionaries at the mission station clearly classes African priests as members of the elite. They share in the Europeans' food and accommodation and all the facilities available to them. Their clerical dress, moreover, sets them into a category apart from the ordinary people. For it is not money in itself which confers prestige but the status symbols which are evident to all.

African priests are accepted as equals by their European colleagues. The educational gap between them is not very great. They have studied for longer years than most members of the African elite, and are acquainted with the European missionaries' cultural values and have adopted most of these as their own. Their acceptance by missionaries gives African priests a security and self-reliance which is often lacking in other members of the African elite.

This acceptance, however, is not automatically granted to them when they mix with other Europeans. None of them recorded ever having been treated discourteously by civil servants, but they generally stated that they reduced their contacts with district commissioners and other government officials to ā minimum. They distrusted them as much as did their European colleagues and the African people among whom they lived. Consequently the contacts of African priests with Europeans seldom extend beyond missionary circles. They know much about Europeans and their culture, but do not personally associate with the average Europeans in Rhodesia.

(c) Relations with Africans

African Catholic priests see themselves first and foremost as pastors, helping their people in their spiritual and moral needs. One said: 'I see myself as a priest, dedicated to the task of saving souls.' They were less concerned with providing social and economic facilities for their people than were their European colleagues. They were interested in direct evangelization, not in pre-evangelization. They thought that their ties with their people were very close. Some admitted that when they first left the seminary they felt somewhat out of touch with their own people and had often to rely on older

European missionaries to re-introduce them to the African way of life. But in all cases the contact was soon re-established.

Many Catholic priests spend most of their time in the African villages, visiting their people, administering the sacraments to them, and participating in their very life. While on district duties, they often sleep in the huts of the Christians they visit and share their food. They soon realize that they stand much closer to their own people than do European missionaries, and the people themselves regard African priests as their 'own priests'. Many priests mentioned how frequently Africans came to consult them about traditional religious beliefs and how they opened such conversations with the phrase: 'Father, you will understand my difficulty because you know that the ancestor spirits require me to carry out this ritual.'

The confidence placed in African priests by their people, and their simultaneous acceptance by European colleagues, place them in an unusually integrated situation. They are neither marginal to the Europeans with whom they live nor to the people whom they serve, but they are insulated from many of the pressures which bear on other members of the emergent African elite.

(d) Relations with chiefs

As members of the African rural elite, fully accepted by Africans and local Europeans alike, African priests feel secure. This security enables them to feel at ease in many types of relationship which cause strain to other members of the elite. Their relationships with African chiefs, for example, are marked by a relaxed and natural recognition. Chiefs respect African priests and call them 'Father', just as the people do, though the chiefs may be old and the priests young. Catholic priests, though seldom related to local chiefs by blood because of their transfers from one mission station to another, are on friendly terms with them. Outwardly priests conform to local etiquette and clap their hands when they approach a chief, but they admit that they merely do this to give a good example to the people, not in order to recognize chiefs as their superiors.

Catholic priests generally regard chiefs as respectable old men, but as of little importance in modern life. One said: 'Chiefs feel very insecure. They have no power; all power is in the hands of the district commissioners. Chiefs today have money but no prestige.' Another said: 'Chiefs are the spokesmen of the district commissioner. They can do little for the people. Since government has tried to increase their power, the real standing of chiefs in the community has considerably fallen. They are feared by their people but not loved.' A third priest recorded an interview with an important chief in which the chief said to him: 'You see, Father, I myself do not like to do the things I am told to do by government. But I have to obey instructions or else I lose my salary which by now is over £50 a month. Without it I cannot give my children as good an education as I would like to do. I dislike the present government as much as you do but I am caught.'

Catholic priests often sympathize with the chiefs' dilemma; they do not condemn them.

(e) Political aspirations

African priests do not directly interfere in politics, but like their European colleagues they often feel bound by their religious commitment to protest against government policies if these infringe human liberties and social justice. Some stated that their sermons were occasionally recorded by members of the Criminal Investigation Department.

Many priests sympathize with African nationalism, though as priests they do not take out membership cards. Some of their close relatives have been active in the nationalist movement and one said that his brother was in restriction. Some related that in the past they were occasionally asked advice by nationalist leaders; they suspected, however, that these questions were more interrogations designed to test their political views than requests for spiritual guidance.

Like their people, African priests feel themselves constantly watched and some complained that they could not give their people adequate guidance because of police informants. One said: 'I cannot even tell my people about their civil rights without being called to the district commissioner to account for my words. As a result our people are ignorant and afraid.'

(f) Conclusion

Catholic priests, then, may be seen as a highly educated group who are fully accepted as equals by their European colleagues and who have also very close ties with their own people, both through their kinship connections with peasant families and through their work which maintains their close contact with the African population. Their one hardship is their low money income which prevents them from being of greater financial assistance to their kinsmen.

There are certain aspects of their life which prevent Catholic priests from becoming a reference group for many people. According to Benoi's criteria for prestige,[1] Catholic priests qualify for elite status because they are objects of admiration and deference, a source of suggestion and a centre of attraction, but they seldom serve as objects of imitation for their manner of life differs from that of most Africans because of its celibacy and voluntary poverty. Consequently not many youths try to live their life.

2. Reformed ministers

(a) Recruitment

Like Catholic priests, African Reformed ministers are locally recruited. They too are frequently sons of peasants, though some come from families of teachers or traditional leaders. After ten years' schooling, most study for four years some philosophy and the Bible; the main emphasis is given to practical theology. Some ordained ministers try to improve their qualifications by studying privately for a university degree.

Most Reformed ministers lay great emphasis on education and try to give their children the best education they can. One minister in his fifties has seven children, three girls and four boys. One of his daughters is a teacher, one a secretary and one a nurse. One son is a mechanic, the others are still in school. Another minister gave the best education to his eldest son who became an extension supervisor, his second son received slightly less education and took up a lower position in the agricultural department. By the time his third son was of school age, the minister was financially unable to pay for his secondary education and the youth had to leave after primary schooling. Since the young man's ambition to become a minister like his father was frustrated because of lack of education, he left the Reformed Church and formed his own African independent Church.

(b) Relations with Europeans

The average Reformed minister receives a salary of some £28 to £30, contributed by the members of his congregation. This compares

[1] Cf. *supra*, p. 105.

positively with the income of African primary school teachers, but is less than a quarter or a third of what European ministers of the Reformed Church are paid by the Mission Board in South Africa. Consequently they cannot afford the same living standards as their European colleagues.

Mission stations of the Reformed Church contain family groups. The homes of European and African mission staff are built on different sites of the mission property and differ in quality. These differences are visible to the African people who consequently argue that African ministers are treated as inferior by European missionaries.

The races mix but little on Reformed mission stations. A leading African minister stated that a European minister came sometimes to see him at his house and that he sometimes saw him at his, but that they did not drop in for social occasions. He felt that he was not wanted and commented:

I would like to mix with European missionaries, but feel that they are very different from me. I refrain therefore from making the approach. When I was in Europe, I felt very much at ease in European company, but here in Rhodesia all is different. Here we regard Europeans as our masters and learn from them. They are superior to us. I personally regard them as my fathers, but in the way that African sons regard their fathers, not as European children regard theirs. Once I met with Catholic missionaries. On that occasion I mixed easily. The Catholic missionaries did not seem as distant to me as do the ministers of my own denomination.

Lack of acceptance by missionaries, who trained them to take over the leadership of their Church, often causes an acute sense of frustration in Reformed ministers and results in great insecurity. They are asked to accept the Christian religion without being allowed to share in the culture which has formed the present shape of that religion.

(c) Relations with Africans

Reformed ministers often take this sense of insecurity with them when they meet the educated members of their congregations. One minister complained that few educated Africans ever attended his services and that consequently he failed to contact the modern African elite. He admitted that educated Africans often looked down condescendingly at him. Yet he felt accepted by the ordinary people. He said: 'One day a week I visit my people in their villages. I think that they understand the Bible better when I preach to them than when a European does so. They even ask me how to deal with their spirits when they trouble them.' Like Catholic priests, therefore, Reformed ministers feel that the members of their congregations confide in them, though Catholic priests feel accepted by educated and uneducated Africans alike.

Reformed ministers emphasized the pastoral aspect of their work which imposed on them the duty to instil in Church members a certain moral code forbidding beer drinking and sexual immorality, including polygyny. They constantly returned to the theme of increased beer consumption among Africans. They blamed government for this because government provides ever better opportunities for the sale of beer. Many complained that even schoolboys already took to drinking.

They realized that their people took exception to their insistence on a strict moral code and one admitted: 'It is my duty to point out their serious shortcomings to my people. But sometimes I am weak and do not want to do it. Then I experience a great inner conflict. I feel that I must insist on the observances of these laws of our Church because I may not neglect my responsibility. I must accomplish the task given to me.'

The Reformed ministers' insistence on abstinence from beer and other moral restrictions does indeed cause a growing resentment among the ordinary Africans towards their ministers. In the past African ministers could tell their people that European ministers had imposed these regulations. Since the late 1960s the local synod consists of a majority of African ministers and their vote determines all issues. With progressive Africanization of the leadership in the Church, African ministers can no longer shrug off responsibility for restrictive regulations.

(d) Relations with chiefs

Reformed ministers expressed themselves cautiously about chiefs. One said: 'Chiefs often appear as irresponsible because they dare not say what they would like to say for fear of being deposed by government.' Another stated: 'Chiefs carry out government orders instead of helping their people. Some chiefs enjoy their close link with government, others do not.' And a third commented: 'The chief in my district does not belong to my Church. I have nothing to do with him. I know that the people of his chiefdom are split into two opposing factions and that many greatly dislike the chief for selling land to outsiders. But this does not concern me.'

Whereas Catholic priests look sympathetically at chiefs as symbols of the past, now manipulated by government, Reformed ministers stand aloof from them. They extend their general attitude of not mixing in politics also to traditional political processes.

(e) Political aspirations

The reluctance of European missionaries of the Reformed Church to discuss the political development of the country with their African clergy creates in the latter the impression that religion and politics are divorced from each other. European missionaries of this denomination regard politics as divorced from Church policies, but not as unimportant. They rather regard political action as the responsibility of the consciences of individual Church members. Because they do not exchange their views on this topic with their African colleagues, few African Reformed ministers hold clearly formulated views on Rhodesian politics. One thought that Africans were still too disunited to make a bid for majority rule and that they dared not unite for fear of arrest.

The political non-involvement of Reformed ministers is not well accepted by the African people, especially not in those communities which have a high percentage of educated Africans. Since Reformed missionaries have laid emphasis on a well-developed school system, many of their Church members are educated. This causes many conflicts between ministers and people. Kuper, studying the position of the Reformed African clergy in South Africa, recorded the following comments of his respondents: 'Minister—at present time does not earn much respect. Lots of people have tended to despise them as instruments of their suffering.'[2] Kuper explains this attitude as follows: 'The Dutch Reformed Churches dispense spiritual sanctions for the secular policies of apartheid. The effect for many Africans is that of clothing naked oppression in Christian vestments. This makes it difficult to separate White oppression from Christian doctrine.'[3]

The political environment in which Reformed ministers find themselves isolates them from both their European superiors and their people. They are reluctant to speak of their personal suffering, and

[2]Kuper, 1965, p. 121.
[3]*Ibid.*, p. 195.

only if they trust a person are they ready to reveal what occupies their minds. One minister stressed on such an occasion the incompatibility between the Christian teaching of the brotherhood of all men and the discriminations to which he is exposed at his own mission station. Another stated that the prohibition to engage in political activities, and even the discouragement to express political views, was felt by him as stifling his aspirations.

Kuper summarizes the effects on African ministers in a similar social setting as follows:

They are encased in ambivalence. There is ambivalence towards Christianity among Africans—the deep spiritual devotion of some and the disillusioned cynicism or, indeed, bitter hostility of others . . . There is ambivalence in the role of the clergyman—the duty to sublimate personal self-interest in spiritual and selfless service and, at the same time, the insistent call for justice and recognition. Perhaps it is by not sublimating their personal dilemma that African clergymen will make their most significant contribution.[4]

(*f*) Conclusion

The findings of the present survey, corroborated by findings of Kuper in South Africa, show that African Reformed ministers are marginal to both their fellow European colleagues and also to their own African society. They have to implement many rules and regulations which the people reject, for which many do not find justification in the Bible—such as the prohibition of beer drinking—and which therefore appear to them as an imposition by members of another race. Yet for all this difficult task African Reformed ministers are not accepted by white missionaries either. They generally stand alone in a no-man's land. Lacking the more thorough education of Catholic priests, and especially the security which the latter derive from their full integration into a multiracial mission community, Reformed ministers feel less sure of themselves, even in their contacts with fellow Africans. They often give the impression of devout, but timid, personalities.

Few African youths try to become Reformed ministers. Celibacy is not demanded by the Reformed Church and so does not prevent young men from joining the ministry. The income is also about the same as that of African teachers, and many Africans study for

[4]*Ibid.*, pp. 214–15.

the latter profession. The lack of imitation of the Reformed clergy seems therefore to be due to the ambivalent position of the Reformed ministers, to their marginality to both African and European society.

Because of their marginality they do not form an important reference group for many Africans. They live a life distinct from that of the African masses and display many prestige symbols of the modern elite, such as good clothing and housing. Yet their juxtaposition to European missionaries, who excel in all these status symbols, reduces their objective values. The lower ranking of African ministers is affected by this marginal position of the African Reformed clergy within their own Church.

3. Methodist ministers

(a) Recruitment

Methodist ministers have a similar social background to many Catholic priests or Reformed ministers. Most are born in the area in which they work and most of their parents are peasants. One minister outlined his life history as follows: His mother died in his early childhood so that he does not remember her. His father died when he was a young boy. At his father's death, his family was in great need. He therefore informed his elder brothers and sisters that he would seek work to support himself. He found employment on a farm and earned four shillings and sixpence a month. After some years, when he was about twelve years of age, the farmer's wife suggested to her husband sending the young boy to school. He attended a local school for four years and then came to a Methodist mission where he completed his primary education, paying for his school fees by working during holidays. He felt called to the ministry and underwent religious training for three years, at the end of which his Church sent him to Europe and America for further studies.

Church assistance helped several Methodist ministers to ordination, just as it helped candidates for the Catholic priesthood.

(b) Relations with Europeans

Methodist mission stations share characteristics with both Catholic and Reformed mission stations. Its missionaries and ministers are mostly married, and free married accommodation is provided for all families. Methodist mission stations are distinguished from Reformed mission stations in that all houses are of identical quality and the races are not spacially separated from each other. In fact, houses are at times inhabited by African, at times by European families, depending on the transfer of staff members.

Europeans and Africans mix perfectly on mission stations. Family feasts, recreational activities and casual visits take place with equal frequency between Africans and Europeans as they do between members of either race. One minister stated: 'When I have to go to town at the same time as the European missionary, we sometimes take my car, sometimes his. Sometimes I buy him a bottle of soft drink in town, sometimes he buys one for me. European store keepers often wonder when they see me paying for him. We are happy together and always call each other by our Christian names.'

The Methodist ministers' acceptance by Europeans is, however, confined to the mission station. Several related that when they went with their European colleagues to town they were not served on an equal basis; then all of them would leave the shop or restaurant and go without food. These experiences strengthen the bonds between Methodist clergymen, but make African ministers the more aware of racial discrimination in Rhodesian society. One said: 'Europeans in general consider themselves much superior to us. They boss us up; they shout at us; they do not give us a chance and do not trust us. They press us down and do not let us improve ourselves. They will never accept us on an equal footing.' Another minister related his experience with district commissioners. He stated: 'District commissioners never trust African ministers. When I write a letter to him concerning the marriage of our Church members, he asks endless questions. He would never do this if a European missionary had signed the letter. I try to like even district commissioners because as a minister of God I must love and help all people. But it is very difficult to deal with such men; they frighten me.'

(c) Relations with Africans

Accepted by fellow missionaries, but feeling deeply their rejection by the wider European community, Methodist ministers have many ties with their own people. They earn about the same salary as Reformed ministers, and therefore less than white Methodist missionaries. Like the African Reformed ministers they are paid by their local congregation, not by a mission board. Yet their intense social intercourse with European missionary families, and the sharing of many social facilities, overshadows their income differences. Methodist ministers have the advantage over Catholic priests that they are able through their salaries to support their kinsmen on a larger scale. Since they come generally from poor families, their relatives often ask for their assistance. One minister stated that his home at times looked like a public place because of the large number of relatives and strangers who came to 'the minister's house to sleep and eat'. He stressed that his house was a home for all people.

Methodist ministers often feel at one with their people. They not only welcome them in their own houses, but they also visit them in theirs. Several stressed that they felt loved and accepted by members of their congregations and often ate with them in their homes. Some stressed their good relations with educated Africans, especially teachers. They did not feel rejected by them as did a number of Reformed ministers.

Methodist ministers stressed their duty to insist on strict sexual morality and abstention from beer just as did Reformed ministers. Several felt this to be a burdensome duty, but none felt that this created a rift between them and the people.

(d) Relations with chiefs

The Methodist ministers' attitude towards chiefs is often critical. One said: 'Many chiefs are as selfish as Europeans. They want everything for themselves. District commissioners support chiefs in everything they do, and they even go as far as to punish unruly villagers who do not obey their chiefs' orders.' Another said: 'Some chiefs are good, some bad. We had a very good chief in our area, but he was deposed by government because he was more influential among the people than the district commissioner himself. He was always with his people and knew what they wanted. As long as he ruled all went well. But our present chief exploits the people.'

(e) Political aspirations

Methodist ministers seemed keenly interested in the political development of the country, though few of them actively participated in political movements. One commented: 'My people hate the government, but dare not say so for fear of being sent to a restriction camp. Consequently they smile and Europeans think that they are happy. But they are very unhappy. So am I. I suffer with them.'

Like most Africans, the majority of Methodist ministers looked forward to majority rule. One said: 'The sooner it comes the better. By now it is already too late to avoid much bloodshed. Africans have become too frustrated.'

These responses reveal that some Africans who have frequent opportunities to discuss politics with well-disposed Europeans have a much clearer and more radical attitude towards politics than those who are discouraged from discussing politics. The political attitudes expressed by European and African clergy of the Methodist and Catholic Churches are much alike, whereas in the Reformed Church no such affinity exists.

(f) Conclusion

Methodist ministers, accepted by both their European colleagues and the African people, constitute a group highly critical of European society in general. Their lively interest in politics constitutes a strong bond between them and their people and prevents the formation of a gap which seems to separate Reformed ministers from their congregations.

4. Seventh Day Adventist pastors

Pastors of the Seventh Day Adventist Church are a group of Protestant clergy rather different from those described above. Their Church is divided into two sections, one dealing exclusively with Europeans, the other with Africans. Consequently African pastors do not generally live on large mission stations with European colleagues, but as individuals in the midst of African villagers. Annually they are visited by ministers in charge of larger territorial units. Most of these visiting ministers are Europeans. Apart from these visits African pastors live alone among the African people. They have very little contact with Europeans.

(a) Recruitment

Seventh Day Adventists distinguish between ministers and pastors. Few Africans are ordained ministers; the large majority of African Church leaders are pastors. They lack an official training in theology but acquired their knowledge in many informal ways. One pastor had been selling Church literature for several years and in his spare

time studied the booklets he sold. Because of their lower qualifications, the scope of pastors is limited. They preach and preside over
the celebration of the communion service, but they do not baptize.
Baptism takes place annually when the ordained ministers visit the
congregations.

(b) Relations with Africans

Their lower educational qualifications, often confined to eight to ten
years' schooling, is reflected in their low and irregular salaries. They
live on what their congregations voluntarily provide, which generally
is far less than Methodist and Reformed ministers receive. One pastor, in order to educate his children, runs a butchery; others follow
other secular occupations in order to support their families. Many
obtain land from the chiefs in whose areas they are stationed in
order to grow their own food. This economic dependence greatly
influences the relationship between pastors and their people, and
especially the relationship between pastors and local chiefs.

Unlike the Catholic, Reformed and Methodist clergy, most
Seventh Day Adventist pastors are not born in the districts in which
they are stationed. Church policy assigns them to areas far removed
from their relatives so that as 'strangers'[5] they are unburdened by
kinship obligations and free to spread the word of God. Yet economic need often replaces kinship ties with dependence on non-rela-
tives. This is illustrated by the following case history.

(c) Relations with chiefs

In one chiefdom people could not decide, on the death of a chief,
who his successor should be. The succession dispute lasted for many
years and divided the chiefdom into two opposing factions. The local
pastor was drawn into the succession dispute. His church was built
in the area of one faction, but the acting chief lived in the other.
The pastor depended on the acting chief for land to grow his food,
but his most active Church members lived around his church and
were members of the other faction. The pastor's support of the acting chief caused tensions between him and his congregation. The
leader of the opposition reacted to his partisanship by removing
his children from the local primary school, run by his Church, and

---

[5]Africans distinguish between *majinda*, relatives of local chiefs, and *vatorwa*,
'strangers', that is, unrelated persons. *Vatorwa* are often at a disadvantage in their
communities because traditional leaders tend to favour their relatives.

Plate II 129

IIa. A Catholic priest addresses a congress of laymen

IIb. A Methodist minister leads his congregation in worship

taking them to a Catholic mission. His action caused a stir among
the people, but the opposition leader declared:

Our Church wants only uneducated and innocent people. It started our
school in 1927, but by now it only provides five years of education while
the Catholic school, which opened only in 1952, already provides secondary education. Our Church has arrested our progress. I have two com-
plaints. We are told not to engage in politics, but only to fight for the things
of heaven. Yet look at our pastor, how heartily he fights for the things
of this earth. He supports my political opponent for the chieftainship.
Meanwhile he tells us to close our eyes and pray. We have been fooled.

Because of their economic dependence, the relationship between
Seventh Day Adventist pastors and chiefs is much closer than is the
relationship of other clergymen with chiefs. Their lack of education,
their lack of income, and their orientation towards village life, as well
as their almost complete isolation from Europeans, induce them to
seek their security in traditional society by being accepted by traditional leaders, the chiefs.

(d) Political aspirations

Because of their close integration into traditional society, Seventh
Day Adventist pastors are little interested in African nationalism
and African self-government. They stress strongly their obligation
to abstain from any participation in politics, from which they
exclude, however, their interest in traditional political processes, that
is, competition for the chieftainship. They argue that all Africans
are 'sons of the soil' and that chieftainship is part of their way
of life.

In spite of their lack of identification with modern African aspirations, Seventh Day Adventist pastors are often well received by their
people because the African communities in which they live are
generally less well educated than other areas so that the people too
are less interested in African nationalism than are the people who
are strongly influenced by other denominations. The reason is that
higher education and interest in African nationalism are closely
related.[6]

---

[6]Cf. Weinrich, *Chiefs and Councils in Rhodesia*. There it has been shown that
higher education and interest in nationalism are directly related. The educational
level of Seventh Day Adventists is often lower than that of Church members of
other denominations, because they lay less emphasis on schooling than other Christ-
tian denominations, partly because of lack of funds, partly because of lack of

(e) Conclusion

The social characteristics of Seventh Day Adventist pastors do not show them as leaders guiding their people towards a new culture. They have become integrated into traditional culture which they are modifying only slightly in order to accommodate within it certain Christian values. Lacking modern prestige criteria, Seventh Day Adventist pastors are neither sources of suggestion and centres of attraction, nor objects of imitation by people aspiring to a modern way of life. But they are loved and paid deference to by those who belong to their congregations and devoutly follow their religious instructions.

5. Evaluation of the African religious elite

This survey of the African clergy in some Christian denominations in Rhodesia shows that priests, ministers and pastors stand in different relationships to both Europeans and their own people. At one extreme stand Catholic priests, highly educated and fully accepted by their European colleagues. They feel secure in their position, and their security gives them confidence in all social contacts. None reported having ever been treated disrespectfully by civil servants or any other Europeans, though they did not go out of their way to meet them.

Among Africans they are accepted as leaders and admired for their learning and familiarity with the European way of life. They are liked by fellow Africans for their political views and are trusted. The African people are proud of their own priests. Consequently they are accepted by local Europeans and Africans alike.

At the other extreme stand Seventh Day Adventist pastors who lack advanced formal training and do not distinguish themselves greatly in their way of life from fellow Africans. They live in well-built houses in the tribal areas, but this, together with their clerical dress, is almost the only mark distinguishing them from peasants. They have very little contact with Europeans and share most of the values of African society.

---

trained personnel. Since in Rhodesia education in rural areas is almost exclusively provided by Christian missions, and since denominations generally respect each other's mission territory, Africans in Seventh Day Adventist areas often lack advanced schooling facilities.

Methodist and Reformed ministers stand between these two extremes. Methodist ministers, like Catholic priests, are fully accepted by European fellow missionaries, but are distinguished from Catholic priests by less education. They suffer no economic hardships as do Seventh Day Adventist pastors, and live at about the same standard as most members of the African elite, as for example school teachers and extension assistants. Through mixing socially with European missionaries, they gain prestige in the eyes of fellow Africans. Because they share the aspirations of most Africans for a new social order in Rhodesia, they feel generally accepted in African villages.

Reformed missionaries, occupying similar educational and financial positions as the Methodist clergy, stand nevertheless in a different relationship to both Europeans and their own people. Because they are socially unacceptable to European fellow ministers, their people hold them in less esteem. The respect enjoyed by African religious leaders seems to be linked to the degree to which they are accepted by Europeans, and above all to the degree that people observe them to be treated as equals by Europeans.

Though the religious elite does not generally constitute a reference group to Africans in the sense that many try to follow their example and become themselves priests or ministers of religion, they do constitute a reference group in the sense that many men, women and children look to their priests, ministers and pastors for inspiration in personal moral behaviour and as models for religious devotion and piety. This too is a form of leadership, the form of leadership, moreover, which the African clergy consciously tries to give. They want to be leaders, influencing their people in their spiritual and moral lives. According to Lloyd's definition of the modern African elite, Catholic priests and Protestant ministers are members of this group of emergent Africans. Pastors of the Seventh Day Adventist Church, however, may better be classed as members of a sub-elite since they lack both the degree of modern education and income which Lloyd considered as a minimum requirement for elite status.[7]

[7] Cf. *supra*, p. 105.

7. The African medical elite

1. Doctors

(a) Recruitment

African doctors tend to come from peasant backgrounds. One or two are the sons of ministers of religion or teachers. One doctor related that he is the only educated person in his family and that his father was a famous diviner and herbalist. His parents were not even Christians, yet his father sent him to school. He excelled in his class and, encouraged by his teachers and relatives, he continued his studies until he graduated in England as a medical practitioner. Looking back at his boyhood the doctor admits to being dazzled at 'the length of the jump' he has taken and wishes it had been achieved more gradually. He is aware of a great cultural gulf between himself and his family.

Like most members of the modern elite, African doctors try to give their children the best education within their means. One doctor has sent his eldest son to a private boarding school, catering for the most affluent section of Europeans in Rhodesia. The high school fees charged, however, prevent him from giving an equally good education to his other children, and these follow the normal secondary education available to Africans.

African doctors tend to remain in touch with their relatives. One doctor stated that his mother occasionally visits him, but that she refuses to stay for any length of time in his house since she does not feel at ease outside her village environment. Most doctors are frequently asked by their brothers and sisters, as well as by more distant relatives, for financial assistance. One doctor estimates that he spends at irregular intervals some £40 to £60 in aid of his kinsmen whenever they experience a sudden emergency. With an annual salary of between £2,000 and £3,000, depending on whether they are in mission or government employment, doctors feel that they cannot refuse help to their needy relatives.

Doctors from peasant families have often to struggle to pay their way through school and rely heavily on missionaries and other benefactors, and later on scholarships, to complete their education. The son of the diviner and herbalist was fortunate that his father was keen to send him to school because African diviners have often enough money at hand to see their children at least through primary and secondary school.

Very few Africans aspire to become doctors because of the long and difficult study course involved. Only very intelligent young men succeed in completing a medical training. Because they are so few, financial assistance is generally forthcoming. By the late 1960s there were less than ten African doctors practising in Rhodesia.

(b) Relations with Europeans

The type of relationship which African doctors have with Europeans depends on the type of their practice. If they set up a private practice, they live in urban areas attending to Africans in European employment. These doctors are excluded from the present study. The majority are employed either in government or mission hospitals.[1] Doctors in government hospitals have mostly civil servants, especially district commissioners, extension officers and the police, as their neighbours. Occasionally they are admitted to their social circle. If they are not, the social life of rural doctors can be very lonely. They have about as little social contact with Europeans as African doctors in private practice.

Those employed on Christian missions have easier access to Europeans in their social life, especially on Catholic and Methodist mission stations. There they mix in the same way as do African priests and ministers. Since there are very few African doctors in rural areas, they are not only treated as quite outstanding men by their own people, but also by Europeans.

Several doctors evaluated Europeans of different nationalities differently. They stressed that Americans[2] were easier to get on with than the English, and these easier than Afrikaaners. They also felt that European men were more polite than European women. One doctor stated: 'European men can be free and easy with you when

[1]Cf. Kuper, 1965, pp. 125, 239, for a similar situation in South Africa.

[2]As stated above, p. 9, the word 'European' is used in Rhodesia for white people, whether they are born in Europe, America or Africa.

they are alone, but if their wives are with them they are much more arrogant and even aggressive. A European woman will always keep you at arm's length.' Others recorded unpleasant receptions by European women secretaries when they called at their offices in the course of their professional duties.

Most doctors made a clear distinction between their contacts with Europeans on mission stations and in the wider Rhodesian society. One doctor said that whenever he went to town he tried to appear as an ordinary African. But when in the pursuit of his business he had to introduce himself as a medical practitioner, attitudes generally changed radically and often he was offered a cup of tea by Europeans. Another doctor, who had studied overseas, recorded that European store assistants often showed resentment when he placed his orders in perfect English, without the accent common to most Rhodesian Africans. He concluded: 'Lower educated Europeans are hostile to educated Africans like myself because they see us as a threat to their own position. This depresses me and I often wonder what will happen to Rhodesian society under these conditions.'

A third doctor, often hurt by disrespectful behaviour of junior European clerks, avoids contact with civil servants as much as possible and submits his requests in writing or sends a messenger to transact his business for him. He concluded: 'This saves me time and frustration.' Another said: 'Europeans have been so insincere to us that little communication is still possible. Africans in turn have reacted by insincerity to them. We now live in different, often hostile, worlds.'

(c) Relations with Africans

If the relationship between African doctors and the wider European society is ambivalent, it is positive with their own people. Since very few Africans succeed in becoming doctors, those who do are very highly respected. The high esteem given to doctors is recognized both by themselves and by Europeans. A district commissioner commented on an African doctor at his station:

When he first came, people stopped coming to the hospital. They could not believe that a black man could do what a white man does. Then one day a serious case was brought in and the doctor had to operate at once. The operation was highly successful. This completely changed the attitude of the people. They came flocking to the hospital and now claim that the African doctor is much better than any European doctor they ever had before. He is now treated as the most important man in the district.

A missionary, familiar with another government hospital in a rural area, observed that since that hospital had an African doctor the relationship between the people and the hospital had greatly improved and that the people trusted the African medical practitioner much more than the former European doctors. The fact that African doctors occupy the houses formerly inhabited by Europeans helps to enhance their standing in the eyes of the African people.

The doctors themselves stress that they receive great respect from the people, that they are often invited to their homes and served with the best food the people can afford. One added: 'They even bring me cakes', a very rare food in African villages.

Yet the African doctors were also aware of a distance between themselves and their people. One stressed that he had to make a very definite effort to keep in touch with his people and admitted that this was sometimes difficult. He said: 'Educated Africans have a great responsibility to contact the ordinary people. Whenever I go to a village, people watch whether I am really genuine in my concern for them. I have to prove to them my sincerity.'

In addition to winning the confidence of ordinary peasants, African doctors have to meet the demands of educated Africans. One doctor reported the difficulties he first experienced when he came back from his studies and was stationed on a mission in his home area where he was well known: Teachers, who had been his boyhood friends, would jump the queue when coming for treatment and demand to be attended to before everybody else, claiming they were friends of the doctor. This caused resentment among the people and embarrassed the medical practitioner.

These educated Africans, moreover, took much more of his time than ordinary peasants, demanded an explanation for every pain and every treatment prescribed, and tried to get the best possible service the hospital could give. In order to avoid disturbances, the doctor recognized the claim to higher social status by teachers and arranged for private consultation by members of the modern elite. He met them by appointment at a time convenient to both, and gave them the full attention they demanded. In return he charged them a higher fee than he charged the ordinary people. The teachers were very satisfied with the arrangement because it underlined their prestige position in the community, and the regular consultation hours for the people were no longer disturbed. As a consequence of this recognition, the relations between members of the elite were harmonious.

(d) Relations with chiefs

The doctors' relationships with chiefs closely resemble those of Catholic priests in their ease and relaxed manner. Most doctors stated that their contacts with chiefs were good. But they also stressed the extreme dependence of chiefs on government. One doctor said:

Government will stop at nothing to remain in power, even if it uses for the time being African chiefs. Chiefs have become our biggest problem. Civil servants, especially district commissioners, regard them as the true leaders of our people and completely by-pass us educated Africans. They go down to the level of the chiefs, sit together with them as friends and inquire into their troubles. They tell them how much government does for them and what difficulties government has with educated Africans. In this way civil servants try to turn the people away from us. It is easier for district commissioners to handle uneducated chiefs than educated modern leaders.

The answers of African doctors show that they maintain friendly relations with chiefs, but that like Catholic priests they do not recognize them as leaders. Rather they painfully experience the fact that government replaces Africans who have knowledge by those who are ignorant and unable to mediate effectively between the races.

(e) Political aspirations

Doctors were often dissatisfied with the present political system of Rhodesia and felt insecure. One said: 'In this country a person like myself can be picked up by the police at any time. The government has many informers. I do not mind being arrested after standing up for a cause which is worthy of my protest. But to think that a careless word may lead to my arrest is demoralizing. Then the sacrifice of my freedom will not be worth anything.' Another doctor of similar convictions stated: 'I have on several occasions stated my views to the district commissioner and the police, but I never go to meetings in the rural areas. People there would call on me to give my opinion, and some would misconstrue what I said and lay false information against me.' A third doctor thought: 'Whatever deference government officials may pay to chiefs, the people know that we are their real leaders. They often come to us and we give them advice in secret.' One of them was convinced of a change in government in the not too distant future. He gave the following reasons for the impending change:

Firstly, there will be more and more educated Africans without employment. They no longer fit into their village communities and will be utterly frustrated. Frustration will build up until it leads to an explosion. Secondly, the African rural areas are far too small to accommodate the ever growing population. Thirdly, depression in industry pushes more and more people back on the land. These landless men form a great problem to chiefs and government. Fourthly, advanced African farmers have resented the recent transfer of African agriculture to the ministry of Internal Affairs.[3] They see their future threatened by it and will rebel.

A very thoughtful doctor compared himself with another African doctor in Rhodesia, who had recently become vice-president of an African nationalist party, and said:

I often wonder whether it is my duty to follow his example and try to lead my people to freedom. But I just cannot see myself as a politician. I could never stand on a political platform and deliver emotional speeches. On the one hand, I think that as an educated man who understands more of what goes on in the country than the majority of people, I have a responsibility towards them; on the other again, I think that it is my duty to care for the sick and help them in a quiet way which is much more in harmony with my temperament. It is a problem posed by my conscience which I find difficult to solve.

(f) Conclusion

African doctors belong to the most outstanding members of the emergent African elite. Their very high education and their high salaries put them in a group apart from other Africans. They are greatly admired by all their people who are proud that some of their own race have obtained a position comparable to that of the more outstanding Europeans. The comment of the European district commissioner about the relations of local Africans to their new doctor highlights this esteem and admiration.[4]

The partial acceptance of African doctors by Europeans, who recognize them as men of ability, contributes to their prestige and

[3] *The Rhodesia Herald*, 15.8.1969.
[4] Cf. also Kuper, 1965, p. 123, for similar reactions by South Africans.

self-confidence. This is borne out by the observation of one doctor who noticed that as soon as he stated his profession to Europeans in business contacts, he was treated with deference.

On the other hand, African doctors share at times the discrimination to which their people are exposed,[5] and this strengthens their bonds with less educated Africans. Doctors cannot but be keenly aware of the social injustices and economic and political inequalities suffered by their people, especially when they attend to the many cases of malnutrition in their hospitals. As highly educated persons they often feel a great responsibility to bring about a juster social order. Yet only those who run a private practice can openly engage in politics.[6] Several doctors, therefore, see themselves as potential, but not actual, leaders in the political sphere. In the realm of general human behaviour all doctors know that they are looked up to as models of conduct, just as do African clergymen.

The doctors' positive connections with other educated Africans, as well as the admiration they receive from peasants, greatly strengthen their influential position. Consequently they are sources of suggestion and centres of attraction to many people, even if few young Africans can follow them in their professional calling.

2. Hospital administrators

The post of hospital administrator has only recently been opened to Africans and there are very few of them in Rhodesia. Most hospitals are administered by doctors, others by orderlies and matrons, or even by chemists who are assisted by clerks. Only a few hospitals employ a full-time hospital administrator. Consequently there are even fewer men in this position than there are African doctors. Two were interviewed for this study. Both worked in mission hospitals.

Hospital administration is a branch of the medical profession which is only beginning to be recognized as a distinct occupation in Rhodesia. Few Africans knew what the position implied and none was able to rank it in the prestige exercise. Nevertheless, the position of the few hospital administrators is so important in the African community that a special consideration of them is justified. Kuper observes that in South African hospitals most resentment of the

[5]Cf. *ibid.*, pp. 240 and 244.
[6]*Ibid.*, p. 242.

African staff is directed against the administration because administrators, who are not directly involved in the work situation, are responsible for social discrimination.[7] African administrators too may often find themselves in situations in which different groups make different demands on them and in which their decision may alienate one group.

(a) Recruitment

The two administrators interviewed are in charge of large mission hospitals. The first studied in Europe, the other in the United States. The latter holds two university degrees in science and psychology and in social administration. The first had gone to Europe for the specific purpose of training as hospital administrator. The second did not choose his subjects with a specific goal in mind, but selected subjects that interested him. His Church had given him a generous scholarship, and when he returned to Rhodesia his Church found him his present employment. Both administrators draw a salary of about £100 a month, that is £1,200 a year.

Both hospital administrators try to give the best possible education to their children. One sends all his children to private schools for Coloureds, which have a better reputation than those for Africans.

Before one of the hospital administrators arrived at his present place of employment, the hospital was administered by the joint efforts of doctors and senior nurses. It took the new administrator some months to collect under his control the various tasks belonging to his work. By the time of the interview he was in full control of the business and administrative sides of the hospital. His hospital staff consisted of three European and one African doctor, four European and twenty-four African nurses, eleven African medical extension workers, fifteen general workers and thirty girls engaged in domestic duties.

(b) Relations with Europeans

Like many other members of the African elite, hospital administrators distinguished between racial contacts at the mission station and in the wider Rhodesian society. One claimed that race relations were

[7]Kuper, 1965, p. 242.

Plate III 141

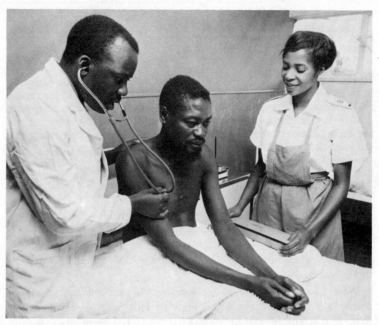

IIIa. An African doctor examines a patient in a rural hospital

IIIb. An African teacher instructs a class of primary schoolchildren

excellent at his mission station. Even in town he encountered less
discrimination than most other Africans. He suggested that his occupation might be responsible for this:

I mainly deal with people in the medical profession who are interested
in business. When I come to one of the great medical stores in the capital,
the European in charge calls on his secretary to prepare tea for me; when
I leave he asks me for my next destination and orders his driver to take
me there. It may be a false pretext and may only be done because of
the large orders I place for our hospital, but I certainly receive first class
treatment on these occasions.

When this hospital administrator goes to town, he stays in one
of the large multiracial hotels, but never extends his stay longer
than is necessary. His fluency in English and slight American accent
often cause people to ask him whether he is a Negro from the
States. They express amazement when they learn that he was born
in Rhodesia.

None of the administrators claim to have personal friends among
Europeans outside the mission station. This lack of social contact
with Europeans is a tacit admission that apart from their occupational acceptance hospital administrators are aware that they are
not welcomed by Europeans.

(c) Relations with Africans

One of the administrators was accompanied by his wife during his
studies overseas. Both he and his wife are more thoroughly westernized than most members of the African elite. This western behaviour occasionally creates a barrier between the couple and their
own people, but like the other administrator interviewed, he claimed
that on most occasions he was well accepted by Africans. Other
staff members of the two hospitals confirmed the administrators'
self-evaluation.

As employers of labour, hospital administrators find themselves
under pressure by their relatives to give them work in preference
to other people who are better qualified. Kinsmen also expect to
be treated free of charge because their 'brother' is in charge of hospital finances. One administrator stated: 'People cannot understand
that a full account of all money transactions has to be given and
that jobs must be offered to the best qualified people so that the

hospital can give the best possible service to all.' The other emphasized another complication deriving from kinship ties. He said:

Many of my relatives come as patients to the hospital and tell me that
they cannot pay. They expect me to take them into my house as long
as they need treatment. I am unwilling to do this because I have children
of my own and do not want them to catch a disease, nor do I want
my home filled with distantly related people. I tell them that they are welcome to stay with me for a visit, but that if they are sick they have to
go to the hospital in the same way as all other patients. This often dis-
pleases them. I help them wherever I can and spend on the average some
20 per cent of my salary on my kinsmen. This is as much as I can afford.

The two hospital administrators have close ties with other educated Africans on the mission station, especially with doctors and
teachers. One of them occasionally visits the African villages in the
company of his friends and like doctors and teachers claimed to
be welcomed and honoured by the villagers.

The distinct relationship between hospital administrators and the
African people stands out most clearly when the reaction of one
of them to his kinsmen is compared with the reaction of one Methodist minister to relatives and strangers. The latter claimed that his
home was the home of all the people, that he welcomed them by
day and that at night relatives as well as strangers slept on the
floors of all his rooms. The difference between these two members
of the African elite is in part due to their different education, upbringing and living standards. Whereas the minister received little more
than primary education and spends all his time in the villages and
homes of his people, the administrator received an advanced university education overseas and both he and his wife are concerned
to maintain on their mission station the living standard to which
they have become accustomed. Though they try not to erect barriers
between themselves and the people, they do not mix with them to
a great extent. Hospital administrators have differentiated themselves from the people and are conscious of belonging to the elite.

(d) Relations with chiefs

Hospital administrators felt at ease in their contacts with chiefs.
They admitted they got on well with some, but occasionally clashed
with others. Like Catholic priests, they stressed that they stepped
back to show deference to chiefs in public, but that chiefs respected
them because of their education. As a result, there was a mutual

give and take. One said: 'I accept chiefs as figure heads. But when it comes to political leadership, the question is different. In this sphere we cannot recognize chiefs as leaders.'

Like other educated Africans the two hospital administrators felt that chiefs were losing prestige. One complained: 'Chiefs have taken to drink. Government is encouraging beer consumption among Africans because beer brings in great revenues. One of the first projects our local community development council completed was a new beer hall. The distict commissioner came for the opening. Beer is undermining the morality of chiefs and people alike.'[8]

In spite of the moral deterioration he observed in chiefs, one administrator believed that chiefs might yet be helpful to their people to establish a better society. Referring to the new powers given to chiefs in Rhodesia's 1969 Constitution, he thought it the duty of educated Africans to instruct chiefs of the true facts of the situation so that chiefs could put pressure on government to do something for the betterment of the people. He concluded: 'This is the only hope we Africans have, for government is determined to listen to no black man except chiefs. This forces us to work through chiefs.'

(e) Political aspirations

Both hospital administrators looked forward to a multi-racial society and one stated: 'There are so many good and reasonable people in Rhodesia, black as well as white, that I think an integrated society can still be established in this country.' The other considered the possibility of a violent uprising but thought it unlikely because of lack of unity among the African people. The administrator who had been in the United States repeated a conversation he had had with American students who had asked him whether something was missing in the personality of Rhodesian Africans because they did not rebel against white domination. He had answered them: 'Nothing is wrong with the African personality, but life is hard in Rhodesia. Everybody who has got some position is keen to keep it and not to lose it. Highly educated Africans holding well-paid posts feel that they can only lose if they come forward as leaders opposing government. Self-interest does not allow them to engage in politics.' Looking to the future he concluded: 'Our generation has not many men

---

[8]This observation is confirmed by a study of African chiefs. Many more chiefs have taken to drink during the last few years than in the past. Cf. Weinrich, *Chiefs and Councils in Rhodesia.*

who are willing to die for their country, but such men will be in the majority in the next generation because the seeds of utter frustration are now being sown.'

(f) Conclusion

Hospital administrators are a new section of the emergent African elite. Their full responsibility for the financial state of hospitals requires great honesty and integrity. Only very reliable men are accepted for the post.[9] The experiences of the two administrators interviewed show that their professional duties are often misunderstood by their own people who expect personal advantages from the position of their relatives. This shows that African hospital administrators may indeed find themselves in positions in which they find it hard to reconcile different demands,[10] yet these differences seem not insuperable. Their success derives from their full acceptance of western values which regard nepotism as corruption, and from convincing their relations through their financial assistance that they are ready to help them as much as stands in their power. The two hospital administrators admitted their desire for a just society, but were concerned about their own position. Because only a few Africans have become hospital administrators, it is impossible to draw any general conclusion about men filling this position.

3. Nurses[11]

Nursing is the occupation most favoured by African women in Rhodesia. Together with teaching it provides one of the few prestige positions open to them in modern society.[12]

(a) Recruitment

Nurses come from a great variety of family backgrounds. Since

[9]Many Africans entrusted with public finances have been found guilty in Rhodesian courts of misappropriating communal funds. The reports of the Secretary for Internal Affairs record repeatedly that treasurers of community development councils stole money. Cf. *Reports of the Secretary for Internal Affairs*, 1963, p. 86, and 1967, p. 21. Cf. also *Chiefs and Councils in Rhodesia*, Chapters 9 and 10.

[10]Cf. *supra*, p. 140.

[11]For an excellent analysis of African nurses in South Africa see Hilda Kuper in Kuper, 1965, pp. 216–33.

[12]The following data are based on a questionnaire administered to two classes of nurse trainees and to a number of fully qualified nurses who have served for many years in either government or mission hospitals.

higher education of girls is a relatively recent phenomenon in Rhodesia, many come from families that have for at least one generation closer contacts with European culture. About half come from peasant families, the rest come from the homes of craftsmen, drivers, clerks and professionals. Their fathers' occupations are set out in Table 11. In this table, the number of nurses whose fathers are working in professional or other white collar occupations is striking because it is far above the national average of men in these occupations. Several nurses are the daughters of teachers and one is the daughter of a surgeon. Most of their fathers, therefore, belong to the sub-elite, if not the elite proper, of African rural society. Because of the relative financial affluence of their homes, most had their education paid for by their fathers.

Fathers' occupation	Number	Percentage
Peasant/unskilled	42	51·2
Craft/skilled	14	17·1
Business	4	4·9
White collar/professional	22	26·8
Total	**82**	**100·0**

Table 11. Occupations of the fathers of African nurses

All had been good students in school because the training hospitals only accept candidates with high pass marks after they have completed primary or several years' secondary education. Most nurses attended school for eight to ten years, and then studied nursing for a further three years. Only a few studied for eleven years and then did a full course, culminating in a general certificate of nursing which entitles them to the status of 'State Registered Nurses'. The majority attended mission training schools and qualified as assistant nurses. African patients are seldom aware of the difference in qualification and status, and honour both groups of nurses alike. An African nurse with the lower qualification earns about £15 to £25 a month. African state registered nurses get the same salary as European state registered nurses, namely between £60 and £80 a month, depending on seniority and additional qualifications.

Most nurses work in the districts in which they were born but others, who cannot find employment near their homes, travel to other parts of Rhodesia, wherever they can find a vacancy. Since more nurses train than there are places for them, competition for posts is becoming acute and several assistant nurses cannot find employment.

State registered nurses are mainly employed in urban areas because the government claims to be financially unable to pay the higher salaries to nurses stationed in country districts. Consequently most nurses in rural areas have only the lower qualification, except some in mission hospitals whose salaries are subsidised by the missions themselves.

Young nurses expect to marry a man with higher education. Many trainees thought that their own education would help them to find a husband among the modern African elite. Their parents too desire them to be married to wealthy Africans and often demand a very high bride-wealth for them.[13] The nurses who are married have generally achieved this goal. There seems to be a high degree of in-marriage within the medical profession because many doctors and hospital administrators are married to nurses. Several nurses are married to teachers.

All nurses are keen to educate their children to as high a level as possible and one, who has been nursing for fifteen years and is married to the headmaster of a school, said that one of her sons intends to study medicine. Since their children will often be third-generation elite members, they are likely to have a good chance to achieve the high academic ambitions their mothers have for them. Since both their parents are in well-paid employment, financial difficulties are unlikely to block their studies. They are therefore spared the struggles which first-generation elite members have to face.

(b) Relations with Europeans

The closest contacts nurses have with Europeans take place in the hospitals themselves. Hospital services are hierarchically ordered according to nursing qualifications and experience. In some mission hospitals nurses with a lower qualification may be given greater responsibilities if after several years in close co-operation with fully qualified nursing staff they have proved their ability. In general, state registered nurses take on positions of responsibility and are in charge of assistant nurses. Since in rural areas most state registered nurses are Europeans, African nurses are often dependent on European nurses. In some hospitals, however, African matrons and ward

[13]Kuper, 1965, p. 239, made the same observation in South Africa.

sisters are in charge and in a few mission hospitals such nurses have some European nurses on their staff. But this is still very rare. European nurses working under an African nurse are generally dedicated missionaries who aim at African social advancement.[14]

Most nurses have some missionary friends, a few have contacts with other Europeans. Several know European farmers' wives on an informal basis because they work together with them in club work among African women. African women seem to find it easier to mix with European women outside the work situation than do African men with European men.

(c) Relations with Africans

African nurses are highly esteemed by their own people.[15] This esteem is especially visible in a society in which men rank traditionally higher than women, and old people higher than the young. Nurses are often very young, yet it is especially older Africans who show a high regard for nurses; young men too respect them, but are more often critical, above all if the nurse is aware that she is better educated and therefore occupies a position of higher prestige than the young men. Then competition for precedence may arise and the young men regard the nurses as 'proud'.[16]

Most experienced nurses on district duties have closer contacts with the people than those permanently working in hospitals because the most conservative section of the African people is still reluctant to bring their sick to hospital. Most of the patients in hospitals are ready to accept some of the values represented by modern medicine. In some remote areas nurses report that old people and children are still frightened of the hospital and of nurses. But in most villages they are welcomed and their visits are eagerly awaited.

Single nurses, who reside at a hospital, are welcomed when they visit their families and often try to spread modern ideas of hygiene and child care in their home villages. In this way many gain an influence they could never have had in the past.

For social activities, nurses invite both teachers and people from the villages. If they live permanently on a mission station they often form an effective link between mission residents and people in the

---

[14]Cf. Kuper, 1965, p. 218. For race relations between European and African nurses in South Africa see *ibid.*, pp. 222–33.

[15]*Ibid.*, p. 113, records a similar position of nurses in South Africa.

[16]Cf. *ibid.*, p. 224.

surrounding areas. Many nurses, however, even in rural areas, try to distinguish themselves from other African women through their dress and behaviour. They straighten their hair and wear smart dresses and high heels. Many lighten their skin with special cream. They are keenly aware of their elite status.[17] Older Africans are not always impressed by this behaviour, but young girls try to imitate them whenever they have a chance.

(d) Relations with chiefs

Young nurses have few contacts with chiefs, and their opinions about tribal leaders generally reflect the opinions held by their families. Older nurses visit chiefs only if they have personal relations with the chiefs' wives. One nurse, for example, related that she went to school with the wife of the local chief and occasionally paid a social call. Another stated that she was the friend of the local chief's wife because both worked together in African women's clubs.

A nurse occupying a responsible senior position in a mission hospital held a clearer opinion about chiefs. She said:

Chiefs are paid by government and only care for their own families. They no longer care for their people. Some of us visit chiefs frequently and try to convince them of the responsibility they have to speak up to government for the majority of their people. I have visited our chief often in the company of my husband, but I have become convinced that it is quite a hopeless undertaking. When I see how abandoned we African people are, I can do nothing but cling to my religious faith.

(e) Political aspirations

A surprisingly large proportion of young nurses showed great interest in political questions. Many stated that they would like to see Africans rule their own country. Only a few said that they were not at all interested in politics.[18] Older and more mature nurses often expressed the wish for a society in which colour restrictions did not exist, but in which all people could meet each other freely. One spoke about a stay in the United States with her family and related how easy their relationship with white people had been there. She explained: 'It took some time before our neighbours got to know us. But then they came and said how much they preferred

[17]Kuper, 1965, p. 227, gives a similar picture of South African nurses.
[18]This contrasts with the lack of political interest observed by Kuper among South African nurses. Cf. Kuper, 1965, p. 232.

to have us as their neighbours rather than some other whites. If only such relationships were established in Rhodesia. I hope that my children at least will be able to live in a socially integrated society.'

Another said: 'When I read the newspaper these days I often hope that what I read is an ugly dream. If Christ died for white men and black men, why can white men and black men not live together as friends?' A third observed: 'Since the country declared itself unilaterally independent in 1965 Africans have lost their senses. Our people have become ever more selfish. No one is ready to help his neighbour. Everybody is afraid of losing his own position and therefore keeps quiet whatever the government does.'

(f) Conclusion

An African doctor observed: 'Our women do not initiate changes, but they back us husbands in what we do.' This observation coincides with the responses of African nurses. Those who expressed strong political views shared them with their husbands or other Africans. Where both husband and wife were interviewed, either because both worked together in a hospital, or because the husband worked as a teacher, a close similarity of views was expressed by husband and wife, reflecting that in the families of these educated Africans politics are frequently discussed.

African nurses have two advantages over men in their quest for elite status. Firstly, many have relatives who are more highly educated than themselves, or a father who is already part of the modern elite, so that they grew up in families orientated towards western culture. None of them experienced as great a discontinuity in her life as did the doctor whose father was an illiterate diviner and herbalist. Secondly, as women many of them found it easier to mix with Europeans than did African men. Church organizations and other women's clubs proved especially fruitful for some of them in establishing friendly ties across the colour line.

African nurses are greatly admired by men and women. To the older people they are objects of deference; to the young objects of imitation. Many young girls aspire to become nurses themselves and try to copy nurses in their dress and behaviour. Many young men look out for nurses as brides so that they can set up families in which their children will be accustomed to a modern way of life. The higher bride-wealth paid for nurses is seen both as an investment for the future salaries earned by nursing wives as also for the modern family atmosphere to which nurses will actively contribute. Nurses therefore form an important element of the African elite. Even if they do not stand in the forefront as political leaders, they provide the homes from which leaders emerge.

4. Evaluation of the medical elite

The medical elite represents one of the most important sections of the African elite in Rhodesia. Doctors occupy the highest prestige positions recognized by Africans. Their high education and high salary greatly contribute to this eminence. Together with Catholic priests and hospital administrators they represent one of the most westernized sections of the African elite. Yet in spite of their high education and their economic affluence, doctors stand closer to the people than the equally westernized administrators.

Administrators work more in the background and are less seen by the people than doctors who occupy the central place in the patients' lives. Doctors restore life, administrators deal with money and employment, two sources of great concern among the African people. They recognize that both are essential for modern life, but see in them also a source of their frustration.[19]

Nursing is one of the very few prestige positions open to African women and therefore greatly coveted by them.[20] Because educated Africans come to realize ever more the essential position of an educated wife and mother in the family, parents are keen to give to their daughters as good an education as they can afford, and prospective husbands are willing to pay a much higher bride-wealth for an educated than for an uneducated wife. Nursing is the easiest way by which girls can achieve occupational prestige.

In their political aspirations the medical profession represents a homogeneous group. Few, apart from some young nurses, express radical ideas. Most look forward to an integrated society in which race does not count. This attitude seems to derive from the high formal education of doctors, administrators and state registered

[19]A survey in an African township of Rhodesia, carried out in 1969, recorded that many townsmen feel that one of the evils Europeans brought to Rhodesia is money, a cultural item unknown to them in the past, but without which life has become impossible.

[20]Cf. Kuper, 1965, p. 216.

nurses. Several of them realized that the more educated a person is, and the better paid a position he fills, the less willing he is to risk his position through political involvement. Nevertheless, to conscientious professionals their abstention from political involvement poses a question of conscience. They feel an obligation to help construct a better society in which everybody can enjoy equal rights of citizenship.

8. The African educational elite

Gouveia, writing about elites in Latin America, observes:

Secondary school teachers, although normally well-educated, are rarely thought of as members of the elite in economically developed societies ... The situation, however, is quite different in most underdeveloped nations. Thus secondary school teachers are an extremely important stratum. Knowledge about their attitudes and values, about differences among them, should tell us much about prospects for social modernization in forthcoming generations of graduates.[1]

If secondary school teachers are not members of the elite in developed countries, but are so in Latin America, in rural Rhodesia even primary school teachers are considered members of the elite, and their values and attitudes exert a very great influence on the rural population. At a Catholic teachers' congress in Rhodesia in 1969, African headmasters were told that they were the key-figures in situations of modern change, and they were contrasted with the forces of traditional culture which are marked by conservatism and so constitute a hindrance to progress.[2]

Foster, who studied the effects of education in Ghana, observes that formal educational institutions serve as differentiating agencies.[3] Africans are keenly aware of the important role of teachers and regard them as the 'way-openers' of children into the modern world.[4]

Teaching has been one of the first white collar jobs open to Africans. Soon after the first missionaries had settled in Rhodesia and won followers among the African people, they trained intelligent young men to help them teach the new religion to their neighbours. After a few decades the first African teachers were formally educated. Later African headmasters were appointed to local primary

[1]Gouveia, 1967, pp. 484–5.
[2]*Moto*, October 1969.
[3]Foster, 1967, p. 6.
[4]*Supra*, p. 107.

schools. In 1957 the Methodist Church appointed the first African school manager and by the early 1960s Catholic, and other missionaries too, handed over this post to experienced African teachers. Government also appointed the first African school inspectors.

1. School inspectors

(a) Recruitment

Like most men of the modern African elite, school inspectors tend to come from peasant background and many have made their way to the top through hard work. Several hold a South African University degree and are married to educated wives, some of whom are South African born and therefore of different tribes from their husbands. Some school inspectors have visited Europe or America. With an income of between £2,000 and £3,000, identical with that of their European colleagues, school inspectors are more affluent than most Africans and tend to send their children to multiracial, predominantly European, schools.

Though most school inspectors are in charge of schools in the rural areas of Rhodesia, their homes are almost always situated in urban areas. They are fully urbanized and generally state their intention never to return to village life. They belong to the few Rhodesian Africans who plan to spend their old age in towns and to be buried there. Consequently they no longer belong to the rural African society. They are included in this study because their work forces them to spend most of their time in rural areas.

(b) Relations with Europeans

Urban residence is often regarded by Africans as a sign of civilization and most members of the Rhodesian elite try to live in towns. European school inspectors live in houses provided by the ministry of Education. African school inspectors desire to be given the same facilities, but since government accommodation for school inspectors is available only in European residential areas—because most inspectors are still Europeans—African school inspectors feel discriminated against when they are told to find their own accommodation in African townships.

One school inspector on his transfer from a large urban centre to a small provincial town sought accommodation in the European section. When this was refused he looked for a house among local Asians, but was told that the Land Apportionment Act forbade him to live anywhere but in the African township. Deeply hurt he shared for some months accommodation with an African teacher until he was able to build his own home on the outskirts of the African township. He complained bitterly that whereas European inspectors are provided with suitable accommodation, he had to incur a heavy financial outlay to live in a home commensurate with his position. He feared that at his next transfer he would have to sell it at a great loss since no local African would be able to pay for it as much as he had invested in it.

School inspectors are often highly esteemed by individual Europeans and claim to co-operate well with their European colleagues. But outside working contacts they are not invited into European social circles. Their wives are often able to establish some contacts with European ladies, especially if they are active in social welfare organizations.

When on district duties in the rural areas school inspectors are denied accommodation in government rest houses used by European civil servants, they again feel humiliated and frustrated. Christian mission stations often give them hospitality in their guest quarters. On most mission stations they mix as equals with European and African mission staff. Their reception there underlines strongly the different kind of treatment they receive by Europeans not engaged in mission work.

To compensate for the racial discrimination they experience both in the execution of their work and in their private lives, several school inspectors visit the capital several times a year with their families and stay in some of the multiracial hotels. One family regularly goes there for Christmas with all its children and spends money freely in order to prove its claim to upper class status.

(c) Relations with Africans

To the upper stratum of the African elite, style of living becomes an important index distinguishing them from ordinary people. One of the school inspectors during an interview pointed to his tastefully decorated and furnished house and said: 'This is *my* colour bar.' This statement clearly indicates that he sees himself as separated from other Africans by a large cultural gulf. Most school inspectors emphasize their different living standards, and the best way of doing this is through displaying their wealth by investing it in European prestige symbols. One inspector, for example, owns two cars, one for himself and one for his wife. In this way, inspectors claim not only to live a 'European way of life', but also the life of the upper stratum of European society.

As a consequence of their affluence, school inspectors often appear as outsiders to their own people. In the rural areas they inspire as much fear in African teachers and pupils as do European inspectors. Their almost exclusive association with mission personnel on their district rounds, underlines their claim to equality with Europeans.

In their African townships inspectors again stand apart from the lives of the people. To maintain their high status they stress their exclusiveness from the masses by following the advice of the African proverb that 'great men must not be seen too often'.

But their reserve alienates them from their people. Once a school inspector attended an urban party given by a businessman on some family occasion. To enliven the gathering the school inspector played some traditional music to the people which he had tape-recorded in the rural areas. The guests were offended and asked whether he despised them as much as Europeans despised them by playing 'country music' to them. This incident reveals a lack of understanding between some members of this social group and the African people.

On public occasions and entertainments, school inspectors are offered the best places. They are greeted respectfully by the people, but few Africans dare to talk to them freely because of the inspectors' high rank.

(d) Relations with chiefs

School inspectors meet chiefs in the execution of their work. One inspector reported that on his visits to rural schools chiefs were frequently present. He said: 'They think that I am a government minister and send a report to head office to tell government whether particular chiefs are doing their duty. Many chiefs ask me to note in my report that they were present during my visit and that they had their people work hard to improve their school buildings.' Another inspector related: 'On one of my visits to rural schools I found the buildings of one in very poor condition. I told the local sub-chief that I would report to head office that his school did not meet government requirements. The sub-chief implored me not to write such a report and promised to improve the buildings. When I came back after a short time, the villagers had worked hard and great improvements had been made.'

All school inspectors stressed that they were greatly honoured by chiefs, but that chiefs regarded them as belonging to European society rather than to their own. One said: 'Chiefs treat me as if I were a European,' and another: 'Chiefs fear me because I am a senior government employee.'

Of those interviewed, all school inspectors rejected chiefs as political leaders. They expressed great concern at uneducated chiefs being guaranteed seats in parliament. Some sympathized with chiefs because, in the words of one, 'Government exploits their ignorance.' Others were less sympathetic. One said: 'Chiefs obey any order from government, whether they understand it or not. At present they struggle to get along with the 1969 constitution which they accepted without understanding it.' Another commented: 'Government has found in chiefs a very effective tool to oppress Africans.'

School inspectors emphasized the changed position of chiefs. They recalled that in the past chiefs had real authority. One remembered a chief who thirty years ago chased a district commissioner from his village because the latter had refused to sit on the floor in front of him. Since modern chiefs have to be approved by the ministry of Internal Affairs before they can assume their office, this inspector argued, chiefs are dependent on government officials. Another inspector thought: 'One day we will have a majority government. Then we can reconsider the whole issue of chieftainship and retain from our old customs what we want to retain. Then we might get again good chiefs. But at present chiefs are brainwashed by government and are of no use to our people.'

(e) *Political aspirations*

Politically, African school inspectors are in a very delicate situation. Because of their influential position, the African people expect them to come forward as leaders and to oppose the European government. Their conditions of service, however, do not allow them to engage in politics. Consequently they are reluctant to mix with their people in order not to be pressurized to accept political leadership positions. Some give financial support secretly to nationalists, both because they are convinced of the justice of their cause, and also because they try to insure their property against destruction in case of riots. But they dare not associate themselves openly with African nationalism.

On one occasion, when the leader of a new nationalist party addressed a public rally in a provincial town, none of the local school inspectors working in the adjoining districts attended the meeting. But at night one of them came to visit the party president in the home of a party member and asked for information about the movement. He left again in the dark in order not to be identified by the people.

Because of the inspectors' apparent lack of involvement in African nationalism, many Africans regard them as 'sell-outs', as men who have profited from and who have a stake in the continuation of the political system of Rhodesia.

Most of the inspectors interviewed expressed very moderate political views. It was only after the 1969 referendum on the new constitution that several showed great signs of distress at the political development of the country. One stated: 'This is the saddest day of my life. Now all hope of African development is gone.'

The very position of African school inspectors places them in a dilemma. Like other Africans, they wish to see Africans governing themselves. But they cannot actively engage in bringing about political change because their security lies in the stability of the government and a gradual transition to African control. They are not revolutionaries. Their position in Rhodesia in the 1960s is similar to that of American Negro leaders in the 1940s of whom Myrdal wrote: 'The ambitious and successful Negro is more dependent upon the whites than upon his caste followers in the lower class. He is more conspicuous. He has more to lose and he has more to gain.'[5] The social leadership positions school inspectors fill often become to them 'a form of escape'[6] from the political leadership they might provide.

(f) Conclusion

African school inspectors are outstandingly successful men who rank socially high above their fellow Africans but who seldom serve as a direct reference group, at least not as a reference group for rural Africans. Their living standards are so high above those of

[5]Myrdal, 1944, p. 769.
[6]*Ibid.*, p. 776.

ordinary people that they have become estranged from them. The frequency with which they marry South African wives underlines the distance between them and the people among whom they grew up.

The incident of the tape-recorded traditional African music shows that some inspectors regard traditional society with a curiosity almost equal to that of Europeans. The fact that their residence is urban but that they work in rural areas, further emphasizes the gulf between them and African villagers. School inspectors are both geographically marginal to rural Africans, and they are also socially marginal to African society as a whole. School inspectors use Europeans as their exclusive reference group. By affirming the values of this out-group both in words and actions, school inspectors widen the gap between themselves and fellow Africans. They have broken their ties with traditional society and they intend never to return to it. Their attitudes towards chiefs resemble those of other high-ranking members of the African elite, such as Catholic priests and doctors.

Yet there are differences between Catholic priests and doctors on the one hand, and school inspectors on the other. Catholic priests and doctors remain in close daily contact with the African people in spite of their high academic qualifications; the school inspectors seem at times to look down on Africans. Priests and doctors actively try to overcome the barrier between themselves and the people by frequent visits. Whereas priests eat and sleep with African peasants in their huts, school inspectors remain at a distance and sleep at mission stations. Though government policies force school inspectors to live in close physical proximity with other Africans, this proximity does not bridge the status gap between them.

The comparison between highly trained mission personnel and school inspectors can be drawn still further. Whereas priests are fully integrated into the community of fellow missionaries, school inspectors are integrated into no community. European society, to whose membership they aspire, rejects them. They are treated by their European colleagues with politeness during working hours, but after work they are avoided and forced to enjoy their splendid homes in the almost exclusive company of their wives and children. Europeans do not visit them, and Africans, apart from a very few highly educated men and women, are afraid to associate with such wealthy neighbours.

School inspectors are admired and have great deference paid to them. Yet they are isolated. They influence African society from a distance, and only from a distance are they sources of suggestion and objects of imitation.

2. School managers

African school managers are in a different position from African school inspectors. They are less conspicuous and less important, and their medium position in the African educational hierarchy gives them some protection. Three Catholic and three Methodist school managers were interviewed for this study.

(a) Recruitment

All three Catholic school managers were born in the chiefdoms in which they are employed, and two of them are distantly related to their chiefs. All three Methodist school managers were transferred to their present post from other districts; one of them married locally so that his in-laws live close to him.

Five of the six school managers come from peasant families. They worked their way up both by their own efforts and with the support of their kinsmen. One of them first studied to become a Catholic priest but interrupted his studies to choose a secular career. Only one manager does not come from a peasant family; he is the son of a school teacher. At the time of the interview his father was teaching in one of the schools under his control.

Whether school managers will maintain such close ties with African peasants in the future depends on the education they are able to give to their children. All try to let their children attend secondary schools and if they succeed their children can start off their careers with a considerable advantage over other rural Africans.

Managers are selected from the ranks of teachers. The selection is made on the basis of academic qualifications, teaching experience and success in their profession. In some districts candidates for the post are chosen by the missionaries from among the teachers whom the missionaries judge most suitable; in other areas all the teachers vote for their managers. In either case the names of the candidates have to be submitted for approval to the ministry of African Education.

(b) Relations with Europeans

School managers stand in a friendly, but not too familiar, relationship with local European missionaries. They are well known to them because they have worked with them for many years and are trusted and esteemed by them. Missionaries stated that their managers were taken from the best teachers they had in their areas. The manager who had attempted theological studies was well received by the missionaries and often joined their recreations in a common room. When school managers come up against problems in their work, they often refer them to the missionaries who had been managers in the past. On such occasions they are given friendly advice, but are left full responsibility for their work. Missionaries do not interfere in the execution of a manager's duties. This trust and acceptance gives school managers a confidence and security which several other members of the African elite lack.

When African school managers visit town, they experience the same discrimination as all other Africans. Their medium salaries of £40 to £60 a month enable them to visit towns more frequently than most rural Africans. Consequently they are more often exposed to the experience of being treated as second-rate citizens than are less educated and less affluent people. Their salaries, however, are too small to allow them to stay in the large multiracial hotels, frequented by school inspectors and other members of the top stratum of the new African elite. Consequently they cannot gain vicarious satisfaction through a conspicuous display of wealth.

(c) Relations with Africans

Through their kinship ties with local Africans, many school managers are closely integrated into the African communities. If their ties with Europeans are tenuous, those with their own people are strong. The four school managers who live close to their relatives help these financially, especially by paying school fees for their younger relatives. This makes considerable inroads in their salaries. Since, however, their relatives paid for their education, none of them is shirking his obligation to pay for his younger kinsmen.

Occupationally, school managers have the closest connections with African teachers. All the managers interviewed felt that they had their teachers' full support. Each of them looks after some twenty to thirty schools, which means that each has about a hundred teachers dependent on him. Their sphere of influence in rural Rhodesia is therefore great.

Their professional duties demand that school managers both support and correct their African staff. Their authority often causes slight tensions, and the earlier quoted report of *Moto*[7] indicates that tensions do exist. These tensions are also reflected in the relatively low prestige ranking of managers. During the interviews, however, school managers played down these tensions or even denied them.

To consolidate their leading positions in local communities, Catholic school managers joined voluntary Church organizations in which they have become chairmen or committee members. In this way they enlarged their sphere of influence and conferred prestige on the organizations, because those organizations, which have a school manager on their executive, gain in local esteem. Methodist school managers are often offered similar positions in their Church, but they generally turn them down for fear that such leadership may complicate their professional relationship with teachers.

School managers, therefore, stand much closer to the African people than do school inspectors. Kinship ties and local residence alike bind them to the communities in which they work. The social gulf between them and the people is not very wide. They are accepted as part of the communities in which they live.

(d) Relationships with chiefs

Some school managers maintain friendly relations with local chiefs. They respect chiefs and state that many of them are respected by chiefs in return. One commented: 'Sometimes I feel a bit uneasy when chiefs get up to show me respect.' Another said:

An educated man does not despise a chief, but helps him to become a better ruler by teaching him how to govern his people in justice. I myself have once been a personal friend of a chief and was able to influence him. In a sense we managers are in the same dilemma as chiefs: like them we are bound to be 'yes-men' because we also receive a government salary and can be dismissed if we oppose a policy which we know is to the detriment of our people.

Yet there exist also tensions between school managers and chiefs, and many school managers criticize chiefs as strongly as do many other members of the modern elite. Several complained that although chiefs are keen to send their children to school, they are

[7] *Supra*, p. 108.

afraid of their educated subjects and discriminate against them during court trials. The greatest objection managers had to chiefs was that chiefs were subservient to government officials, especially to district commissioners.

School managers realize that they need at least the tacit approval of chiefs for the smooth running of local schools; and the chiefs' active consent is required if they want to open new schools. One manager said:

In the past, chiefs were the leaders of the people, but now they are so no longer. I was once called by a chief to settle a dispute between him and one of my headmasters about an action taken by a school committee. I judged between them and showed to the chief that he was wrong and that the headmaster had faithfully followed the regulations laid down by the ministry of African Education. The chief had expected me to side with him, and when he heard my decision he went away in anger. Yet he abided by my judgment.

In situations like these, the prestige of traditional and modern leaders is tested. Chiefs can be made to realize that they are unfamiliar with, and incompetent to judge, issues arising from modern administration. Each time chiefs have to bow before their educated subjects, the power relationship between them undergoes a slight shift.

To increase their own influence over local schools, some chiefs support the government policy of community development[8] which allows them to assume control over local primary schools. Most schools are still under the control of missionaries of the various Christian denominations, and teachers and school managers alike are keen to remain under mission control rather than to come under the direct control of chiefs. The desire of chiefs to transfer mission schools to council control often causes acute tensions between chiefs on the one hand and school managers and teachers on the other. On these issues parents generally support teachers and school managers and oppose their chiefs. Chiefs desire control over schools, both in order to extend their influence and in order to control school funds. Teachers fear that a transfer will make them subordinate to illiterate elders and claim that academic standards will fall if chiefs have a say in the running of schools. Parents fear that a transfer of schools may arrest the expansion of educational facilities for their children and reduce their own influence on the school committees.

[8]*Supra*, p. 12.

One school manager stated proudly that in his area, which has a very powerful council, he has been able to prevent the handing over of any school, and that one school, which had passed under council control before his managership, had so much deteriorated in its buildings and the examination results of the pupils, that parents begged him to organize its transfer back to mission control. This, however, is impossible because of government policy to hand over all African primary education to councils.

If chiefs compete for control over schools and school funds, the relationship between them and school managers sometimes reaches breaking point. One manager stated bluntly:

I am unpopular with chiefs because I do not allow them to take money from the school committees to use for their personal interests. I place all money as soon as it has been collected in the bank in the name of the mission, but on a special account, called 'School Fund'. Nobody but myself can draw it and so the money is safe. This greatly annoys the chiefs. Chiefs are afraid of us educated men because we are clever and able to scrutinize their administration and point out their injustices.

Another manager stated the general complaint: 'Chiefs are indoctrinated by district commissioners. They are their spies and constantly watch and report on us in order to ingratiate themselves with their masters.'

The general attitude of school managers towards chiefs is therefore ambivalent. On the one hand they recognize chiefs as important local leaders; on the other hand they are aware of the chiefs' self-interest, their submissiveness to government, and their inadequate knowledge of modern administration. This greatly lowers them in their esteem.

(e) Political aspirations

In spite of their criticisms, school managers are less politically outspoken than teachers. Standing in a slightly more prominent position than ordinary teachers, they are more closely watched. Most managers gave the impression of being very responsible men. One said:

Men like myself have been strongly influenced by western values and we have accepted many of them. I consider it my task to change my fellow Africans and to lead them towards a fuller understanding of modern life. We educated Africans desire for our people an education identical with that received by Europeans so that we can compete with them on an equal footing. Should a Bantustan type of education be introduced in Rhodesia, that is, an education which gives different curricula to African and European schools, I and many of my colleagues shall protest and resign. We do not reject all aspects of the traditional system; some we want to keep and integrate into the new society we are striving to build up. But we want to choose for ourselves. We shall not allow ourselves to be dictated to as to what we have to accept from the past and what not.

This comment of a Rhodesian school manager recalls Kuper's findings that South African teachers object to becoming 'instruments of a modernized tribalism'.[9]

Occupationally, school managers feel very insecure and their precarious occupational position disinclines many to take a stand on political issues. Their post is less well paid than that of permanent headmasters and can be held for only ten years in succession. If at the end of their term of office no headmastership is vacant, they have to return to the rank of ordinary teachers. To improve their position, African school managers wrote a joint letter to the ministry of African Education, complaining of the unsatisfactory conditions of their service and asking for better pay and greater security. It is in order to safeguard themselves that they prefer to remain fully involved in education and keen to leave political leadership to others.

(f) Conclusion

The position of school managers is one of mediation between the traditional society and modern culture. Being fully integrated into local African communities and being yet familiar with western values, they are less marginal to their own people than school inspectors who have completely broken away from tribal life. Though they lack the high education of doctors and priests, they are welcomed by local missionaries. But European society as a whole does not admit them, and their lower social standing prevents them from making as strong a bid for acceptance as do some members of the religious or medical elites.

School managers share in common with the higher strata of the African elite their moderate attitude towards politics and their relative respect for African chiefs. Their occupational insecurity affects the plans they have for their children's education and prevents them from assuring them of as good a future course of studies as parents of the upper strata of the African elite can offer their children. None

[9]Kuper, 1965, p. 177.

of them has sent his children to multiracial schools. School managers belong to the middle strata of the emergent African elite.

3. Teachers

Teachers represent the largest and most powerful group of the modern elite in rural Rhodesia. The prestige rating has shown that they rank very high, both in their own eyes and in the eyes of rural Africans. In one African area with a population of 45,000, there were over 200 African teachers. These form a powerful body influencing public opinion.

(a) Recruitment

In most areas teachers are locally recruited. Many are distantly related to chiefs, others are unrelated. But even those who have no kinship ties with chiefs have generally grown up in the chiefdom in which they are employed. The genealogy of a Rhodesian chiefdom (Figure 5, opposite) sets out the kinship ties of those teachers who are related to chiefs. These ties are important because they illustrate the positions of those who opt out of the traditional framework.

This genealogy indicates that all members of generations A, B, C and D are dead. Generation D provided the first chief, and in his generation the local group divided itself into distinct branches, called 'houses', two of which are only putatively linked to the chieftainship. Close agnates of the chief claim that the founders of these houses had been unrelated friends of the first chiefs; members of the houses concerned, however, claim to have a common ancestor with the chief's family.

Several of the eleven houses of the chieftainship, founded in generation D, have provided teachers for local schools; others have not done so. House 1, which provides the present chief, has no teacher sons; one of its members had been a spirit medium long before the present chief was elected. Houses 2 and 3, which are closely linked because they are brothers having a common mother and now have few people, hold a sub-chieftainship in the area. House 4 has died out. House 5 provides a spirit medium concerned with rain ceremonies. Houses 6, 7 and 8 have teacher sons: the teacher of House 7 was the first school manager in the area, and two teachers of Houses 6 and 8 are headmasters. House 9 provided

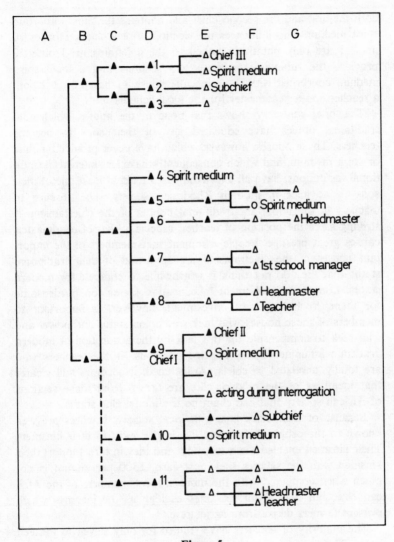

Figure 5

both the first and the second chief and contains the most important spirit medium who influences the election of new chiefs. Houses 10 and 11 are only putatively linked to the chieftainship: House 10 provides the sub-chief for these two sections and a local spirit medium concerned with the rain cult; house 11 has provided both a teacher and a headmaster for the local schools.

This brief summary shows that none of the houses which hold traditional offices have educated any of their sons to become teachers. Those houses, however, which have never provided a chief or spirit medium, and which consequently have less interest in traditional institutions, have all endeavoured to train at least one of their sons to advance in modern Rhodesian society. The absence of teachers in the important traditional houses of the chieftainship is striking since the position of teacher, especially that of headmaster, carries great prestige. People comment that members of the important houses of the chieftainship are so proud of their traditional status that they do not think it worthwhile to compete for modern status. Long term investment in education seems too burdensome for them. Such long term investment, however, is important to members of those houses who lack traditional status and power and who seek to compensate for this lack by the acquisition of modern academic attainments and prestige positions. If the teachers who are totally unrelated to chiefs are included, it becomes still clearer that members of the modern elite are drawn from those sections of African society that can claim no traditional elite status.

Because of their close link with local society, teachers are well known to the people and mostly live in the midst of their kinsmen. Their kinsmen enabled them to study, and they in turn support their kinsmen with the salaries they now earn. £300 per annum is not much when compared with the more affluent members of the African elite, but it is about six times as high as the incomes which peasant farmers derive from agriculture.[10]

The majority of teachers have studied for only eleven to thirteen years. Their course of study is well within the means of many people so that a large number of Africans, men and women alike, aspire to this position. Africans believe that intelligent young people have good chances of completing a course culminating in a teacher's diploma, and the more enterprising regard teaching as a stepping stone

[10]*Supra*, p. 23.

to higher education. Many teachers continue their studies privately and some find their way later to the university.

(b) Relations with Europeans

Since primary school teachers obtained all their training at mission stations, they have close ties with missionaries. Missionaries supervised their early schooling and taught them in teacher training colleges. In addition, many teachers received personal assistance from missionaries during their studies. This help often resulted in lasting friendships. Ties between missionaries and teachers are further intensified in that most teachers are leaders of voluntary Church organizations. In Catholic mission areas, for instance, every village school has branches of several Catholic Church organizations whose chairmen are often local teachers. These teachers meet every month with missionaries at the central mission station to co-ordinate the work of their organizations throughout the chiefdom.

Through these contacts teachers are often initiated into the aims of mission work, and work hand in hand with the missionaries. For example, when government began its campaign for community development, the Catholic bishops of Rhodesia issued a 'Pastor Letter'[11] warning their Christians against the new policy. Missionaries at once communicated the letter to African teachers and the teachers, realizing the effects which this policy was likely to have both on African education in general and on their own position in particular, engaged in an active campaign among chiefs and people dissuading them from accepting the new policy. They were listened to. One sub-chief said: 'We elders appreciate our teacher sons because they warn us of the tricks of the white man which we are not clever enough to understand.' Teachers, therefore, form an important link between missionaries and the people.

With government officials, however, teachers have very different relationships. In some districts these relationships are tense. It is reported that one district commissioner repeatedly beat teachers who disagreed with him. At last teachers took him to court. The district commissioner was found guilty and fined £150 for assault. He resigned from the civil service.[12] Such actions, however, are exceptional. Verbal disagreements, on the other hand, are frequent.

During several community development campaigns launched by

[11]Catholic Bishops of Southern Rhodesia, 1963.
[12]*The Rhodesia Herald*, 21.3.1968.

the ministry of Internal Affairs, teachers came forward as the spokesmen of their people and tried to boycott the implementation of the new policy. Teachers frequently adopted a highly academic line of argument. On one occasion they quoted Hobbes, Rousseau and other political philosophers to prove to a district officer the immorality of the new policy. The civil servant, however, was unable to follow their arguments and declared that theory was good for the lecture room but out of place in an African rural area where practical matters had to be settled. On another occasion teachers disputed with an official of the ministry of Internal Affairs that community development meant separate development and domination by a white minority; they claimed that this was immoral. The civil servant allowed himself to be drawn into polemics and hurled at the teachers examples of African misrule in independent African states. The teachers answered with examples of undemocratic governments in Europe, both in the past and at present. All attempts to establish a reasoned argument between the administrator and the teachers proved fruitless.

Teachers often regard themselves as the guardians of African interests in rural areas, ruling out the leadership of chiefs as incompetent, and so see themselves as the opponents of district commissioners and their assistants.

(c) Relations with Africans

The occupational rating has shown that African teachers enjoy a prestige in rural areas quite out of proportion to their educational achievements and their salaries. Although many of them are very young, more deference is shown to them than to their elders. Whenever teachers come to drinking parties in the villages, chairs are fetched for them and beer is offered them free of charge. The reason for this esteem is well expressed in a letter published in the Catholic African newspaper *Moto*. A reader asked why teachers were accorded so much honour, and another reader replied:

I would like to enlighten Mr. Waddicor Bee who wants to know why teachers are always given the places of honour at meetings, the best food at parties and the biggest cups of beer at 'beer drinks'.

If a teacher refuses to accept the position which he is offered, it would not befit him and would embarrass those who offered him the position. A teacher is not honoured simply because he has acquired a title which is popular with the people. He is respected like mothers are respected. Indeed, he is like a parent who propagates life. See how the world is blossoming with new life in class rooms everywhere. Why then should the people not honour the givers of this life.[13]

Because of their kinship connections with the people and their easy association with them in their daily lives, teachers are a powerful force in the rural villages. They are at the same time very close to the people and yet very exalted in their eyes. Because of the very great emphasis laid by Africans on education, teachers are in a very influential position. In fact, their local acceptance, and the regard in which people hold them, often turn them into rival leaders of chiefs.

(d) Relations with chiefs

The high prestige of teachers in village communities, which in the early 1960s equalled that of chiefs but by the late 1960s far outstripped the esteem given to the traditional leaders, turns them into rivals of chiefly power. Excluded from traditional office because of their genealogical positions, they aspire to modern leadership. Consequently teachers have for many years been most outspoken in their rejection of chiefs.

Teachers claim that chiefs discriminate against them and impose higher fines on them than on other litigants when they come to the chiefs' courts. Several said: 'Chiefs charge us more than others because they are jealous of us and think that because of our regular salaries we are able to pay more.' Teachers made the following comments about chiefs: 'Chiefs are old and illiterate; they are sell-outs of the people.' 'Government wants only uneducated chiefs who do not know right from wrong and who always say "yes" to what government wants.' 'Government is afraid of young men because they have the courage to speak up for the truth. Therefore government tells chiefs that young men want to displace them and so deprive them of their salaries.'

Although teachers are highly critical of chiefs, when occasion arises they are willing to win chiefs to their side. This became clear in several chiefdoms during the community development campaign. The opposition of teachers to chiefs is therefore not hard and fast.

[13]*Moto*, May 1965.

The fact that teachers still bring their court cases to chiefs shows that they continue to see in them leaders of a kind. With increasing powers granted to chiefs by government, the influence of teachers in many rural areas has decreased. The most outspoken critics among them of chiefly power and government have been sent to restriction camps.

(e) Political aspirations

In many areas teachers formed the backbone of the nationalist movement almost from its beginning. This was especially the case in areas where one political party was dominant. Where the people were divided between two rival parties[14] teachers were less active in politics.

The first nationalist leader who powerfully appealed to African teachers was Benjamin Burombo. Burombo, originally interested in the rights of urban workers, turned his attention in 1949 to rural areas where the delayed implementation of the Land Apportionment Act caused great dissatisfaction. Government tried to move 4,482 families from land formally classed as European areas. Burombo encouraged the people to stay on the land on which they had lived for generations, and government was able to remove only 1,569 families. With this success the prestige of Burombo soared in rural areas.[15]

In 1953 Burombo visited one of the rural areas in which most of the present research was done. He collected money from the people to pay for his planned trip to England to represent the aspirations of Rhodesian Africans to the British Government. In a very short time the people collected between £150 and £200 for his journey. He roused great enthusiasm. The teachers followed his advice to organize themselves into a committee which set itself up as a watchdog of African interests. When in 1957 the Southern Rhodesian African National Congress was reconstituted, the teachers were ready to join. Soon they actively led local opposition to the introduction of the Land Husbandry Act[16] which changed the African land tenure system, enforced soil conservation and cattle de-stocking. They received the moral support of European missionaries and became the leaders of the people in opposition to government. One

---

[14]The split in the nationalist movement occurred in 1963.
[15]Cf. Gray, 1960, p. 327.
[16]*Land Husbandry Act*, 1951, cap. 103.

teacher in particular distinguished himself during this campaign, and through his open hostility to the Act brought its implementation in his area to a halt. This conferred great prestige on him among the people.

African teachers want to see an African government as soon as possible. Many were paid-up members of the nationalist party and several kept their membership cards even after all nationalist activity was made illegal. This is proved by the following incident related to the investigator by an African teacher after a police raid in the area. The teacher reported: 'Yesterday the police visited me and they shouted at me: "You have been a party member. Surrender your membership card." I answered: "Sir, I have never been a party member, only a sympathizer. If you do not believe me, you may search my house." The police looked doubtful, but finally they left. At their departure I tore up my membership card.' The investigator expressed regret at the destruction of the card, having never seen one. The teacher smiled and said: 'You may have my card, if you like,' and got up to fetch it. At handing it over, however, he asked that his name be thoroughly erased so that no police could identify him. While erasing the name with a pocket knife the investigator suddenly stopped: 'But teacher, one day you might need it again. If you can later on prove that you have remained loyal to the party throughout these troubled times, you may get a high position in the party.' The teacher smiled again and said: 'I have a second membership card.'

(f) Conclusion

Teachers form the most outspoken critics of the European government and the strongest supporters of African nationalism in many areas. The restriction of several teachers has turned them into local heroes in the eyes of the peasants who support their teachers' families economically. Teachers reached the height of their influence in the early 1960s when the nationalist movement was strongest. With the banning of nationalist parties and the active support by government of the chiefs, the teachers' political leadership is slightly declining. Being aware of government informants they are less outspoken in public than they were in the past, but in private conversations they still express their nationalist sympathies and their frustration at the political development of the country. Education has broadened their interests, and although they are still fully integrated in their local communities, yet their interests are nationwide. Kornhauser argues that 'individuals who relate themselves to large scale social events, rather than to the "proximate" concerns of family, community, occupational groups, and so forth, may be more susceptible to the appeal of extremist politics'.[17] This explains the position of African teachers in Rhodesia.   Unlike school inspectors, teachers have little to lose in their championship of the national cause. They have not obtained so high a position that they have lost contact with their own people. They are still fully integrated in village life and should they be discharged by the ministry of African Education, or even be restricted, their families are cared for by their relatives. In case of deposition, some may find more remunerative employment in industry. Many teachers have voluntarily retired from teaching in order to find better paid employment in other occupations.

Because of their great influence, teachers are crucial to the development of African areas. They are the central mediating agents between African and European culture. Because they are fairly familiar with western culture and yet still fully integrated into African rural life, their role merits much attention in the study of race relations. Through their work and esteem in classroom and community, they exert a strong formative influence on African opinion.

4. Evaluation of the teaching elite

School inspectors, school managers and teachers share similar professional interests, but partly because of their different salaries, partly because of their different relationships with their own people, both of which are the result of different educational achievements, their outlook on life and their interests vary.

School inspectors belong to the most westernized section of the African elite, the section which has the least ties with traditional African society. Having built their permanent homes in towns and visiting rural areas only in the course of their professional duties, they have few social connections with rural Africans. The frequency with which school inspectors marry South African wives and send their children to non-African schools further underlines their separation from local African society. Their reference group is European, and not merely Europeans in general but members of the upper strata of European society.

[17]Quoted in Parkin, 1966, p. 161.

The school inspectors' rejection by the out-group to whose membership they aspire frustrates them, but this frustration is not strong enough to throw them back to seek acceptance by their own people. They are tied with golden fetters to the established social order and can envisage only loss by joining revolutionary movements.

African teachers stand at the other pole of the educational professional hierarchy. Their full integration into village life and their living standards which are not greatly above those of the majority of rural inhabitants, do not alienate them from the people, though they enjoy enough prestige to be looked up to as leaders by the masses. Their frequent opposition to the implementation of new government policies, such as the Land Husbandry Act and community development, shows that they actively seek for leadership positions in the field of black–white relations. Since European society is clearly closed to them—they are far less qualified than school inspectors to mix as equals with Europeans—they can only hope for advancement through changing the present social structure. Since they have little to lose and much to gain, they are ideal leaders of a revolutionary movement. The frequency with which teachers have been restricted for political activities[18] shows that their structural position inclines them to radicalism.

School managers occupy an intermediate position. Educationally, salary-wise, and according to their integration into rural communities, they stand closer to teachers than to school inspectors. Yet they have begun to climb the ladder of promotion and so have a greater stake in the teaching profession than ordinary teachers. They are fully imbued with a professional ethos and want to lead their people towards a modern way of life. Some give the impression that they regard teaching more as a way of life than as a means of economic personal advancement.

School managers seem to be ideal mediators between traditional and modern society. They have a stake in both, and because they cannot afford the luxuries of school inspectors, they are not yet as marginal to the society of their birth as their superiors in the teaching profession.

The educational elite constitutes one of the most important sections of African society. Admired and accepted by the African people, most of its members are dedicated to lead Africans towards

[18]Unfortunately no official figures of teachers in restriction are available, but several restricted teachers are known to the research worker.

a new society in which they can meet Europeans as equals. Several have witnessed publicly to their conviction and suffered the loss of their freedom. Peasants regard them as the leaders of the future. Dedicated to social change, they are the natural opponents of chiefs, the guardians of the past, whom government has put at present into leadership positions.

9. The African agricultural elite

1. Extension officers

(a) Recruitment

Rhodesia has one agricultural college which trains Africans for the posts of extension officers if they have completed eleven years' schooling. Even though the department of conservation and extension in the ministry of Agriculture admits more Africans to officer level than any other branch of the Rhodesian civil service, many graduates from the training college find themselves without employment. The few who do obtain a post in the ministry of Agriculture consider themselves as pioneers. One of them said: 'We are the first African extension officers in the country and therefore we must be very successful. If we fail, the door will be closed for further Africanization. We must show to all men that we are able to do the same work that Europeans do, and that we can do it equally well, if not better.'

The post of extension officer, only recently opened to Africans, seems to attract men from families slightly more affluent than ordinary peasant cultivators. Several have fathers who own purchase area farms; others are the sons of craftsmen. A number have other educated relatives. One, for example, is the brother of a physician, another of an extension supervisor. Like nurses, therefore, African extension officers come from families slightly better off than many other sections of the African elite. When they marry, they look for educated wives. The last extension officer interviewed is engaged to a nurse. Most African extension officers are still very young men.

Even more than European extension officers, African extension officers feel insecure in their profession. They lack a university degree and so have few promotion possibilities. In order to secure future promotion, many of them study privately for a degree. Most expressed great concern that African agriculture was to be

177

transferred back to the ministry of Internal Affairs. They feared that they might lose their positions to Europeans, since Internal Affairs has been very reluctant to allow Africanization in its ministry.

(b) Relations with Europeans

African extension officers earn the same salaries as European extension officers, that is, about £1,000 per annum, and they live in staff houses occupied by either Africans or Europeans. In work situations their European colleagues treat them as equals and many European extension officers stressed that African extension officers understood African peasants better than they did and so could help them more effectively. Some European extension officers accept their African colleagues into their homes and mix with them socially, others prefer not to do so. One African extension officer explained: 'It is difficult for Europeans to accept us socially because even if they would like to do so, their neighbours often discriminate against them when they find us in their homes. Europeans friendly to Africans are despised by members of their own race. This distresses me very much.' Another recalled with pleasure several parties he had attended in the company of European civil servants; at one even a district commissioner had been present. He commented: 'At first it is a bit difficult to mix with Europeans. But I carefully observed how they behaved and it did not take me very long to do as they did.'

Extension officers know that their social acceptance in European circles never extends beyond a few well-meaning European colleagues. They cannot gain admittance into the larger European society. As civil servants they have few contacts with missionaries.

(c) Relations with Africans

Extension officers divide their contacts with fellow Africans into three groups: contacts with relatives, contacts with African peasants, and contacts with educated Africans. Because of their civil service posts, they are subject to frequent transfers. Consequently they seldom, if ever, live close to their relatives so that they can very rarely interact with kinsmen. This, however, does not mean that they do not assist their relatives. One extension officer stressed that his brother has a family of twelve children whom he is no longer able to feed. He therefore took one of his brother's sons and sees to his food, clothing and education.

Isolation from kinsmen also means that extension officers live as strangers in African communities. In this respect they resemble European extension officers who are also forced to live as strangers in a society in which kinship ties determine all social relationships.[1]

The extension officers' contacts with ordinary peasants varies. One complained about the peasants' dirty food and beer and admitted reluctance to share their unhygienic meals. Another stressed that he was only successful because he accepted every African peasant as his equal and showed him great respect.

Yet whether extension officers felt repelled or attracted, all tried to maintain friendly relations with the ordinary people. One even stressed that he went out of his way to give Africans a lift to town whenever he saw them standing by the roadside. The extension officers' relationships with ordinary Africans, therefore, approach those of well-meaning Europeans who also give help wherever they can, but who do not normally mix socially with them.

Extension officers prefer to mix with their social equals. If they cannot find them on their stations in rural areas, they feel lonely. Some try to overcome their social isolation by visits to nearby towns, but even these visits often cause them frustration. One related:

We educated Africans have nowhere to go. Until recently we had a multi-racial hotel in the nearby town, but since the Prime Minister was there and heard an African band playing at the hotel, Africans have been forbidden admittance. We are told to go to the African township which has a beer hall with cocktail bar. But I do not like going there. The bar is always overcrowded. I now buy my drinks there but then take them home to drink in peace.

Another extension officer commented in a similar strain:

In order to have a place to retire to which is appropriate to our status, several of us educated men tried to form an exclusive club. To prevent the ordinary people from just coming in and watching us we charged a five guinea entry fee. But we failed in our objective because wealthy but uneducated Africans, such as businessmen, came to join us. I wish we Africans had already evolved a full class structure. This would be the first step towards progress. Everybody would know then at what to aim: namely to membership of the social class above him. This would give us all a place to stand. At present we are onlookers on society.

[1] Several peasants stressed that they saw no difference between African and European extension officers.

(d) Relations with chiefs

Few extension officers hold extreme views about chiefs. All said with conviction that they would never compete for the office of chief, nor support their fathers, had these a chance. Some found chiefs co-operative when they approached them in the course of their professional duties. One was more precise. He said:

About a quarter of all chiefs act responsibly in regard to soil conservation, the others do not. One chief in my area collected money among his people to build contour ridges, but when he had the money he used it for his personal needs. Another built contour ridges, but they were so small that they could not perform their function. It is futile to force chiefs to act more responsibly because force merely makes them suspicious.

Many extension officers respect chiefs. One said: 'If I were together with a teacher, a fellow extension officer and a chief, I would honour the chief most.' Another said: 'Young and old people seem to respect chiefs; so why should not I?' But a third commented:

In the past chiefs were quite different from what they are at present. They were chosen by the people and had no financial profit from their position. They were truly interested in the well-being of their people and did not accept bribes. Today they are appointed by government, receive a government salary, and in addition extort much money from their people. Modern chiefs are selfish.

Most extension officers inform chiefs of the new plans in their agricultural extension work. Though they deplore the land deterioration which has spread since chiefs have been given power to allocate and control land, as civil servants they cannot actively oppose current government policy which tries to recreate a powerful image of African chiefs.

(e) Political aspirations

Extension officers expressed less interest in politics than many other members of the African elite. Most thought that there was no hope for African political advance. One said: 'There will be no African parliament for a very long time,' and another: 'African political advancement must be shelved; there is just no chance at present.' A third said: 'We Africans are very unhappy at present, but we are also afraid. What can we do?'

Most extension officers pointed to their own very insecure professional position and added: 'We dare not speak.' One said: 'I am worried to lose my job. We are living in very difficult circumstances, full of insecurities. We are not allowed to talk. If something goes wrong, we African officers will be told that we have not done our duty.' Another commented: 'Africans can get education but no work. The longer this state of affairs continues, the more cruel Africans will become. But revenge will not bring us progress.'

(f) Conclusion

Moderate and frustrated, mainly because of professional insecurity, African extension officers stand in a no-man's land. Their position as officers in the civil service does not allow them to voice their political views. Their social circle is very narrow, confined to a few well-meaning colleagues and members of the African elite. Traditional African society is no longer congenial to them.

Ndabaninge Sithole, leader of an African nationalist party in Rhodesia, and at the time this book is written in a Rhodesian prison, wrote to the author about Africans in a similar position to extension officers:

You are right in suggesting that the educated African is at home neither in the African society nor in European society. My own observation is that the present educated African will of necessity have to go through this interim period of frustration until there are sufficient numbers of educated Africans who will form a third culture which is neither predominantly African nor European, but which will satisfy the needs of the educated African.[2]

Like other members of the African elite, therefore, extension officers feel marginal to both traditional and European society. Refusing to be integrated into the one, and being refused acceptance by the other, they stand alone. As pioneers in a branch of the civil service which only recently admitted Africans to its rank, they dare not openly criticize government. Like school inspectors and other well-paid members of the elite, they are bound by economic rewards and interests to the European-controlled society of Rhodesia and cannot challenge the establishement.

2. Extension supervisors and assistants

(a) Recruitment

A significant number of extension supervisors and assistants are

[2]Letter from prison, Salisbury, 1.9.1968.

sons of purchase area farmers; the rest tend to come from ordinary
peasant families. All of them, therefore, come from farming backgrounds. The minimum education required for extension assistants
is a completed primary education plus a three-year course in agriculture. In recent years, two years of secondary education have been
asked for before allowing young men to undergo their agricultural
training.

After some ten years as extension assistants, men may be promoted to the rank of extension supervisors, but with this their promotion possibilities are exhausted because for the next rank, that
of extension officer, a higher formal education is required. Many
extension assistants feel frustrated about their lack of promotion
possibilities, and in the early 1960s a large number joined the ministry of Internal Affairs as community advisors, a new post created
during the community development campaign which brings a higher
salary than that of extension assistant but does not necessitate
higher education.

Extension supervisors and assistants belong to the middle rank
of the African elite. They earn a salary of about £25 to £30 a
month, just as do teachers and most Protestant ministers of religion.
Most are able to pay for their children's complete primary education, and some even for a few years' secondary education. But this
exhausts the financial ability of most extension staff.

(b) Relations with Europeans

Extension supervisors and assistants have very little contact with
Europeans. Stationed in African rural areas, the only Europeans
they meet regularly are their superiors in the civil service, the extension officers who pass on their instructions to them and whom they
have to obey. Extension officers appreciate efficient members in their
teams but do not treat them familiarly. Extension supervisors and
assistants address extension officers by the title 'Sir' and show them
respect. Few members of the extension staff ever visit mission stations. Civil servants and missionaries seem to be divided by an invi-
sible barrier.

(c) Relations with Africans

Extension staff are civil servants employed by a minority government. Their task is to alter traditional farming techniques, a hazar-
dous undertaking in any peasant community. Their professional

duties, therefore, put extension supervisors and assistants in a difficult position. In the 1950s they had to implement the Land Husbandry Act, a task which made them very unpopular. This upopularity is reflected in the relatively low ranking of extension staff in the rating exercise, set out in Table 9.[3] Kuper writes about the dubious position of African civil servants: 'Bureaucracy demands unconditional loyalty from its African civil servants, while Africans expect such educated persons as civil servants to lead their people, to challenge the very laws they are expected to administer.[4] Extension workers belong to that section of the civil service whose orders were often felt most burdensome by African peasants. When this study was undertaken, they had no particular policy to implement and some succeeded in establishing friendlier relations with peasants. But their past image still hung over them like a cloud.

Like extension officers, extension supervisors and assistants are frequently transferred and so do not live among their relatives. As strangers in African chiefdoms, they lack many chances of local leadership which are open to teachers. A few extension workers are temporarily able to free themselves from these restrictions. One supervisor married locally and became a close and trusted friend of a sub-chief. As long as he was stationed in his area, conservation works expanded fast and modern farming techniques were adopted by a large number of peasants. At his transfer, however, agricultural development came to a standstill and the supervisor had again to live as a stranger in his new area.

Extension workers seek to be accepted by the local people, but like government itself they remain outsiders in the life of local communities and are socially less influential than mission trained teachers. They are seen as agents of government and their acceptance depends on current policies they have to implement. Their civil service position causes a gulf between them and the people. Because of their link with government, which is not offset by a large salary as is that of extension officers and school inspectors, people often wonder why they have chosen such an invidious occupation.

For social companionship extension workers are confined to their equals. One supervisor said: 'When I give a party, I invite other

[3] *Supra*, p. 106, Table 9.
[4] Kuper, 1965, p. 254.

extension workers and the African police. Sometimes an African teacher is willing to come. But few other people ever join.'

(d) Relations with chiefs

All extension workers try to maintain reasonably good relations with chiefs, though not all agree with the administrative practices of individual chiefs. Several pointed out injustices and irresponsible actions on the part of chiefs, both in trying court cases and in the allocation of land. One said: 'Our chief is utterly irresponsible. Since he has been given power to allocate land, conservation works have seriously deteriorated and land is ploughed which should never have come under the plough. When I talk to the chief, he does not listen.' Another extension assistant said: 'Chiefs do not know their responsibilities. They have been given new powers too fast. They often misuse their power to allocate land and give much to outsiders who pay them more than their own people. People often resent the actions of their chiefs, but they are afraid to criticize them openly.' Still another commented: 'Chiefs treat educated and uneducated Africans differently. Unless they are the chief's relatives, uneducated men never get what is their right. Educated men get what they want more easily because chiefs know them to be cleverer than themselves.'[5] An extension supervisor stated:

Chiefs are of little use to us in extension work because they are too uneducated. We often call them for training courses at our agricultural institute to explain to them their duties. When we ask them whether they understand, they always say 'yes'. But when they return to their people they can explain nothing. They simply tell the people: 'You must do so and so because the Europeans and the district commissioner want it.' In this way they throw the responsibility on others.[6]

(e) Political aspirations

Some extension workers are very frightened to express any political opinion. Since most of them are supervised by European extension officers, they feel more frequently watched than many other members of the African elite. Their civil service position places upon

---

[5]This statement differs from that of teachers (cf. *supra*, p. 171), that chiefs discriminate against educated subjects.

[6]The chiefs' endeavour to throw the responsibility for new agricultural practices on others need not be due to lack of understanding, but may derive from the desire to dissociate themselves from practices which they know their people will resent.

them a strong obligation to conform. Teachers, who are also civil servants, do not experience as great a pressure because they work generally under missionaries who sympathize with their political aspirations. Extension supervisors and assistants lack the cushioning which teachers receive from European priests and ministers. Consequently extension workers and teachers often react differently to government policies.

When in one area the ministry of Internal Affairs started the community development campaign, extension supervisors and assistants distinguished themselves from teachers in their much more rational and co-operative attitude towards the new policy. They did not ask for the ultimate purpose of the new policy, but put factual questions, concerning their role in community development.

A number of extension workers would like to be as outspoken about their political aspirations as teachers are, but few have the courage. One extension assistant felt so committed to African nationalism that he could not in conscience avoid political involvement. During the implementation of the Land Husbandry Act he violently disagreed with its policy and resigned his post. With money he had saved he opened a store and supported his family as a businessman. Not satisfied by protesting through resignation, he led the peasant discontent in the area in which he had worked and in which he had opened his store. He encouraged the villagers to stone the cattle dip tanks and to burn hide sheds. He was brought to court, found guilty and imprisoned. During his imprisonment customers continued to buy at his store, then run by his wife. His neighbours gave his family all the support needed until he had served his prison sentence and was able to return to his business. Such decisive action among civil servants, however, is rare. Also, few of them are financially able to support their families if they lose their employment, and this financial dependence forces them to conform.

(f) Conclusion

This analysis shows that men in the lower ranks of the extension service are as marginal to African society as are extension officers, not because of their superior living standards but because of their connection with government. Having in the past frequently been obliged to implement policies resented by the peasants, they are often as much rejected by the people as are European government

officials. Although they have about the same degree of education
as teachers and earn about the same salary, they are not accepted
as teachers are accepted. Unrelated to the people because recruited
from a pool of experts trained in a government institution, they
remain outsiders in the communities in which they work. Their contacts with Europeans are negligible.

The extension workers' relationships with chiefs are less strained
than those of teachers because in their detached view of chiefs they
resemble more the higher echelons of the African elite than the views
of men with similar education and income. Their general reluctance
to take a clear stand on politics marks them as outsiders to local
communities. They are members of the elite, remote and relatively
well-to-do, but few Africans try to imitate them. They are not
centres of suggestion and objects of attraction. They are government
employees.

3. Cash crop farmers

Cash crop farmers are distinguished from the other members of
the African elite in that they are at times very wealthy but lack
higher formal education and close contact with western civilization.
Most, but not all, have bought farms of about 200 acres in size
in land classified as 'purchase areas', that is, land set aside for Africans under the Land Apportionment Act in which they can own
land under freehold title. Such farms are outside the control of local
chiefs. All farmers in these purchase areas are immigrants who left
their chiefdoms for the express purpose of going in for cash crop-
ping. Their communities are administered by democratically elected
committees. These farmers are proud of having left behind them
tribal life and many of its customs, especially the dependence of
tribesmen on chiefs. Prominence in these communities goes to two
types of men: to those who are economically most successful, and
to those who rise to positions of local leadership on important committees. Few of them have completed more than primary education.

The following section on successful farmers follows a different
pattern from the previous sections dealing with the African elite.
Since there are very many African farmers, but only a few who
can claim membership of the modern African elite, or at least sub-
elite, three case histories of successful farmers are set out, and then
some general observations are made. The first two case histories

are typical of outstanding farmers in purchase areas. The third case history tells of the career of an exceptional farmer in a chiefdom.

(a) *Case history of a successful farmer*

In a purchase area in which the average farmer has an annual income from his farm of about £200, this farmer has an income of about £1,000. He is the wealthiest man in his community. The reasons for his success are varied and his background is unusual.

After completing primary education he claims to have done a correspondence course with a Californian University in philosophy and psychology, a claim in which he takes great pride but which could not be proved. His father bought himself a European-sized farm on unreserved land and later helped him to pay for his 200-acre farm. In addition to his father's help, he had saved £800 as a labour migrant before he applied for his farm, a saving which is far in excess of the £300 required by government for prospective African settlers on purchase area farms.

During twelve years of occupation, he spent £1,700 on opening up and improving his farm. Among other capital investments, he built a dam and installed a pump; he built himself a house worth £500 and bought a new truck to bring his vegetables to surrounding towns. He needs the truck because unlike most farmers he irrigates part of his land and grows vegetables for sale throughout the year. This brings him in more than half his annual income.

For many years he has been chairman of the local co-operative society and vice-secretary of the African Farmers' Union committee through which the purchase area is administered. He is greatly respected by his fellow farmers as well as by the extension staff. Extension assistants often use his farm to demonstrate to other farmers modern farming techniques. He is regarded as an innovator who experiments with the latest findings of agricultural research.

In order to farm his land intensely, he married three wives to help him in the fields, and he also employs some six to eight hired labourers from nearby chiefdoms during the months when work is pressing. These he pays in vegetables, sometimes in money.

Progressive farmers look to him as a source of suggestion and an object of imitation. They admire him greatly and again and again offer him leadership positions in local associations. He is the rich man whom many would like to be.

(b) Case history of an exceptional farmer

This farmer differs from others in his background. Son of a European father and an African mother, he worked in his youth as a Coloured and earned good wages as a teacher, store-keeper and cattle buyer. His father, however, disowned him and he grew up with his mother in an African chiefdom. There he married an African wife. When the area in which he lived was declared a purchase area and families living there under chiefs had to move out, he applied for a farm. Being told that as a Coloured he was not allowed to own a farm in an African farming community, he changed his racial classification to 'African'. His children took exception to this step and went to the district commissioner, claiming that they were of Coloured ancestry and superior to African peasants. In registering as Coloureds they disqualified themselves from inheriting their father's farm.

When the new purchase area was opened, this farmer became one of the first settlers. He was unanimously elected as the first chairman of the local African Farmers' Union committee, a post which he held from 1956 to 1967. He distinguished himself through his excellent farming methods and European civil servants often commented that the streak of European blood in his veins made him superior to his neighbours. They often asked him to convince his fellow farmers of the advantages of certain government policies, and he often succeeded in winning their co-operation. Through his assistance an Intensive Conservation Area committee was established and many local improvements initiated.

Yet people did not consider him as an outsider. From his mother he had learned the value of medical herbs and had become a famous herbalist. His willingness to cure his sick neighbours often won him their gratitude. He shared their cultural values.

In the eyes of Europeans this man was an ideal mediator because of his racial background. In the eyes of his African neighbours he was a suitable spokesman not only because he was acceptable to Europeans, but also because he shared intimately in their own culture. In addition to his links with both Africans and Europeans, and his success in mediating between diverse interests, this man was a distinguished farmer. His income of over £400 from farming was double that of the average farmer in his area, and like the farmer in the first case history he experimented with modern farming techniques as soon as they became known. He was the first farmer in his purchase area who began stall feeding his cattle, and the beasts he sold fetched higher prices than had ever been paid to local farmers. His farm became a little experimental station for beef production in the area.

This farmer won his leadership position through long association with the area in which he lived, his respect for traditional custom, his farming expertise, and his acceptance in civil service quarters. His neighbours trusted him to represent their interests to the best of his abilities.

(c) Case history of a cash crop farmer in a tribal area

This farmer differs from those of the preceding case histories in that he refused the offer of a purchase area farm because he occupied a leading position in the chiefdom in which he was born and hoped to win the chieftainship for his father's brother.

Having completed primary schooling and worked for many years as a bricklayer, he was convinced by the arguments of an extension assistant that he could make more money through intensive farming than through working for Europeans. As a young married man, therefore, he gave up labour migration and concentrated on agriculture. He joined a course run by a local extension assistant on modern farming techniques and soon obtained a certificate for progressive farming.

After the Land Husbandry Act was implemented in his area, he bought from a neighbour the latter's right to cultivate land so that his own holding was twice the standard size, namely twelve acres. He followed all the advice the extension staff gave him, and in addition sent a sample of his soil to a laboratory in the capital to obtain instructions on the exact type of fertilizer needed. As soon as cotton was recommended to African farmers, he planted a large field with the new cash crop and reaped a bumper harvest. On his fields devoted to the staple crop, maize, he harvested on the average twenty bags per acre. His neighbours reaped three to five bags, and Europeans in the same district ten bags.

This man was recognized as the best farmer in the area and the most eager innovator whom the extension staff, especially the European extension officers, frequently visited in order to use his lands for demonstration purposes.

Apart from European extension staff, this farmer also cultivated the friendship of nearby Catholic missionaries, though he himself belonged to a Protestant denomination. Every year he hired the missionaries' tractor to plough his fields and frequently sold his produce to them, thus avoiding the low prices paid by the Grain Marketing Board and its agents. Many economic ties bound him to the nearby mission station.

Economic wealth is especially useful if it can be transformed into social prestige. The successful farmer drew around him a group of other farmers interested in modern farming methods. These tried to copy his farming techniques and competed with each other in imitating him. He himself became the head of a local farming club. From this modest leadership position he was soon able to be elected to other positions of leadership. He became a village headman, chairman of a kind of co-operative society, and when community development was introduced he became the representative of his ward.

His wife likewise holds a leadership position in the community. She is chairwoman of the oldest African women's club, started by a European farmer's wife. Through her club she has learned modern house-keeping, sewing, cooking and child care. Her home resembles that of Europeans in the lower income brackets. It is clean and simple, but distinctly different from that of other peasants. Her husband's income and her own skill enable her to model it on that of Europeans. During one of frequent visits, husband and wife asked the research worker: 'How does your father treat your mother? We would like to treat each other exactly as European spouses do because we are the first family in this district.'

All his children attend lower secondary school and his eldest son is training as an extension assistant.

Politically, this farmer is not at all interested in African nationalism. Instead he competes with his father's brother for the chieftainship, and this competition was the major reason why he refused the offer of a purchase area farm. He regards chieftainship as a valuable institution of the African way of life.

(d) Conclusion

Outstanding cash crop farmers, whether in purchase areas or in chiefdoms, come from peasant families. They have few contacts with Europeans, except with European extension staff and occasionally some nearby missionaries. But even these contacts are strictly confined to agriculture and no social mixing takes place. No farmer expressed a great desire to be socially accepted by Europeans because all their ties are with their African neighbours.

Successful cash crop farmers are admired by their neighbours because their surplus enables them to buy many goods which other men would like to purchase, but have no means of doing so. If they live in purchase areas, far away from their relatives, few kinship demands are made on them and most can invest their profits in their land. In chiefdoms re-investment of profits is slightly more difficult, but outstanding men succeed even there to use their capital economically.

Wealth is highly esteemed by Rhodesian Africans, more so than education if education does not bring with it well-paid employment.[7] Successful farmers are admired by many peasants and form a group apart from other people. Their economic interests may account for their lack of concern about political development.

Their ties with traditional social values are still strong. Whether they compete with a close relative for the chieftainship, invest their money in a plurality of wives, or distinguish themselves as herbalists, all have one or other characteristic which shows that they have not rejected traditional values.

Successful cash crop farmers do not qualify as members of the modern emergent elite in the same way as do clergymen or men in the medical professions or teachers, because their contacts with western culture are minimal and their education rudimentary. Yet they stand out locally. They may be classed as forming a sub-elite in communities aspiring to enter the market economy.

4. Evaluation of the agricultural elite

The agricultural elite and sub-elite differ from most African elites through their relative political neutrality. As members of the civil service, extension workers differ from the mission-recruited elite both in their loyalties and aspirations. The gulf between them and the African peasants is much larger than the distance between priests, doctors and teachers and the African people. Their association with government prevents the same ties of trust developing between them and the people as exist between the people and the mission-

---

[7]This statement is based on research findings from an urban study. Publication forthcoming.

influenced elite. Consequently African civil servants are much more isolated than other educated Africans in rural areas.

Outstanding cash crop farmers stand in a group apart, being hardly distinguishable from the ordinary people in regard to education and acceptance of western cultural values, but yet being fully absorbed into the European controlled market economy. Their African neighbours accept them because of the many ties uniting them with ordinary villagers.

With a few exceptions, the African agricultural elite and sub-elite are politically less articulate than other sections of the emergent African elite. Their civil service ties or economic interests prevent them from criticizing government. As pointed out above,[8] teachers, though also civil servants, are cushioned from the impact of government control in a way the extension staff is not. Because extension workers are strangers among the people for whom they work, they are both less trusted and less trusting. Should they express political views, they are less sure than teachers of who the local informants are, since they do not know their neighbours well enough. Consequently the agricultural civil service elite remains marginal to the communities in which they are stationed.

The agricultural sub-elite suffers from no such marginality. Living in a community of farmers, they are accepted and their leadership positions turn them into local objects of admiration and imitation in a sense that the extension staff is not. Many peasants who want to improve themselves economically, copy advanced fellow farmers rather than consult extension workers.

[8]*Supra*, p. 185.

10. The African commercial elites and sub-elites

1. The business elite

In rural Rhodesia, a few African businessmen have received an education comparable to that of members in the middle ranks of the emergent African elite, but others have received little or no schooling. Education is not strictly speaking necessary for an African businessman, though it is helpful.

The African business elite are men constantly introducing new aspects into traditional African life. Like other members of the modern elite, they follow an occupation introduced into African society by Europeans.[1] Many Africans first encountered shops when they migrated to urban areas in search of employment. Soon some of the more enterprising among them attempted to start their own little stores.

Through their stores, African businessmen provide peasants with many goods unknown in traditional society. European food, such as tea, sugar, bread, and clothing for men, women and children in the form of dresses, shirts and trousers, as well as capital equipment like ploughs and sewing machines, are introduced by traders into the economies of Rhodesian chiefdoms. The ever greater supply of these and many other goods, and the growing dependence of villagers on them, are rapidly transforming village life. Businessmen, through their stores, are a key factor in this transformation.

African businessmen are a dynamic force for change in still another sense. Most of the more important traders own cars to fetch their goods from their wholesalers in urban areas, and through the transport at their disposal they provide African villagers with important links with the outside world. Indeed it can be stated that

---

[1] In addition to Europeans, Asians control a large section of Rhodesian trade. But the proportion of Asians in the total population is only 0·2 per cent and therefore little reference is made to them in this study.

businessmen derive one of the major sources of their power from their control over the network of communication in rural areas. Their stores are always situated on important roads, either near bus stops or at cross roads, but never in villages. Many stores are built near mission stations, schools or chiefs' residences where many people gather. They are always situated at strategical points to give easy access to a large number of people. The central position of their stores contributes to the influence of local store owners.

African stores may be built in places officially designated by government as 'African Business Centres', that is, areas in chiefdoms or purchase areas set aside for the development of rural townships; or an important man may open his own store or stores near his home and so establish his own business centre. The officially designated business centres attract both important businessmen and small traders who try their luck in opening a store, but often go out of business again if they fail to make a profit. A business centre may take its name either from the nearby residence of a chief or from its most important businessman.

(a) Recruitment and case histories

Businessmen fall into two groups. Though all come from peasant families, some have taken to business after some years in a profession which enabled them to accumulate capital with which to open their stores; others lack formal education and capital of their own and attempt a business enterprise with some money contributed by their kinsmen. Success does not seem to depend on formal education.

The following case histories of businessmen and women represent a typical cross section of the more successful African store owners in rural Rhodesia.

(i) A teacher turned store owner

This store owner started off as a mission-trained teacher.[2] In 1950 he opened the first store in the chiefdom and situated it next to the bus stop at the mission station at which he was teaching. His store prospered and by 1955 he retired from teaching in order to devote himself full time to his business. He opened a second store some miles away and placed it in charge of his younger

[2] Cf. Kuper, 1965, p. 294. Kuper also notes a tendency among South African teachers acquiring commercial interests.

brother. His brother, however, handled the money dishonestly and the store went bankrupt.

About the time the second store failed, the mission opened a new hospital and the first store experienced a boom. The teacher, turned businessman, acquired a car which he used as a taxi to bring patients to the hospital. In 1960 he opened a bottle store and bakery, and in 1962 a butchery, all next to his store. His home therefore became a business centre in which he himself owned all the stores. His wife helped him to run the centre efficiently, for since he felt let down by his brother he employed no other relatives.

By 1963 he had installed a telephone at his first store and acquired a postbag. The head of the bus company, which served the businesman's area, was related to his wholesaler. Through belonging to the same political party as this man, the store owner had some influence with the bus drivers and conductors. By the early 1960s, therefore, he controlled all the means of communication and could provide the local community with services which no other African could provide. Up to that time only the mission possessed a telephone and postbag.

With these acquisitions, however, the businessman reached the height of his social and economic power. Soon afterwards he divorced his wife and placed his stores in the hands of unrelated women assistants who stole much of his money. His business went bankrupt and by 1965 he was a manager in the stores he had built, working for his former wholesaler.

This teacher, turned store owner, is distantly related to the local chief.

(ii) *A café house owner*

This man also started his business enterprise with money saved from teaching. In fact, he remained a teacher through all his life. In the 1950s, after some family quarrels, he left his father's village and built a café house near a mission station at which he was headmaster, and placed it in the hands of his wife. His café house soon became the meeting place of local teachers. Through the combined income of teaching and business he was able to give his children a good secondary education, and one of his daughters became the first state registered nurse in the chiefdom. Like the first teacher turned store owner, he was distantly related to the chief.

(iii) *A teacher turned butcher and grocer*

This businessman also belongs to the educated elite. He was one

Plate IV. Typical store in an African chiefdom

of the first teachers trained in his local community. In 1950 he opened a butchery at an area designated as a business centre which, however, at that time did not yet contain any stores. During the cattle de-stocking under the Land Husbandry Act in 1956, his butchery went almost bankrupt. Since he had given up teaching, he was faced with an economic crisis. In his difficulty he took another risk. An unsuccessful petty trader was trying to sell his store, and the butcher bought it. It was situated near the residence of a sub-chief, some miles from his butchery. He turned this store into a grocery and the grocery prospered. With its profits he was able to keep his butchery solvent. By 1963 both stores flourished and he bought himself a secondhand lorry for £600.

He put his transport at the disposal of villagers, petty traders and the mission when it needed additional transport to cart sand from a river to one of its building sites. This brought him in a substantial amount of money.

His business also received a boost through trading links with the mission station. He provided the mission regularly with meat and received a standing order to provide a local women's association with uniforms. For this purpose he employed a tailor who in addition to sewing uniforms made dresses for local women.

In 1963, when his sister was divorced, he opened a bakery for her at a not too distant business centre so that she could support herself. This earned him great esteem among his neighbours.

As a stranger in the chiefdom, his relatives lived further away, but whenever they came to him he assisted them with goods. In return he asked them for little services around his stores. Thus he honoured his kinship obligations without being overburdened by them.

(iv) *An extension assistant turned businessman*

This man left the civil service in 1956 in protest at the implementation of the Land Husbandry Act.[3] Like the teachers who took to business, he had accumulated capital while in employment and with this capital he opened a general dealer's store near a major outstation of a mission. After some years he added a butchery to his store. Christians coming to religious services frequented his stores. His profits enabled him to buy a lorry which he used for a variety of purposes.[4] He is a stranger in his community.

(v) *Business of an educated stranger*

This trader immigrated from another chiefdom, in which he received full primary education, in order to be far away from his relatives and able to re-invest his profits in his store. For many years he was one of the most successful businessmen in his district, but in 1964 he went bankrupt, having accumulated debts in the region of £3,000.

(vi) *The son of a diviner turned entrepreneur*

This man's case history differs from those of the preceding businessmen in that he started off without any formal education. In fact, he has never been to school and is unable to read and write. Like his father, a diviner, he is deeply rooted in traditional African culture and accepts many of its values. As an immigrant from another chiefdom, he is a stranger in the area in which he opened his stores.

[3]Cf. *supra*, p. 185.   [4]Cf. *infra*, p. 203.

In 1954, his father advanced him money and with this money he opened a mill. At that time his was the only mill for many miles and many women came to have their grain milled by him. He was soon able to repay his father's loan. In 1955 he opened a general dealer's store with his own money near an important bus stop. Not only do buses from the capital and other important towns pass his store, but most stay there overnight so that he is able to sell much food and drink to passengers in transit. In 1957 he bought himself a secondhand lorry and built another mill at a distant business centre. In 1958 he opened a butchery near his first mill and in 1962 a tea room. That year he also bought himself a new lorry costing £2,000. In 1963 he opened a bakery in yet another business centre and a store near the chief's residence. By 1963, therefore, he owned seven businesses.

This successful entrepreneur also has seven wives, and he placed each of his establishments in the hands of a wife who is able to write and do simple book-keeping. After he experienced some initial failure by placing stores in the hands of his brothers, he decided that polygyny was the most efficient system to run stores. He realized that wives may steal small amounts of money, but found that their petty thefts could not be compared with the major thefts of brothers who consider their brothers' goods as their own. He therefore had a similar experience as the teacher turned store owner.

(vii) *A businesswoman*

One important trader is a woman who built a chain of stores through her own efforts. At her husband's death she inherited a house in an urban African township. This she rented out to lodgers and with a gradually accumulating capital she opened one store after another. Her chain of stores stretch through three chiefdoms. She is greatly respected by all the people in these chiefdoms because her stores are well stocked and the service provided is exceptionally polite. She gives out many goods on credit so that many peasants and rural white collar workers are economically dependent on her. At one stage she was suggested as a councillor for a community development council. She is a stranger in the communities in which she runs her stores.

(viii) *Many small traders*

In addition to some of the outstanding African rural businessmen described above, there is a large number of petty traders who with the help of their kinsmen are able to collect some capital to start a store, but lacking business expertise soon go bankrupt or at best manage to keep a little store open without making much profit. Since these men received capital from their kinsmen, they feel obliged to support them with goods free of charge so that they frequently run their stores at a loss.

Bankruptcy is common among all classes of African traders because no adequate government loans are available to them. But it is especially widespread among small traders. These rely on more successful traders for transport to carry their goods from the wholesalers, and then have to compete with them for customers.

(b) Relations with Europeans

Businessmen have two major contacts with Europeans:[5] with wholesalers and with missionaries. Their contacts with wholesalers are frequent and regular, but exclusively confined to business transactions. Friendly relations exist between them as long as the traders are able to pay. If they cease to be solvent, wholesalers attempt to rescue as much of their capital as possible, and this breaks the relationship.

Some businessmen have friendly relations with missionaries. This is especially the case among former teachers who after retirement maintain close contacts with the mission. The case history of the teacher turned butcher and grocer shows how such contacts can have economic advantages for a businessman. This particular businessman also occupied leading positions in voluntary Church organizations, in one of which he was a diocesan secretary. Yet in spite of their friendly ties with missionaries, businessmen do not mix socially with them.

Occasionally some businessmen meet with well-meaning civil servants and European businessmen who try to teach and organize them so that they may run their stores at greater profits. One such meeting took place in 1969 when rural and urban traders of a province were called to a provincial town for a seminar at which the formation of an African traders' association was discussed. The meeting was opened by the mayor of the town and speeches were given by the provincial extension officer who stressed the need for rural development in which businessmen could play a major role, and several European businessmen who lectured on the various aspects of business management.

[5] And some Asians whom they meet in the wholesale trade.

Such gatherings are isolated attempts which aim at imparting knowledge to Africans and not at bringing the races closer together. The medium of the English language, which many African traders find difficult to follow, and the great gap in wealth between African and European businessmen, prevent them from meeting on an informal basis.[6] In fact, neither African nor European traders look for such contacts. None of the rural African businessmen interviewed seemed to aspire to integration into European society. They realize that the cultural gap between them and Europeans is very great.

(c) Relations with Africans

If the businessmen's relations with Europeans are very tenuous, those with fellow Africans are strong. Integration into an African community, however, need not necessarily mean that all businessmen are loved and trusted. They may also be objects of fear. But fear is an integral part of African life.

Most businessmen, not only the one businesswoman mentioned, give out goods on credit, and this credit forms a very strong bond between store owners and customers. In 1964 the teacher turned butcher and grocer estimated that his customers owed him among themselves some £500. He knew that he would never be able to recover all his money, but he also knew that this calculated risk would bring him many advantages and pay dividends in the form of great popularity and power.

The reason is that businessmen, who advance goods on credit, make their debtors dependent on them. Most rural Africans have become used to goods imported by traders, and these goods are only available for ready cash or credit. Since few villagers have ready cash at hand, most are indebted to local store owners. Most store owners willingly hand out credit to teachers and other white collar workers who receive a regular monthly salary because they are sure to retrieve their money. If outstanding debts have not been repaid after a long time, traders refuse further credit and, in extreme cases, send the police to collect the money for them. This alternative, however, occasionally resorted to by some traders, rapidly decreased their local popularity. Traders only use this means if they are near bankruptcy.

[6]It is interesting to note that although this meeting took place in an African urban township which has many African businessmen, most businessmen who attended came from rural areas. Urban businessmen stayed away for fear that the new organization might impose monetary obligations on its members.

African store owners also help peasants in buying up their surplus grain for a statutory body, the Grain Marketing Board. The significant profit they make from this transaction frequently arouses local resentment. Yet they are the only channel through which small-scale peasant producers can acquire money.[7] Through the credit systems most store owners are able to regain this money as soon as they have paid it out.

Popular traders are the social kingpins of their communities because their stores are the social centres where men gather to discuss local events and politics. Here housewives, peasants, teachers and travellers meet and rapidly pass on the information circulating in the districts. Teachers especially like to chat at stores because there they can buy cigarettes and drinks to enliven their conversation. Stores are therefore centres of local gossip, and through the eager discussions of men and women, which generally centre round the trader himself, public opinion is formed.

Their stores, therefore, provide traders with many opportunities to convert their economic power into social influence. Many are leaders in voluntary associations. One started the scout movement in the chiefdom while still a teacher, and continues to keep in close touch with its leaders. Ex-teachers who turned to business generally maintain close links with teachers and so are well informed of events in local schools and at mission stations. Their associations with members of the educational elite preserve their own elite status in the eyes of peasants for, as the occupational rating showed,[8] businessmen are not generally accorded high prestige by local Africans.

The reason for the low scores given to businessmen is due to a variety of factors. Many people claim that African businessmen are far less polite than European businessmen, and that they charge higher prices in their stores than do Europeans. These accusations are often true because many African businessmen reason that they make a larger profit from selling a few goods at higher prices than many goods at lower prices. Many peasants also claim that as agents of the Grain Marketing Board, African store owners underpay them. One peasant said: 'African businessmen charge us high prices for their goods, but they pay us little for the grain we sell them.'

More important in causing a barrier between businessmen and

---

[7] Most successful farmers tend to be members of co-operative societies and through these are able to sell their surpluses at greater profits.

[8] Cf. *supra*, p. 106.

villagers than cute practice is the belief that successful traders are witches. Rural Africans in Rhodesia believe that if a man becomes exceptionally successful in business, he must have killed a close relative and buried his heart under the counter in order to attract customers. Murder stories are circulated about several of the successful businessmen listed in this chapter. In spite of careful investigation, no such accusation could be substantiated. The belief is very widespread.[9]

Sometimes this belief profits the businessmen, sometimes it has a devastating effect. For example, it ruined the business of a prospective trader even before he could open his store. While he was building it, a lorry passed the building site and killed a man. The news spread that the businessman had caused the death by his magic. When he opened his store nobody came to buy from him. On the other hand, witchcraft beliefs may profit a successful businessman because they instil fear in his customers, make them hesitant to accumulate too large debts, and induce them to court his friendship. No African would openly dare to invite the hostility of a person he suspects of witchcraft.

(d) Relations with chiefs

Few of the outstanding businessmen are related to local chiefs; most are strangers in the chiefdoms in which they run their businesses. Many stressed that distance from kinsmen enabled them to avoid kinship obligations and to re-invest their profits in their stores. In contrast, most petty traders are local men who have some kinship ties with their chiefs.

In the 1960s, most businessmen were critical of local chiefs on economic as well as political grounds. Before they could open their stores, they had to offer gifts to the chiefs to obtain the chiefs' recommendations to the district commissioners for a licence. In having both to offer gifts and then pay a government official for a licence, African businessmen claimed that they had to pay twice for the same permission. Also, most of the businessmen interviewed were nationalistically inclined and resented the leadership positions given by the European-controlled government to chiefs. During the time of fieldwork, store owners often fomented local opposition to

[9]Cf. Chidyausiku, 1969. It forms part of the plot of the first African drama ever written in Rhodesia.

traditional leaders and generally joined teachers in their criticism of chiefs. The ties which many of them had with the teaching profession may be responsible for this alliance.

Only one of the businessmen known to the investigator kept in close contact with his chief. The chief, in whose area his store was situated, was uneducated, given to drink, and afraid of civil servants. He relied on the businessman in all his contacts with the district commissioner and the businessman was able to make the chief utterly dependent on him. Since the chief desired to buy more goods than his salary allowed, he became also economically dependent on the businessman. Because he could neither read nor write, he also needed the businessman to read and write his letters so that the businessman was fully informed of the chief's actions and was able to manipulate him according to his interests. Such a relationship between chief and trader continued for many years. This businessman, even more than others, publicly criticized chiefs as incapable, illiterate, and mouthpieces of government.

(e) *Political aspirations*

Most businessmen are keenly interested in politics.[10] One of them had joined the United Federal Party in the 1950s when a significant number of Africans believed in multiracialism. But by the early 1960s he joined a nationalist party. Several of the other businessmen too were paid up members of a nationalist party. One had personally organized the incipient nationalist movement in his chiefdom, and another resigned from the civil service because of his political convictions.[11]

The possession of cars and lorries turned businessmen into effective supporters of the nationalist parties. When rallies were announced in the early 1960s, the businessmen were ready with their transport to bring villagers to the meeting places. The speakers on such occasions were often teachers, but the organizers businessmen. Consequently businessmen enjoyed not only strong economic but also political influence in their chiefdoms, a political influence, that is, in the sphere of modern politics, not in traditional power struggles. A few leading businessmen, however, tried to keep out of politics.

[10]For a similar interest of Kenya businessmen in African nationalism, before that country reached independence, see Kariuku, 1963, pp. 44, 135.

[11]Cf. *supra*, pp. 185, 197.

On one occasion a nationalist businessman organized a school strike at a local mission in order to teach the people what could be achieved in black–white relations through unity. He and his colleagues waited for a cause of complaint among school children to give to the villagers a demonstration lesson. When for two weeks meat rations had been in short supply, the businessmen told the parents to instruct their sons to boycott lessons. Classes came to a halt and at an appointed time four leading businessmen brought local villagers with their lorries to the mission station to complain to the missionaries. The nationalist businessman who acted as main speaker had himself no child at the school. He put forward certain grievances of the parents, such as that school children were at times asked to help making bricks for school extension. The first meeting did not achieve its aim. When the police came and investigated the strike, many teachers sided with the people. After each inquiry, they gathered at a local store to discuss further action. After several meetings the parents were granted most of their requests. The businessmen, who had organized the strike and had been supported by the teachers, had scored a victory in the name of nationalism and their influence in the community rose.

By the mid-1960s, when all nationalist activities had been banned, businessmen in two adjoining chiefdoms formed a local businessmen's association which overtly aimed at protecting their trading interests. Its hidden function, however, was to keep alive nationalist aspirations. The executive positions of its committee were filled with former members of a nationalist party.

(f) Conclusion

In spite of the low scores accorded to businessmen in the occupational rating exercise, businessmen clearly form an essential section of the rural African elite. They enjoy prominent positions and are objects, if not of admiration, then at least of envy. Many peasants try to imitate them by opening their own stores. Consequently they form a reference group to a large section of the rural population that lacks education and hopes through business to improve its economic position.

Businessmen are an integral part of rural African society, in spite of their tensions with villagers. The frequent but subdued accusations of witchcraft prove that they are still considered part of local communities, for complete outsiders, such as Europeans or even men of the upper section of the African elite, are never accused of witchcraft. The businessmen's tacit acceptance of their believed witchcraft, which often works to their advantage, is a further indication that businessmen are part of the people.

Since their ties with Europeans are minimal, and non-existent in the social field, they cannot be regarded as marginal to European society. They clearly do not belong to it.

Yet businessmen do feel dissatisfied with their position. Government regulations impose restrictions on them by limiting their credit facilities and regulating where they may open their stores. When African businessmen compare their own opportunities with those of Europeans, they often feel discriminated against. Many can see only one way out of their difficulties: an African government. Whereas economic rewards tie higher civil servants to the establishment, economic need spurs many African store owners to support nationalist movements.

The similarity of political aspiration and involvement of leading businessmen and teachers has its roots in many social similarities between the two sections of the African elite, and results in many bonds of friendship between them. Not only does a significant proportion of African traders come from the teaching profession, but teachers and businessmen share also, more or less, the same income. Their incomes differ mainly in that those of teachers are more regular than those of traders. Like teachers, businessmen are very influential in local communities, mainly because of their control over the money transactions of villagers. Though frequently living apart from their kinsmen, successful and popular businessmen have many friends who are willing to support their wives and children, should they themselves be arrested. In the early 1960s African traders felt that the risk they ran in supporting African nationalism was just one more of the many risks in the life of an African entrepreneur. Since all of them were entrepreneurs on a very small scale, all were threatened by bankruptcy at one time or another.

Petty traders, who have been mentioned only in passing, do not form part of the elite proper. They go bankrupt more frequently than those discussed above and start again with the help of relatives. They share most social characteristics with African craftsmen who are discussed in the following section.

2. Craftsmen

(a) Recruitment

Craftsmen, such as builders and carpenters, are not members of the elite proper because they have generally received very little education and do not earn a regular income from their crafts. Most rural craftsmen are peasant farmers who practise their crafts to gain income additional to farming. This income varies between some £20 and £150 per annum.

Most craftsmen are mission trained. They acquired their technical skills after only five or six years' schooling at a mission station where building, carpentry, tailoring or other crafts are taught. Those who come from the poorer section of the African population and have no land to cultivate, find it impossible to feed their families. These often leave the rural areas for European employment.

(b) Relations with Europeans

During their training, craftsmen were well known to missionary craftsmen who initiated them into their skills, but as young men with little education they did not associate with them in their free time. Those who leave the rural areas to seek work in regular European employment, meet Europeans only in the work situation. Their status as skilled labour migrants is too low to give them social access to Europeans.

(c) Relations with Africans

Those craftsmen who have land to cultivate, generally remain in the rural areas. Their self-employment gives them some prestige in the eyes of fellow villagers. Ordinary peasants have rarely enough money to employ a builder or carpenter, but most successful farmers desire to live in brick houses and to have these furnished with tables, chairs, cupboards and beds. Their regular customers are members of the rural elite. Teachers and men of similar standing are unwilling to live in any but European-styled accommodation. The elite proper, therefore, looks favourably at craftsmen. Among all sections of the rural population the work of craftsmen is appreciated because it enables rural dwellers to enjoy some of the comforts of urban residence.

Craftsmen are structurally important. They are hardly distinguished from ordinary villagers in their style of life and mix easily with them. As members of a sub-elite, of which Lloyd writes that 'through their close contact with the masses . . . they may be . . . more significant as reference groups to the masses than are the elite',[12] some of them gain status through associating with the elite proper and copying their behaviour. Some craftsmen, for example, join voluntary associations, and like teachers and businessmen gain leading positions in them. Church membership too may raise their status. One well-known carpenter, for example, is the father of a Sister in a religious congregation. This confers great prestige on him in a predominantly Catholic community.

(d) Relations with chiefs

Craftsmen, like peasants, have to conform to the rule of chiefs, but many of them are as critical of traditional leaders as are teachers and businessmen, especially if they are interested in African nationalism. These regard chiefs as 'stooges of the government' and 'sell-outs'. Many craftsmen are openly critical of chiefs at local beer drinks, but they dare not challenge the chiefs' leadership directly.

(e) Political aspirations

In the early 1960s, several of the rural craftsmen were eager supporters of the nationalist movement. They regularly attended local beer drinks and even religious services because these provided them with occasions to meet large numbers of people. They tried to win party members whenever they had a chance to contact people. One carpenter in particular distinguished himself in organizing a branch of an African nationalist party in his chiefdom. His endeavours earned him the esteem of nationalistically-inclined teachers and businessmen and gave him some access to their company.

(f) Conclusion

If craftsmen want to become members of a sub-elite, they cannot derive status solely from their craft, but must acquire in addition social, religious and especially political prestige criteria. Leadership in voluntary associations, especially esteem by members of the elite, which in the early 1960s was earned through active political involvement, enabled some craftsmen to rise in prestige above their fellow villagers. Consequently prestige does not derive solely from income and education but from a configuration of roles in the various spheres of social life.

[12]Lloyd, 1966, p. 13.

Craftsmen are not centres of attraction and objects of imitation because their income is low. Few fellow villagers try to imitate them. But they are considered useful neighbours and are well accepted in their communities. Yet if they capture the leadership positions open to them, they can become outstanding figures in their communities and an effective link between villagers and the modern elite.

3. Evaluation of the business and craft elites and sub-elites

Rural African businessmen and craftsmen differentiate themselves from the emergent African elite through frequent lack of higher formal education. Their contacts with western culture are tenuous, and hardly any of them meet Europeans socially. None of them consciously seeks to be accepted into European social circles. Their reference group is not Europeans but rather other members of the African elite. They therefore copy European behaviour only indirectly.

Together with teachers, businessmen and craftsmen form the largest section of the rural elite or sub-elite. Because of their numerical strength, they are a very important section of village life. Though they still stand close to the people and are accepted by them as part of the community, many of them stand sufficiently above the ordinary peasants to be accepted as leaders. They are often men with ability and ambition, but they know that their chances of making a great career are very small. Consequently they are highly interested in politics. They form a natural leadership of the rural population. Because they profit little from the European-controlled society, they do not experience the ambivalence felt by members in the higher echelons of the African elite. Unlike senior civil servants, they are not bound by golden fetters. Apart from disadvantages and restrictions they can lose but little. But they hope to gain much.

11. A comparison of the rural Rhodesian and urban South African elites

Throughout chapters six to ten, frequent reference has been made to L. Kuper's study of a South African bourgeoisie. As the term 'bourgeoisie' indicates, Kuper was mainly concerned with urban Africans, and only in passing referred to members of the rural South African elite. Kuper's study shows many similarities with this present study: both analyse situations in a multiracial society in which Africans are severely limited in their political, economic and social opportunities. As the overall policies of the Rhodesian government approximate ever more closely to those of the South African government, Kuper's study may be a useful pointer of future development in Rhodesia. A study of race relations in Rhodesian towns is now called for to show whether there is a gradual transition from the race relations in the rural areas of Rhodesia, over race relations in Rhodesian towns, to race relations in South African cities. This chapter gives a brief outline of South African elites, emphasizing their similarities to, or divergences from, Rhodesian African elites.

1. The religious elite

According to the 1951 census, 60 per cent of all Africans in South Africa were Christians.[1] This is a higher percentage than in Rhodesia, and yet in spite of this high percentage the attitude of South Africans towards Christian Churches is not always positive. Kuper observes that although many people value Christianity, they are often highly critical of Christian Churches because of the Churches' close identification with the government. Both in response to a prestige rating undertaken by Kuper,[2] as also in his collection of case histories of African ministers of religion,[3] Kuper was told that Christian Churches were seen as the instruments of white oppression. Consequently African ministers were ranked rather low because

[1]Kuper, 1965, p. 201.   [2]*Ibid.*, p. 121.   [3]*Ibid.*, p. 195.

many interpreted their work as instrumental to their suffering. Only 6 per cent of the young people interviewed by Kuper aspired to become ministers. Hence, far from being centres of attraction and objects of admiration and imitation, ministers of religion were avoided by many South Africans.

Yet attitudes towards Churches varied by denomination. Ministers of the Reformed Church found themselves in the most ambivalent situation. One Reformed minister reported that he used to address mostly illiterate congregations. He deeply disagreed with the policies of his own Church which actively supported apartheid.[4] Reformed ministers also resented being paid differential salaries from European ministers, a practice unknown in the Anglican Church.[5]

Anglican and Catholic priests[6] were happier about their position in their own Churches because they enjoyed a greater co-operation with Europeans than did the ministers of the Reformed Church. Anglicans expressed satisfaction that their bishops had spoken out against racial segregation, and the Catholic bishops' pronouncements were widely applauded.

Of all denominations, Methodists were recognized as the most militant group. Perhaps because of this, Methodists had the largest African membership in the country.[7]

This brief summary shows many similarities with the Rhodesian scene. These similarities indicate that denominations, having an international membership, follow a uniform Church policy in the various territories in which they work. Consequently a Church's attitude towards race relations in any one country can be predicted, and, given identical political, economic and social circumstances, African reactions to various denominations are also likely to follow a uniform pattern.

2. The medical elite

(a) Doctors

Kuper's study differs from the Rhodesian study in that he was mainly concerned with doctors working in large urban hospitals, not with doctors living in rural areas. He analysed race relations in circumstances much more humiliating to African doctors than

[4]Kuper, 1965, p. 196.   [5]*Ibid.*, pp. 210–11.
[6]*Ibid.*, pp. 196, 213.   [7]*Ibid.*, pp. 212–13.

occur in Rhodesian rural hospitals. Kuper mentions constant petty discriminations which irritate African doctors in urban hospitals.[8] He was told how African doctors feel constantly on trial because any mistake they may make is not regarded as a normal human failure but attributed to ethnic inferiority,[9] and how they feel their second class citizenship when collegial relations with European doctors cease after working hours.[10]

Within African society, African doctors are very highly esteemed. Kuper reports how Africans can hardly believe that some of their numbers have achieved such high positions.[11] In contrast to the high prestige accorded to African doctors by their own people, the discrimination they suffer from Europeans is felt the more acutely.

This discrepancy between an African doctor's standing in African and European society seems to contribute to their political involvement. For although African doctors could avoid such involvement, many consider it a duty to help organize their people to resist white policies which treat them as second-class citizens. As a consequence, many doctors have been brought to court and found guilty of various charges, ranging from leadership of deputations which failed to disperse, the destruction of reference books, to high treason.[12]

Kuper's account reveals that South African doctors are faced with the same moral dilemma as Rhodesian doctors. They feel torn between the desire to assist their own people to regain their health, and the desire to help them to social justice. Their eminent position in African society makes them conspicuous and respected leaders, should they dare to risk their professional position.[13]

(b) Nurses

Nursing is one of the few professions open to African women. Like L. Kuper's study of doctors, so H. Kuper's[14] study of nurses refers mainly to those employed in large urban hospitals. Consequently similar racial tensions mar the life of nurses as mar the lives of African doctors.

[8]*Ibid.*, p. 240.   [9]*Ibid.*, p. 243.
[10]This situation is similar to that of Rhodesian African school inspectors who too work well with European colleagues in their offices, but are ignored after working hours.   [11]Kuper, 1965, p. 123.   [12]*Ibid.*, p. 245.
[13]African hospital administrators seem to be non-existent in South Africa. Kuper's only reference to hospital administration concerns European administrators. Kuper, 1965, p. 242.
[14]The book, *An African Bourgeoisie*, is written by L. Kuper, except for the chapter on nurses which his wife, H. Kuper, contributed.

Christian missionaries who provided the first health services to the African people, first opened the nursing profession to African women. Later on the state took on responsibility for African health.

In government hospitals, the nursing personnel is stratified both according to professional qualifications and also according to race. By South African law, no African may be placed over a European nurse.[15] Consequently many Afrikaans nurses with low qualifications, who could not hope for fast promotion in a European hospital, willingly serve in African hospitals because there they are more easily promoted and placed in control of an African staff. This causes great resentment among experienced African nurses who resent being ordered about by inexperienced white nurses. Discrimination takes place not only with regard to promotion, but also in salaries, for even if an African and a European nurse have the same qualification and perform the same work, the African nurse is paid less than her European colleague.[16] Like African doctors, African nurses complain that any mistake they may make is attributed to their racial inferiority.[17]

The Rhodesian study has shown that in mission hospitals in Rhodesia's rural areas no such discriminations take place. In fact, in mission hospitals African nurses are at times placed over European nursing staff. Kuper has only one reference to South African mission hospitals, and in this she states that discrimination is unknown in these institutions, and that all facilities for staff members are shared in common.[18] The different race relations which are revealed in the two studies of the Rhodesian and South African members of the medical elites may therefore be due to the different types of employers: missionaries or the wider European society.

Nursing is the most prestigious occupation open to South African women. Hence they enjoy a very high status in their own society. They dress smartly and are eagerly imitated by other women who aspire to elite status.[19] In this respect, South African nurses closely resemble Rhodesian nurses.

Kuper gives little information about the family background of African nurses. She merely states that many of their relatives are illiterate and unskilled workers, but that most nurses listed professionals among their friends.[20] It is likely that their family background is similar to that of Rhodesian nurses.

[15]Kuper, 1965, p. 218.   [16]*Ibid.*, p. 222.   [17]*Ibid.*, p. 224.
[18]*Ibid.*, p. 226.   [19]*Ibid.*, p. 227.   [20]*Ibid.*, p. 229.

In spite of these similarities, there is one important point in which South African nurses differ from their Rhodesian colleagues: they seem much less interested in politics than Rhodesian nurses, and are cynical of any attempt Africans might make to bring about a betterment of their people.[21] This difference too may be due to their different social environment. The study of rural Rhodesian elites has shown that African teachers, employed by Christian missionaries, are much more outspoken in their condemnation of the government than African civil servants in occupations requiring a similar education, and earning a similar salary. Fear of dismissal for political action may well be the cause for the South African nurses' neutrality in politics. They have much to lose.

3. The educational elite

L. Kuper nowhere mentions African school inspectors, but he gives great attention to African teachers. His study focuses on Bantu Education, a policy of the South African government which aims at giving a separate education for African children, fitting them for the subordinate positions which they are expected to fill in South Africa.

Like health services and the training of nurses, African education and the training of teachers was started by Christian missionaries, but was later on taken over by the state. This transfer of control led to the shift from a broad, universal education to an education linked with tribalism.[22] The implementation of Bantu Education led to a rapid fall in academic standards. Experienced teachers left the service or were dismissed, and young African women with low qualifications took their places.[23]

Missionaries were replaced as school managers by school committees and school boards. These bodies, consisting mainly of tribesmen with very little, if any, education, had the power to employ or dismiss teachers.[24] Teachers bitterly resented being dependent on parents who understood nothing about education,[25] and frequently charged the school boards with bribery and corruption. European inspectors, however, never accepted these charges.[26]

Teachers were forbidden to engage in politics. This prohibition included any criticism of Bantu Education[27] and so forced those,

[21]*Ibid.*, p. 232.   [22]*Ibid.*, pp. 168–70.   [23]*Ibid.*, p. 172.   [24]*Ibid.*, p. 175.
[25]*Ibid.*, p. 185.   [26]*Ibid.*, p. 184.   [27]*Ibid.*, p. 177.

who remained in the service and desired to become 'light bearers'
in their communities,[28] to become 'instruments of tribalism'.[29]
Teachers commented to Kuper: 'We are no longer teaching, but
we are poisoning the children.'[30] They felt that they were debasing,
not uplifting their people.[31]

As a result of these changes, the status of South African teachers
has fallen very considerably. Kuper writes: 'In the process of imple-
menting Bantu Education, the status of the African teacher has been
graded downward. Previously he was a member of the new elite,
leading his people outward into the world. Today he is forced back
within the group and subordinated to it. The official reference group
is the tribal or ethnic unit, distinct and inferior, not the dominant
White group.[32]

The light in which many South African teachers evaluate their
own position may be seen from the comment of many teachers who
stated that they only became teachers because they failed to get
another job.[33]

The status of Rhodesian teachers is still higher than that of their
South African colleagues. Both in their own estimation and in that
of their neighbours they rank among the most respected members
of the rural elite. But whether they can maintain their present prestigious position for long is doubtful, since in 1969 government
advised all Christian missions to hand over African primary education to African councils unless they were willing to pay an increasing
proportion of the teachers' salaries. The mission churches, being
financially unable to raise these large sums of money, gave in 1970
notice to all African teachers that their contracts would be ter-
minated by the end of that year.[34] It seems therefore that the South
African situation will repeat itself in Rhodesia.

4. The agricultural elite

Kuper's study is mainly confined to urban Africans. Consequently
he did not interview members of the African agricultural elite. He
gives, however, some information on African civil servants, that section of African employees to which the agricultural extension staff
belongs.

[28]Kuper, 1965, p. 181.   [29]*Ibid.*, p. 177.   [30]*Ibid.*, p. 186.
[31]*Ibid.*, p. 187.   [32]*Ibid.*, p. 174.   [33]*Ibid.*, p. 181.
[34]This development in Rhodesia occurred after the rest of the book had been
written.

Kuper writes of civil servants that Africans are aware that these earn large salaries, but that because of their close identification with the South African government their economic affluence does not bring them respect but hatred.[35] Rhodesian Africans do not look at their extension workers with hatred. They accept them rather with indifference, knowing that it is wisest to conform in some degree, if they want to live in at least relative peace.

5. The business elite

Again there is a great difference between South African towns and Rhodesian rural areas in regard to African business adventure. In Durban, where Kuper undertook a special case study of African traders, he found competition between European, Indian and African traders for the African market.[36] Especially between Indian and African businessmen competition was intense, and because of their limited resources African businessmen felt very insecure. They resented that European and Indian traders were given greater credit facilities which enabled them to make greater profits than Africans.[37] As a consequence, African trade contribute very little to the city's business transactions,[38] and the majority of African traders found it difficult to survive.[39] Moreover, African businessmen were confined to African townships so that they could not profit from the brisker trader in other sections of the town. The fact that legislation forbade them to hand on their shops to their sons prevented them from investing in their stores.[40]

In order to gain some strength as an occupational group, many businessmen tried to establish a link with the Bantu National Congress.[41]

In spite of these difficulties, traders and even craftsmen were respected by their neighbours, mainly because of their independence of white employers.[42] The esteem in which South African craftsmen and businessmen are held seems to be greater than that enjoyed by Rhodesian business- and craftsmen. This is most likely due to the more acute racial discrimination in South Africa, since the reason for prestige is couched in terms of independence from Europeans. Taking into account the many differences between a South Afri-

[35]Kuper, 1965, p. 121. [36]*Ibid.*, p. 289. [37]*Ibid.*, p. 293.
[38]*Ibid.*, p. 191. [39]*Ibid.*, p. 300. [40]*Ibid.*, p. 292.
[41]*Ibid.*, pp. 304–5. [42]*Ibid.*, p. 121.

can township and Rhodesian rural communities, the presence of Indian competition in the one and its absence in the other, several significant similarities nevertheless stand out, predominantly that of the great financial insecurity of all African traders. Great similarity exists also in the recruitment pattern of Rhodesian and South African businessmen. Of the sixty traders interviewed by Kuper, five had been teachers and two demonstrators, that is, extension assistants in the Rhodesian terminology. Apart from seven who came from business families,[43] all were the first in their kinship groups who ventured into business.

Interest in nationalist politics seems to be stronger among Rhodesian businessmen than among South Africans, but it is not absent among the latter either, as their appeal to the Bantu National Congress shows.

6. Conclusion

The South African and the Rhodesian studies, though both dealing with race relations and emergent African elites, focus on different aspects of interracial contacts and elite attitudes. Certain questions essential to village life, such as attitudes towards chiefs, were naturally not asked of urban dwellers. On the other hand more attention was given to legal aspects of race relations in the urban context where many Europeans who were not missionaries had frequent contacts with members of the African elite.

The overall impression emerging from the comparison of the two studies is that racial aversion is more acute in South African towns than in Rhodesian rural areas. Yet to determine whether this greater tension is due to different government policies in the two countries, or rather to the urban–rural contrast, a study of race relations in Rhodesian towns is required. From the few hints given by Kuper on race relations in rural mission institutions in South Africa it appears that the difference is less a difference between practices in the two countries, nor even between town and country, but rather a difference between contrasted ideologies motivating various groups of Europeans: an ideology of the brotherhood of all men, accepted by most Christian denominations, and an ideology of inequality between the races, accepted by many Europeans in the multiracial societies of both Rhodesia and South Africa.

[43]Kuper, 1965, pp. 294–5.

Conclusion

Banton's framework, as set out in the Introduction, has been used in this book in order to systematize the data on the European and African elites in rural Rhodesia. This Conclusion aims to draw some deductions from these data and so to deepen the understanding of race relations in a multiracial society.

1. The importance of first contacts in shaping future race relations

Chapter one indicated the extent to which the first part of Banton's hypothesis applies to the Rhodesian situation. It traced changes in the economic and political power of Europeans and showed that these directly shaped race relations between them and Africans. For example, when in the late 1960s the proportion of Africans to Europeans was again as high as it was in the 1930s, the emphasis on separate development which characterized the 1930s, but was overlaid by a policy of multiracialism in the 1950s, re-emerged. Economic resources have been allocated in such a way in the passage of time that the gulf between the races' incomes has not been appreciably reduced. The disparity in educational and occupational opportunities reinforced this gulf. Because of the reversion of European racial attitudes to those current in the 1930s, a new power balance between the races, predicted by Banton, has been slow to evolve. Political and economic power still rest unquestionably in the hands of Europeans.[1]

To maintain their dominant position in the face of such a challenge, Europeans passed legislation to enforce separate development,

---

[1]Lofchie observes that economic crises reinforced the pluralistic and ethnically fragmented character of Zanzibar society, and that this in turn led to political agitation on the part of the underprivileged African section of society. Lofchie, 1965, p. 95. The first part of this observation applies equally to Rhodesia.

thus protecting themselves against African competition.[2] The eleva-
tion of African chiefs into parliament is one of the outstanding
moves in this direction, because by stipulating that half of all African parliamentarians must be traditional leaders or their representatives, the modern and progressive element of the African people is
able to exert very little pressure in parliament.[3]

Consequently the first part of Banton's hypothesis remains unaltered: *Race relations in a society are determined by the historical
events surrounding the first extended contact between members of
different races.*

2. The impact of racial contact on members of the dominant race

This book has paid little, if any, attention to the psychological
effects of racial domination on the characters of Africans and Europeans, such as were studied by Manoni.[4] Instead it has analysed
in detail the attitudes of members of the dominant race towards
Africans, and so indirectly thrown light on the psychological impact
of racial attitudes on Europeans and also on Africans.

Moreover, the book has concentrated exclusively on race relations
in the rural areas of Rhodesia where there are eighty Africans to
every one European. The suggestion was made that in areas where
the numerical strength of races differs so greatly, Europeans might
try to increase their strength through associating with the African
elite. This book has shown that apart from some missionaries this
is not generally the case. Racial identity seems to be one of the
most important concerns of Rhodesian Europeans.

A comparison between the Europeans interviewed for this study,
and those questioned by Rogers and Frantz, shows that the rural
elite expressed more liberal views than did average Rhodesians.[5]
Consequently rural Africans seem to live in an environment in which
race relations are more friendly than in towns, a suggestion made
in chapter one.[6]

[2]Cf. *The Rhodesia Herald*, 25.10.1969: the caucus meeting of the government
party pledged itself to a rigid enforcement of racial separation.

[3]The attitude of the African elite towards chiefs has been studied in this book.
Chapters five to ten have shown that chiefs are not generally accepted as representatives and leaders of the African people. This also holds true for African peasants,
as the ranking exercise set out in Table 10, page 198, indicates.

[4]Cf. *supra*, pp. 3–4.

[5]Cf. *supra*, pp. 83–5.

[6]*Supra*, pp. 31–2.

Yet formidable racial barriers remain in rural Rhodesia, and most Europeans, especially district commissioners, try consciously to remain independent of the African elite in their contacts with the African masses. The conscious fostering of racial antipathies by some,[7] expressed both in their attitudes towards African advancement and in the stereotypes they entertain of Africans, may be seen as a protection against the possible inclination of some for departing from generally accepted norms of racial interaction. Ritualized interaction helps Europeans to guard the *Massenehre*[8] of white Rhodesians, and in this way the caste status and pollution barrier between Europeans and Africans is maintained.

The differences in racial attitudes between rural Europeans, in which district commissioners and missionaries stand at two extreme poles, and persons engaged in the various forms of agriculture in intermediate positions, is very deep indeed. With the proportional decline of Europeans in Rhodesia's population, and their consequent stricter insistence on conformity to ritualized race relations,[9] tensions between the wider European society and missionaries have become more frequent. Since missionaries of various Christian denominations oppose racial separation and freely associate with Africans, thus breaking the self-imposed exclusiveness of the European race, they are becoming ever more marginal to European society. In not sharing the Superman attitude of average Europeans, missionaries are seen by Europeans as a danger to their social security because missionaries aim at making the many privileges enjoyed by Europeans the common property of all the people of Rhodesia, which means that these will cease to be privileges.

In spite of this deep difference between missionaries and the wider European society, there exists nevertheless many similarities between missionaries and other Europeans. Since the stand taken by district commissioners, extension officers and European farmers resembles closely that postulated by Banton in his hypothesis, the following paragraphs concentrate on the position of missionaries in rural Rhodesia.

[7]Cf. *supra*, pp. 39, 175–6, *et alia*.
[8]Cf. *supra*, p. 11.
[9]Cf. *The Rhodesia Herald*, 25.10.1969: Members of the government party severely criticized private schools for admitting Africans into establishments originally opened for European children. Other factors in addition to demographic imbalance, also contribute to the Europeans' reaction, for example, the threat to internal security in the early 1960s and international ostracism in the late 1960s. These factors caused the decline in the European population.

Contacts across the colour line are in all occupations most frequent in work situations and between colleagues. This holds true
for missionaries as well as for other members of the European rural
elite. A large number of missionaries make no racial distinction
between fellow missionaries and the African clergy of their own
denominations; they also accept into their company other educated
Africans with whom they have professional contacts, such as doctors, school inspectors, managers and occasionally even teachers,
most of whom are mission-trained. The missions' contribution to
African education, which results in personal ties of friendship
between many members of the emergent African elite and missionaries, is a major factor contributing to the understanding
between missionaries and Africans.

In contrast to this mission-trained elite, missionaries do not have
such close social ties with Africans trained in government institutions, or with less educated Africans. Indeed, the aversion of many
missionaries to government seems at times to extend to African civil
servants. Thus missionaries seldom, if ever, mix socially with African extension officers, though they do with members of the African
elite who have the same, or even less, education than these men.
Their selectivity resembles in part that of European extension
officers who are also at times ready to mix with African colleagues,
but not with other educated Africans.[10]

The responses of members in the lower echelons of the African
elite and sub-elite have shown that missionaries do not normally
meet socially with Africans who possess very little education and
whose cultural environment is very different from that of Europeans.
Though they frequently visit Africans in their villages and even join
them at their meals, they do not reciprocate the hospitality of the
rank and file of their Church members at the mission station. Thus
they too are selective in their social contacts. In this they again
resemble other Europeans. It may, therefore, be suggested that the
difference between missionaries and other members of the European
rural elite is not an essential difference, but rather that the threshold
of permissive social intercourse is much lower among missionaries
than among other rural Europeans. Though championing the cause
of African advancement in every sphere of life, and often consciously identifying themselves with the African people, missionaries
are not really part of African society. They are deeply committed

[10]Cf. *supra*, p. 178.

to western culture, that is, to a culture which transcends those values selected by European society in Rhodesia.

Whereas district commissioners are leaders in European and African rural society, and whereas extension officers and farmers mix easily with fellow Europeans, most missionaries are marginal to their own racial group. The stronger their criticism of the discriminatory social order of Rhodesia, the more they are rejected by fellow Europeans. Only missionaries who support, or are believed to support, a separate development of racial groups, remain acceptable to members of their own race.[11]

In addition to becoming ever more marginal to European society, most missionaries also remain marginal to African society. Only those missionaries who are acceptable to European society—but who are least acceptable to the Africans because they keep themselves socially apart from them—are not marginal to African society. Like district commissioners, extension officers and farmers, they clearly do not belong to it.

Those missionaries on the other hand, who are marginal to European society because of their conscious identification with Africans, are in a different position. Having endangered their ties with European society, they seem to remain in a no-man's land. They clearly do not seek full admission into African society. On their mission stations, however primitive these may be, they live as on little islands of western civilization. To these islands they admit as social equals those Africans who share their cultural values. The emphasis here lies on cultural, rather than on religious, values because many of the ordinary peasants in the villages surrounding mission stations share the Christian religion with the missionaries, but they do not mix with them socially. The lack of contacts between missionaries and businessmen, craftsmen or successful farmers illustrate this point. Missionaries are friendly to most people, but associate with only a few. This lack of submersion into African society shows that missionaries to a great extent also remain marginal to African society as well as to that of Europeans.

Missionaries seem to aspire to full membership of neither the European nor the African society. They are members of world-wide organizations and form a distinct layer[12] in Rhodesian society.

[11]For a similar position of missionaries in the early history of Rhodesia see Gann, 1965, pp. 242, 317.
[12]Cf. Eberhard, 1968, pp. 20–5.

Within Rhodesia they often experience their position as that of aliens. They feel socially isolated and so they form a closely knit in-group which determines their social norms. Though until recently most clergymen of various denominations had a marked in-group rather than ecumenical orientation, their identical situation *vis-à-vis* the larger European society has brought them into closer co-operation with each other, thus widening their social circle. This co-operation, though coinciding with world-wide ecumenism, is not strictly dependent on that world movement. It is forced on them by their marginality to Rhodesian white society. Were they fully accepted by fellow Europeans, inter-denominational contacts might be fewer. This is borne out by the lack of participation of members of the Dutch Reformed Church in ecumenical meeting in Rhodesia. The Reformed clergy, more acceptable to Rhodesian Europeans, need not seek allies among clergy of other denominations.

Though most missionaries stand literally between the two major racial groups in Rhodesia, they no longer occupy a mediating position. They have no influence in European power politics and as far as the government is concerned, there is a preference to deal with African chiefs rather than with any other section of the population, black or white, which tries to speak for the African people.

The peculiar position of European missionaries makes them easily accessible to many Africans. Mission educated Africans in particular have many opportunities to associate with them and observe them in their daily lives. But in modelling their image of Europeans on missionaries, many Africans obtain a distorted impression of the dominant race, and many are greatly disillusioned when they come into contact with other Europeans.[13] All sections of the African population are aware of the different racial attitudes of missionaries and other Europeans. To those who freely associate with missionaries, their rejection by the wider European society is especially painful.[14]

Although the Europeans in Rhodesia are a governing elite, they are not as unified an elite as Pareto expects governing elites to be,[15] nor as unified as many Europeans would like to believe that they are. They are divided to the degree to which rural Europeans subscribe in varying degrees to the dominant ethos of racial superiority. Those who are most sensitive to popular white attitudes tend to restrict

[13]cf. *supra*, p. 99.
[14]Cf. reaction of school inspector, *supra*, p. 155, *et alia*.
[15]*Supra*, pp. 33–4.

their own range of association most severely. This is borne out by the remarks of educated Africans, such as that of an extension officer who commented that though some European colleagues welcomed him to their homes, should other Europeans find him there, their own social status would fall.[16]

The data presented in this study show that the second part of Banton's hypothesis applies to a large section of the European rural elite: *The character, attitudes and behaviour of many members of the dominant race, such as district commissioners, extension officers and farmers, are to a certain degree formed by unequal race relationships, and the freedom of the men who submit to popular norms is restricted.*

This statement, however, does not explain the position of most European missionaries in the rural elite. Banton's hypothesis may therefore in the Rhodesian context be expanded as follows:

(a) *In racially composite societies, members of the dominant race who violate the normative expectations of their group, become marginal to their own racial community.*

(b) *Deviants from the dominant racial group do not really seek full admission and integration into the society of the subordinate race. Consequently they are not fully accepted by members of this race and so remain marginal to them as well as to the communities of the dominant racial group and incapsulate themselves in their in-groups.*

(c) *Their marginality to, and lack of power in, the socially dominant group disqualifies them from effective mediation between the races because they are not fully trusted by the dominant race.*

(d) *The existence of a significant number of deviants from racial norms in the dominant race divides the ruling group. Social ostracism of the deviants does not restore the unity of the governing elite because the skin colour of the deviants irrevocably stamps them as members of the dominant race.*

3. Racial cleavage gives rise to an elite structure in the subordinate race paralleling that of the dominant race

This third section of Banton's hypothesis has been tested in the second part of the book. Although Rhodesian history in the 1960s

---

[16]*Supra*, p. 178.

seems to repeat what happened in the 1930s, this movement is best described as spiral-like rather than as circular. For occupational diversification has taken place among the African people and members of the emergent elite have shown signs that they are determined to push against the barriers separating them from the affluent white section of Rhodesian society. Some have succeeded in doing work mainly done by Europeans and work side by side with European colleagues.

Throughout the second part of the book the assumption has been that those Africans enjoy elite status in their own society who have most thoroughly accepted European values and behaviour patterns. The reason for this assumption is that the emergent African elite itself regards Europeans as their reference group. The very definition of elite in terms of western education and income[17] is based on this assumption.

According to these criteria, the African elite can be divided into three social strata: a top stratum, a middle stratum and a lower stratum which is identical with the sub-elite and thereby no longer belongs to the elite proper.

The top stratum tends to be comprised of people such as Catholic priests, doctors, hospital administrators, school inspectors and extension officers. The middle stratum is typically comprised of Protestant ministers of religion, school managers, primary school teachers, nurses, extension supervisors and assistants, and successful businessmen. To the lower stratum, which coincides with the sub-elite, belong pastors of some Churches, like the Seventh Day Adventist pastors, successful farmers, petty traders and craftsmen who, in addition to their occupation, obtain status through activities in various social fields.

Members in the top stratum distinguish themselves through a way of life which closely resembles that of Europeans. Most of them receive high salaries, and all are well educated. Many of them have visited Europe or America. They try to preserve the elite status for their children by sending them to the best schools in Rhodesia. The most affluent section send their children to integrated European private schools, those with slightly lower incomes to private schools for Coloured pupils. All of them seek admittance to European social circles and suffer keenly when this is refused to them. Those who cannot often mix with Europeans seek vicarious satisfaction by visit-

[17]Cf. *supra*, p. 104.

ing multiracial hotels and displaying their wealth in conspicuous ways.

Members of this top stratum who are employed by government try to reduce their contact with uneducated Africans, and those employed on Christian missions often make conscious efforts to remain in some contact with their own people. All feel that a great social gulf separates them from members of their own race. The ordinary concerns of African peasants are practically alien to them. Because of their rare contacts with chiefs, they can afford a more relaxed relationship with these traditional leaders than those who have closer contacts with them.

Politically, they are often neutral, or at least inactive, because either their religious commitment does not allow them to engage in active politics or their economic rewards bind them to submit passively to a social order which discriminates as much against them as against the less educated members of their race.[18]

The middle stratum, like the top stratum, includes members of all occupational groupings, such as the religious, medical, educational and business elites. Few of these, however, have received post-secondary education, and few have ever been outside Rhodesia. Only a small proportion of them can afford an education for their children resembling that of members of the top stratum, but all send their children to school, and many try to see them through secondary education.

Financially unable to afford the luxuries of members in the top stratum, members of the middle stratum find it more difficult to compensate for the discrimination they suffer at the hands of European society by visiting multiracial hotels or driving expensive cars. Their exclusion from European society is much more complete than is that of the higher ranking men in their professions. Because they have less to lose than the wealthier members of the elite, many of them criticize European dominance in Rhodesia if they are not prevented by religious commitments or close supervision by European superiors. A significant number are willing to participate actively in political movements which seek to bring about a changed

[18]Lofchie observed a similar situation in Zanzibar. There very few Africans had received a university education, and those who had were employed in full-time professional occupations or as government civil servants, and so were unable to participate actively in nationalist movements. Cf. Lofchie, 1965, p. 159. For a similar lack of participation in nationalist movements by an educated elite in Kenya see also Kariuku, 1963, p. 133, *et alia*.

social order. Being less alienated, their commitment to African society is much more intense than is that of members of the top elite.

Standing half-way between traditional African and modern western society, some members of the middle stratum of the emergent African elite, especially school managers, see themselves as mediators between the two racial groups in Rhodesia.

Numerically, the middle stratum of the African elite is the strongest section of the emergent elite in Rhodesia, and because their educational achievement is within the reach of many Africans they are a most important reference group for villagers.

Members of the sub-elite aspire to prominence in their own local communities, but not to acceptance by Europeans. This saves them many of the frustrations suffered by members of the elite proper when these try to lift the barrier keeping them in the lower section of Rhodesia's double caste system. Their children go to village schools and they make little distinction between themselves and their neighbours. Their own reference group is the middle stratum of the African elite, and in modelling their lives on that of teachers and businessmen, they represent an intermediate transitional step between the elite proper and the African peasantry.

The stratification of rural African society described in this book is only incipient. Most members of the elite come from peasant background. But already their children are second-generation elite members. With the greater educational advantages of children of educated parents, this stratification is likely to be perpetuated and to develop, in time, into a class structure resembling that of European society.

The third section of Banton's hypothesis, that *Racial cleavages give rise to a stratification within the subordinate race parelleling that of the dominant race*, is therefore confirmed. But this statement does not fully explore the implications of the changes taking place in African society. The study of the emergent African elite raises further issues: the first concerns the marginality of the emergent elite to both European and African society, and the second the influence of occupation on the racial attitudes of the emergent elite. Both of these issues are related to the positions of individual elite members in the elite hierarchy.

All members of the top stratum of the African elite seek admission to European society. Few, if any, are awarded full acceptance.

Some mission-employed elite members are accepted in missionary circles on a basis of equality, but are rejected by the wider European society. Government-employed members of this stratum are at best socially accepted by a few close colleagues. These Africans often suffer from isolation and experience their rejection most strongly.

Members of the top stratum no longer cultivate land. Their deliberate divorce from the land is a sign of their uprootedness from traditional society. They have consciously separated themselves from peasant life and chosen Europeans as their exclusive reference group. Rejected by Europeans, and themselves rejecting African village life, they are marginal to both European and African society. In their exclusion from both European and African society they strongly resemble many missionaries. Consequently there exists potentially a close affinity between them, and this affinity accounts for the mutual acceptance and even ties of friendship between these members of the African elite and some European missionaries.

Members of the middle stratum of the African elite have adopted some western values and strive eagerly to acquire western prestige symbols, but they have been far less successful than members of the top stratum. Their ties with Europeans are remote, but their ties with fellow Africans are still strong.

The sub-elite has very few ties with Europeans and is fully integrated into rural African communities. Its members are marginal neither to European society because they clearly do not belong to it, nor to African society because they are an integral part of it.

The examination of the marginality or integration of the elite to, or into, both European and African society leads to a consideration of occupation as a factor influencing racial attitudes. Among the European rural elite it has been shown that occupation, more than any other criterion, forms racial attitudes.[19] Among the African elite this does not seem to be the case. The chapters in part two examined different professional groups, yet attitudes towards Europeans or political aspirations did not coincide with religious, medical or educational occupations; they rather coincided with the rank position of Africans in the elite hierarchy.

Thus members of the top stratum were in general less interested in African nationalism and more relaxed in their attitudes towards traditional political office holders, the chiefs, than members of the middle stratum. In fact, it was teachers and businessmen who were

[19]Cf. *supra*, p. 96.

most critical of European domination and most determined to bring about a political change in Rhodesia. The middle stratum of the elite, not the most educated men, came forward as political leaders and were supported by the sub-elite. Members of the top elite gave, at the most, support to nationalism secretly in order not to endanger their position. In Barakat's terms, the top elite, though sharing with other Africans the discrimination suffered by all Africans in Rhodesia's caste society, are the 'compliars' in the social system, the middle stratum the 'activists'.[20]

The third part of Banton's hypothesis may therefore be expanded as follows:

(a) *Social stratification in the initial stages of its development results in different degrees of marginality of the various sections of the emergent elite, both in regard to the dominant racial group and in regard to their own racial group.*

(b) *Positions in the stratification system, rather than occupation, determine the political views of members of the emergent elite. Radicalism is most widespread among those who have had contacts with western culture but are barred from any significant participation in the European way of life and are least alienated from their own people.*

4. Conclusion

This book has examined the racial attitudes of some Europeans and Africans holding important positions in rural Rhodesian society and shown that these attitudes are to a very large extent determined by the structural positions of individuals. Whether occupation strongly influences the European stereotype of Africans, or whether rank in the new elite hierarchy determines the social and political aspirations of members of the modern emergent elite, most people, African and European alike, are unable to obtain an image of the other race that closely approximates that race's self-evaluation, because of the caste barrier between the dominant and subordinate races. D. H. Reader gives a reason for this 'fact distortion' when he writes:

We all go through life equipped with a defensive filter which is served by a memory bank. Through the filter are transmitted and received all communications with others, even in cases when we think that we are pas-

[20]Barakat, 1969, p. 9.

sive spectators . . . Fairly obviously, when two people interact, the shared communication has to go through their two filters, which means that fact distortion is usually magnified . . . It is thus all too easy for information through any filter to follow stereotyped patterns and run irretrievably along rails which have been laid by the individual's experience and psychological make-up.[21]

If 'fact distortion' takes place whenever two individuals communicate, the possibilities of distortion are greatly multiplied and misunderstandings still more frequent if these individuals come from different racial backgrounds. If, in addition, members of the dominant and subordinate race see in each other a danger to their own security, 'fact distortion' is increased because situations of contacts are marked by suspicion. The dominant race suffers less because it enjoys many privileges. Members of the subordinate race, on the other hand, often share the sentiments of the Ghanian poet G. Awooner-Williams who wrote:

I am on the world's extreme corner,
I am not sitting in the row with the eminent
But those who are lucky sit in the middle and forget
I am on the world's extreme corner.
I can only go beyond and forget.[22]

[21]Reader, 1969, pp. 7–8.
[22]Quoted in Moore and Beier. See also the American Negro writer Du Bois who describes the relationship between a dominant and a subdominant race in the following words: 'It is difficult to let others see the full psychological meaning of caste segregation. It is as though one, looking out from a dark cave in a side of an impending mountain, sees the world passing and speaks to it; speaks courteously and persuasively, showing them how these entombed souls are hindered in their natural movement, expression, and development; and how their loosening from prison would be a matter not simply of courtesy, sympathy, and help to them, but aid to all the world. One talks on evenly and logically in this way but notices that the passing throng does not even turn its head, or if it does, glances curiously and walks on.' Du Bois, 1940, p. 130.

Appendix

Age	District commissioners	Extension officers	Missionaries	Farmers	Total
20–29	—	4	2	—	6
30–39	5	6	3	2	16
40–49	2	2	5	1	10
50–59	7	2	3	2	14
60–69	—	—	1	3	4
Total	**14**	**14**	**14**	**8**	**50**

Table 12. The age of agents of change

Age	District commissioners	Extension officers	Missionaries	Farmers	Total
15–19	6	—	6	5	17
20–24	7	10	6	2	25
25–29	1	3	2	—	6
30–34	—	1	—	—	1
40	—	—	—	1	1
Total	**14**	**14**	**14**	**8**	**50**

Table 13. The age at which agents of change took up their occupation

Education in years	District commissioners	Extension officers	Missionaries	Farmers	Total
8–11	6	—	—	8	14
12–14	4	5	—	—	9
15–16	4	9	3	—	16
18–20	—	—	8	—	8
23–25	—	—	3	—	3
Total	**14**	**14**	**14**	**8**	**50**

Table 14. The education of agents of change

Religious affiliation	District commissioners	Extension officers	Missionaries	Farmers	Total
Roman Catholic	1	1	6	—	8
Anglican	8	3	—	1	12
Protestant	1	9	8	5	23
None	4	1	—	2	7
Total	**14**	**14**	**14**	**8**	**50**

Table 15. The religious affiliation of agents of change

Country of origin	District commissioners[1]	Extension officers	Missionaries	Farmers	Total
Rhodesia	4	2	2	5	13
South Africa	2	1	3	2	8
U.K.	6	4	3	1	14
Commonwealth	2	3	—	—	5
Other	—	4	6	—	10
Total	**14**	**14**	**14**	**8**	**50**

Table 16. Country of origin of agents of change

Year of arrival	District commissioners	Extension officers	Missionaries	Farmers	Total
Birth	4	2	2	5	13
1920–9	3	—	—	2	5
1930–9	2	—	1	1	4
1940–9	1	3	3	—	7
1950–9	4	5	5	—	14
1960–9	—	4	3	—	7
Total	**14**	**14**	**14**	**8**	**50**

Table 17. Length of stay in Rhodesia of agents of change

[1]For comparative data on a further thirty-seven commissioners see Holleman, 1968, p. 26.

Occupation of father	District commissioners	Extension officers	Missionaries	Farmers	Total
Farming	3	4	2	6	15
Civil service/ Church	9	3	4	1	17
Crafts	2	3	3	1	9
Business	—	3	3	—	6
Professional	—	1	2	—	3
Total	**14**	**14**	**14**	**8**	**50**

Table 18. Occupation of fathers of agents of change

Bibliography

Abraham, D. P., 1962, 'The Early Political History of the Kingdom of Mwene Mutapa'. *Historians in Tropical Africa*. Salisbury, Leverhulme Inter-Collegiate History Conference, University College of Rhodesia and Nyasaland, 1960. Pp. 61–92.

Abraham, W. E., 1967, *The Mind of Africa*. London, Weidenfeld & Nicolson.

Aquina, Sister Mary O. P., 1964, 'The Social Background of Agriculture in Chilimanzi Reserve'. *Rhodes–Livingstone Journal*, 36, pp. 7–39,—1966, 'Christianity in a Rhodesian Tribal Trust Land'. *African Social Research*, 1, pp. 1–40.—1967, 'A Sociological Study of a Religious Congregation of African Sisters in Rhodesia'. *Social Compass*, XIV, 1, pp. 3–32.—1967, 'The People of the Spirit: An Independent Church in Rhodesia'. *Africa*, XXXVII, pp. 203–19.—1969, Zionists in Rhodesia. *Africa*, XXXVIII, pp. 113–37.—(See also Weinrich, A. K. H.)

Arrighi, G., 1967, *The Political Economy of Rhodesia*. The Hague, Mouton.

Banton, M., 1969, *Race Relations*. London, Tavistock Publications.

Barakat, H., 1969, 'Alienation: A Process of Encounter between Utopia and Reality'. *The British Journal of Sociology*, XX, 1, pp. 1–10.

Barber, J., 1967, *Rhodesia: The Road to Rebellion*. Oxford University Press.

Benoit, E., 1966, 'Status, Status Types, and Status Inter-relations', *in* Biddle, B. C. *and* Thomas, E. T., *eds.*, *Role Theory*. New York, Wiley & Sons, Inc., pp. 77–80.

Blumer, H., 1965, 'Industrialisation and Race Relations', *in* Hunter, G., *ed.*, *Industrial Relations and Race Relations*. London, Oxford University Press, pp. 220–53.

Bottomore, T. B., 1964, *Elites and Society*. London, Watts & Co.—1966, *Classes in Modern Society*. New York, Pantheon Books.

Chidyausiku, P., 1969, *Ndakambokuyambira*. Gwelo, Mambo Press.

Davidson, B., 1964, *The African Past*. London, Longman, Green & Co.

Davis, K., 1967, *Human Society*. New York, Collier–Macmillan Student Edition.—1968, 'Demographic Factors in National Efficiency', *in* Young, L. B., *ed.*, *Population in Perspective*. London, Oxford University Press, pp. 180–4.

Dickie-Clark, H. F., 1966, *The Marginal Situation*. London, Routledge & Kegan Paul.

Du Bois, W. E. B., 1940, *Dusk of Dawn*. New York, Harcourt, Brace & Co.

Eberhard, W., 1968, 'Problems of Historical Sociology', *in* Bendix, R., *ed.*, *State and Society*. Boston, Little, Brown & Co.

Erikson, E., 1968, *Identiy: Youth and Crisis*. London, Faber & Faber.

Foster, P., 1967, *Education and Social Change in Ghana*. London, Routledge & Kegan Paul.

Gann, L. H., 1965, *A History of Southern Rhodesia*. London, Chatto & Windus.

Gerth, H. H. and Wright Mills, C., 1961, *From Max Weber: Essays in Sociology*. London, Routledge & Kegan Paul.

Gouveia, A. J., 1967, 'Education and development: Opinions of Secondary School Teachers', *in* Lipset, S. M. *and* Solari, A., *eds.*, *Elites in Latin America*. London, Oxford University Press, pp. 484–513.

Gray, R., 1960, *The Two Nations*. London, Oxford University Press.

Holleman, J. F., 1969, *Chief, Council and Commissioner*. London, Oxford University Press.

Houghton, D. H., 1967, *The South African Economy*. London, Oxford University Press.

Kariuku, J. M., 1963, *'Mau Mau' Detainee*. Penguin African Library, 15.

Kay, G., 1964, *The Distribution of African Population in Southern Rhodesia: Some Preliminary Notes*. Lusaka, Rhodes–Livingstone Institute.

Kuper, L., 1965, *An African Bourgeoisie*. Yale University Press.

Lee, J. M., 1967, *Colonial Development and Good Government*. Oxford, Clarendon Press.

Leys, C., 1960, *European Politics in Southern Rhodesia*. Oxford, Clarendon Press.

Lloyd, P. C., 1966, *The New Elites of Tropical Africa*. Oxford University Press.—1967, *Africa in Social Change*. Penguin African Library, 22.

Lofchie, M. F., 1965, *Zanzibar: Background to Revolution*. Oxford University Press.

Mannoni, O., 1968, *Prospero and Caliban*. New York, Frederick A. Praeger.

Mead, G. H., 1967, *Mind, Self and Society*. Chicago, University of Chicago Press.

Merton, R. K., 1964, *Social Theory & Social Structure*. Illinois, Free Press.

Mills, C. W., 1968, *The Power Elite*. Oxford University Press.

Moore, G. and Beier, U., *Modern Poetry from Africa*. Penguin Africa Library.

Mphahlele, E., 1962, *The African Image*. London, Faber & Faber.

Myrdal, G., 1944, *An American Dilemma*. New York, Harper & Bros.

Nadel, S. F., 1956, 'The Concept of Social Elites'. *Inter-National Social Science Bulletin*, 8, 3, pp. 413–24.

Ngcobo, S. B., 1968, 'African Elite in South Africa'. *Inter-national Social Science Bulletin*, 8, 3, pp. 431–40.

Organski, A. F. K. and K., 1968, 'Nations and Numbers', *in* Young, L. B., *ed.*, *Population in Perspective*. London, Oxford University Press, pp. 170–80.

Palmer, R. H., 1968, *Aspects of Rhodesian Land Policy 1890–1936*. The Central African Historical Association, Local Series 22. Salisbury.

Pareto, V., 1935, *The Mind and Society*. London, Jonathan Cape.

Parkin, F., 1968. *Middle Class Radicalism*. Manchester, Manchester University Press.

Ranger, T. O., 1968, *Aspects of Central African History*. London, Heinemann.

Reader, D. H., 1969, *Social Distortion: An Approach to Race Relations*. Inaugural Lecture, University College of Rhodesia. Salisbury, Mardon Printers.

Rogers, C. A. and Frantz, C., 1962, *Racial Themes in Southern Rhodesia*. New Haven, Yale University Press.

Roman Catholic Church, 1963, *Catholic Bishops of Southern Rhodesia: Problems of our People*. Gwelo, Catholic Mission Press.

Seligman, L. G., 1966, 'Elite Recruitment and Political Development', *in* Finkle, J. G. *and* Gable, R. W., *eds.*, *Political Development and Social Change*. New York, pp 329–37.

Selous, F. C., 1881, *A Hunter's Wanderings in Africa*. Richard Bentley.

Smelser, N. J., and Lipset, S. M., 1964, *Social Structure and Mobility in Economic Development*. London, Routledge & Kegan Paul.

Solari, A., 1967, 'Secondary Education and the Development of Elites', *in* Lipset *and* Solari, A., *eds.*, *Elites in Latin America*. London, Oxford University Press, pp 458–82.

Southern Rhodesian Christian Conference, 1964, 'Survey Report on Adult Literacy and Christian Literature in Southern Rhodesia'.

Stokes, E., 1964, *The Southern Rhodesian Tangle*. New Society, 6–8.—and Brown, R., 1966, *The Zambesian Past: Studies in Central African History*. Manchester, Manchester University Press.

Summers, R., 1961, 'The Southern Rhodesian Iron Age'. *Journal of African History*, 2, 1–13.—1962, 'Archeology and History in South Central Africa'. *Historians in Tropical Africa*. Salisbury, Leverhulme Inter-Collegiate History Conference, University College of Rhodesia and Nyasaland, 1960. Pp. 41–56.

Tanner, R. E. S., 1966, 'European Leadership in Small Communities in Tanganyika prior to Independence', *Race*, 7, 3, pp. 289–302.

Tindall, P. E. N., 1968, *History of Central Africa*. Longmans.

Van der Horst, S. T., 1965, 'The Effects of Industrialisation on Race Relations in South Africa', *in* Hunter, G., *ed.*, *Industrial Relation and Race Relations*. London, Oxford University Press, pp 97–140.

Weinrich, A. K. M., 1971, *Chiefs and Councils in Rhodesia*. London, Heinemann.—(See also Aquina, Sister Mary O. P.)

Weisman, A. D., 1965, *The Existential Core of Psychoanalysis*. Boston, Little, Brown & Company.

Wilson, M. and Mafeje, A., 1963, *Langa: A Study of Social Groups in an African Township*. London, Oxford University Press.

Wrathall, J. J., 1969, 'The Tribal Trust Land: Their Need for Development'. Salisbury, *NADA*, X, 92–9.

Acts of Parliament

(All published by the Government Printer, Salisbury, Rhodesia.)

Southern Rhodesia, *The Land Apportionment Act*, cap. 257 (1931) (amended 1941).—*The Industrial Conciliation Act*, cap. 246 (1934)– – *The African Land Husbandry Act*, cap. 103 (1951)

Rhodesia *Tribal Trust Land Act*, No. 9 (1967)—African Law and Tribal Courts Act, No. 24 (1969)—*Land Tenure Bill*, 1969

Other government publications

(All published by the Government Printer, Salisbury, Rhodesia.)

Southern Rhodesia *Second Report of the Select Committee on Resettlement of Natives*. Presented to the Legislative Assembly on Tuesday, 16th August 1960.—*Southern Rhodesia Constitution 1961*. Presented to Parliament by the Secretary of State for Commonwealth Relations by Command of Her Majesty, June 1961.—*1961 Census of the European, Asian and Coloured Population*. Central Statistical Office, Salisbury.—*Final Report of the April/May 1962 Census of Africans in Southern Rhodesia*. Central Statistical Office, Salisbury. 1964.

Rhodesia *Report of the Secretary for Internal Affairs, for the years 1963 to 1967*. Published 1964–8.—*The Constitution of Rhodesia*. 1965.— *Local Government and Community Development: The Role of Ministries and Co-ordination. Statement of Policy and Directive by the Prime Minister, 1965.—Rhodesia, Its Natural Resources and Economic Development*. Salisbury, Collins, 1965.—*African Education Annual Report* by the Secretary for the Year 1967.—*Annual Report on Education for the Year 1967.—Economic Survey of Rhodesia for 1965–1967.—Rhodesia in Brief*. Salisbury, Ministry of Information, Immigration and Tourism. 1969.—*Report of the Constitutional Commission, 1968* (Whaley Report).—*Proposals for a New Constitution for Rhodesia*. 1969.—*Monthly Migration Statistics for June 1969*. Central Statistical Office, Salisbury. 1969.

Newspapers

Moto. Gwelo, Mambo Press.
The Rhodesia Herald. Salisbury, The Rhodesian Printing & Publishing Co.
The Sunday Mail. Salisbury, The Rhodesian Printing & Publishing Co.

Index

Abraham, W. E., 8n, 44n, 104
abstinence, Dutch Reformed doctrine, 121
acceptance, of Europeans by Africans, 53 ff
acculturation, 2
achieved status, 103, 171
'activists', 228
Acts to protect European interests, 10, 11, 22
administrators in education, 108
advancement opportunities, 8 ff
African advancement, European attitudes to, 68 ff
  economic
    district commissioners, 72
    extension officers, 73
    farmers, 74
    missionaries, 74
  political
    district commissioners, 69
    extension officers, 76
    farmers, 78
    missionaries, 71
  social
    district commissioners, 75
    extension officers, 76
    farmers, 78
    missionaries, 77
African business centres, 194
African Education, ministry of, 162, 165
African Education 1967, 29
African elite
  agricultural
    cash crop farmers, 186 ff
    extension officers, 177 ff
    extension supervisors and assistants, 181 ff
  commercial
    businessmen, 193 ff
    craftsmen, 206 ff
  educational
    school inspectors, 154 ff
    school managers, 160 ff
    teachers, 166 ff
  medical
    doctors, 133 ff
    hospital administrators, 139 ff
    in South Africa, 210
    nurses, 145 ff
  religious
    Catholic, 115 ff
    Dutch Reformed, 119 ff
    Methodist, 124 ff
    Seventh Day Adventist, 127 ff
  relations with doctors, 136

relations with European elite, 22, 25, 29 f, 33 ff, 75 ff, 97 ff, 101 ff, 136
African Farmers' Union, 187 f
African Land Husbandry Act, 11n
African Law and Tribal Courts Act, 100n, 111n
African National Congress, 172
African rural councils, 28
Africans
  effect of education on views, 112
  relations with African agricultural elite, 182
  relations with African commercial elite, 200
  relations with African educational elite, 155, 161, 170
  relations with African medical elite, 135, 142, 148
  relations with African religious elite, 116, 120, 125, 128
  shortcomings in Europeans' eyes, 39 ff
age
  as determinant of racial attitudes, 62 ff, 88
  distribution of population, 22
  of district commissioners, 54, 62, 73, 76, 88
  of extension officers, 64
  of farmers, 67
  of missionaries, 65
agricultural elite, African
  cash crop farmers, 186 ff
  extension officers, 177 ff
  extension supervisors and assistants, 181 ff
  in South Africa, 214
agriculture, 46
  African traditional and European industrial, 23
Agriculture, Department of, 34, 74, 80, 92, 109, 177
alcoholism, chiefs', 144n
American Methodist Episcopal Church, 61n
Anglican priests in South Africa, 210
Annual Report on Education for the Year 1967, 27n, 29n
apartheid, 6, 12, 70, 122, 210, 218
Arab traders, 8
ascribed status, 103, 168

Banton, M., 1 ff, 9, 14, 30, 37, 61, 217 ff
Bantu educational system, 165, 213
Bantu National Congress, 215

DATE DUE			
DEC 1 9 1975			
AP 29'85			